The Cambridge Program for the Writing Skills Test

CAMBRIDGE Adult Education
Prentice Hall Regents, Englewood Cliffs, NJ 07632

The editor has made every effort to trace the ownership of all copyrighted material, and necessary permissions have been secured in most cases. Should there prove to be any question regarding the use of any material, regret is here expressed for such error. Upon notification of any such oversight, proper acknowledgment will be made in future editions.

Published by Prentice-Hall, Inc.
A Division of Simon & Schuster
Englewood Cliffs, New Jersey 07632

Printed in the United States of America

10 9 8 7 6 5 4 3 2

ISBN 0-8428-8701-6 01

Prentice-Hall International (UK) Limited, *London*
Prentice-Hall of Australia Pty. Limited, *Sydney*
Prentice-Hall Canada Inc., *Toronto*
Prentice-Hall Hispanoamericana, S.A., *Mexico*
Prentice-Hall of India Private Limited, *New Delhi*
Prentice-Hall of Japan, Inc., *Tokyo*
Simon & Schuster Asia Pte. Ltd., *Singapore*
Editora Prentice-Hall do Brasil, Ltda., *Rio de Janeiro*

The Cambridge GED Program

Consulting Editors

Mary Ann Corley
Supervisor of Adult Education
Baltimore County Public Schools

Del Gratia Doss
Supervisor, Adult Basic Education
St. Louis, Missouri

Ron Froman
Administrator of Adult Education
Orange County Public Schools, Orlando, Florida

Lawrence Levin
KNILE Educational & Training Association.
Former Director ABE/ESL/HSE Services
New York City Board of Education

Noreen Lopez
Adult Educator
Illinois

Dorothy Hammond
Coordinator
New York State Writing Project

Arturo McDonald
Assistant Superintendent—Adult Education
Brownsville, Texas

Cheryl Moore
Curriculum Director, Windham School System
Texas Department of Corrections

Carrie Robinson Weir
Director, Adult Education Resource Center
Jersey City State College

Harold Wilson
Director of Adult Basic Education
Indianapolis Public Schools

Jane Zinner
Director of Grants and Curriculum
Association for California School Administrators

Contributing Editors

Gloria Cohen, Ed.D.
Consultant, Curriculum & Gifted Education
New York Metropolitan Area

Carole Deletiner
Adult Basic Education Teacher
Formerly, New York City Technical College

Don Gerstein
Academic Educator
Wyoming State Penitentiary 1981–1986

Nathaniel Howard
Senior Training Representative
Consolidated Edison, New York City

Joan Knight
Former City-wide Supervisor of Staff Development
New York City Board of Education Adult program

Bonnie Longnion
Dean of Continuing Education
North Harris County College, Kingwood, Texas

Joe Mangano
Research Associate
State University of New York at Albany

Ada Rogers
Adult Education GED Program
Broward County, Florida, School System

Ann Rowe
Education Specialist
New York State

Elois Scott
Reading Specialist
University of Florida, Gainesville

Stephen Steurer
Correctional Academic Coordinator
Maryland State Department of Education

Dr. Jay Templin
Professor of Biology
Widener University, Delaware Campus

Jeffrey Tenzer
Auxiliary Services for High Schools
New York City

The Cambridge GED Program

Writers

Gary Apple
Owen Boyle
Jesse Browner
Phyllis Cohen
Carole Deletiner
Randee Falk
Don Gerstein
Peter Guthrie
Alan Hines
Jeanne James
Lois Kasper
Rachel Kranz
Gloria Levine
Amy Litt
Dennis Mendyk
Rebecca Motil
Susan Muller
Marcia Mungenast
Thomas Repensek
Ada Rogers
Ann Rowe
Richard Rozakis
Elois Scott
Sally Stepanek
Steve Steurer
Carol Stone
Lynn Tiutczenko
Robin Usyak
Kenneth Uva
Shelley Uva
Tom Walz
Willa Wolcott
Patricia Wright-Stover
Karen Wunderman

Executive Editor

Jerry Long

Senior Editor

Timothy Foote

Project Editors

James Fina
Diane Maass

Subject Editors

Jim Bedell
Diane Engel
Randee Falk
Scott Gillam
Rebecca Motil
Thomas Repensek

Art and Design

Brian Crede Associates
Adele Scheff
Hal Keith

Contents

Practice

Simulation

Introduction

The following pages will introduce you to the Writing Skills Test and to the organization of this book. You will read about ways you can use this book to your best advantage.

What Is the Writing Skills Test?

The Writing Skills Test of the GED Tests examines your knowledge of the conventions of written English and your ability to write.

What Kind of Questions Are on the Test?

The Writing Skills Test is composed of two parts. Part I tests your knowledge of the conventions of written English: usage, sentence structure, and mechanics (punctuation, capitalization, and spelling). Part II tests your ability to write an expository essay.

In Part I, you will read paragraphs made up of ten to twelve sentences. Each sentence in each paragraph is numbered. Most of the items ask you to locate and correct errors in the sentences. The errors may be in spelling, punctuation, capitalization, usage, or sentence structure. Other items ask you to select wording that is less awkward than that used in the paragraph. Some items ask you to rewrite parts of sentences that are poorly constructed.

In Part II, you will be asked to write an essay in which you state your opinion about a certain topic or explain something. You will write a 200-word essay in which you support your opinion or defend your explanation with specific details. There are no correct answers for this portion of the test. Your essay will be judged for its overall effectiveness. Readers will not be critical of the opinion you present: they will be interested in how effectively you present it. The score given to your essay will be based on how clear, well-organized, and generally free of errors it is.

As with all the other GED tests, all of the 55 questions in Part I of the Writing Skills Test are in multiple-choice format.

What Are the Paragraphs and Essay Questions Like?

The paragraphs you will read on Part I of the Writing Skills Test are from ten to twelve sentences long. When corrected, they are examples of good writing. The errors they contain are the kind that beginning writers are most likely to make; thus, as you use this book to study writing skills, you should learn to avoid those types of errors.

About 35 percent of the items on this part of the test will check your knowledge of correct sentence structure. Another 35 percent will test your knowledge of usage. The remaining 30 percent concern the mechanics of writing: spelling, punctuation, and capitalization.

The composition topic is Part II of the Writing Skills Test will be presented in a short paragraph. You may be asked to explain something or give your opinion about a particular issue. If you are asked for an opinion, you may present any opinion you like. The opinion you express will not be a factor in your essay's score.

What You Will Find in This Book

This book gives you a four-step preparation for taking the Writing Skills Test. The four steps are as follows:

Step One: Prediction

In this first step, you will find the Predictor Test. This test is very much like the actual Writing Skills Test, but Part I—the part that tests your knowledge of the conventions of English—is about half as long as the actual Writing Skills Test, Part I. Part II, the part in which you write a composition, is the same length as the actual GED.

By evaluating your performance on the Predictor Test, you will get a sense of your strengths and weaknesses. This information will help you to plan your studies accordingly.

Step Two: Instruction

The instruction section has two units. The first unit, "Writing Skills, Part I: Grammar," covers the conventions of English usage, sentence structure, and mechanics (punctuation, capitalization, and spelling). It also shows you how to edit writing, that is, how to locate and correct errors in usage, sentence structure, and mechanics.

The second unit, "Writing Skills, Part II: Essay Writing" provides a variety of writing activities to prepare you to practice the writing process. Instruction in the writing process itself takes you through the steps by which you plan, organize, write, revise, and edit a successful essay.

Both units of the Instruction section are divided into chapters. The four chapters in Unit I each cover one of the aspects of writing skills that will be tested in Part I of the Writing Skills Test: usage, sentence structure, mechanics, and editing. The chapters, in turn, are divided into skills, such as subject-verb agreement, complete sentences, and spelling. Each skill begins with a Preview and ends with a Review. The Previews and Reviews are made up of questions that cover the material taught in that skill. There are very few multiple-choice questions in Unit I, in order to give you the maximum amount of practice in writing sentences correctly.

Unit II is made up of three chapters. The first chapter provides a variety of writing activities to prepare you to learn the writing process. The second chapter explains and provides practice with the writing process. The third chapter reviews the writing process. Each chapter is divided into lessons that include writing activities.

Step Three: Practice

This section gives you valuable practice in answering questions like those you will find in Part I of the actual Writing Skills Test, and in writing the type of essay required in Part II of the test. There are two parts to this section: *Practice Items* and a *Practice Test*. Both are structured very much like the actual Writing Skills Test. Both types of practice activities have 55 items in Part I, the same number of questions as are in Part I of the GED Test, and one essay question in Part II, as in the real GED. You can use your results to track your progress and to give you an idea of how prepared you are to take the real test.

Step Four: Simulation

Finally, this book offers a simulated version of the Writing Skills Test. It is as similar to the real test as possible. The number of questions, their level of difficulty, and the way they are organized are the same as you will find on the actual test. Taking the Simulated Test will be useful preparation for taking the GED. It will help you find out how ready you are to take the real exam.

The Answer Key

At the back of this book, you will find an Answers and Explanations section. The answer key contains the answers to the items in all the Previews, Exercises, Reviews, Quizzes, and the Test in Unit I, and the answers to the items in Practice Items, the Practice Test, and the Simulated Test. It not only tells you the right answers for grammar items, but it also explains why the answers are right. It names the topic in grammar you need to know to answer a question successfully. The answer key contains model essays and guidelines to help you score essays you write. You can benefit a great deal by carefully consulting the answer key.

USING THIS BOOK

The book has been designed to give you several choices. Whether you are working with an instructor or alone, you can use this book to prepare for the Writing Skills Test in the way that works best for you.

Take a Glance at the Table of Contents

Before doing anything else, look over the Table of Contents and get a feel for this book. You can compare the headings in the Table of Contents with the descriptions found in the preceding pages. You might also want to leaf through the book to see what each section looks like.

Take the Predictor Test

Next, you will probably want to take the Predictor Test. As the introduction before the test explains, there is more than one way to take this test. Decide which is best for you. It might be best for you to take the test in two separate sittings: take Part I one day and Part II on another day.

Your performance and score on the Predictor Test will be very useful to you as you work with the rest of this book. It will help you identify your particular strengths and weaknesses, which can help you plan your course of study.

Beginning Your Instruction

After you have an idea about what your strengths and weaknesses are, you are ready to begin instruction. You may begin with either Unit I or Unit II, or you may wish to work on both of them at the same time.

Likewise, you may approach the first three chapters in Unit I in any order you like. We recommend, however, saving Chapter 4 until after you have completed the first three chapters.

Each of the first three chapters of Unit I is divided into three skills. Each skill begins with a Preview and ends with a Review. To find out whether you need to study the lessons that make up a skill, take the Preview. If you score 80 percent or better on the Preview, skip ahead to the Review. If you score 80 percent or better on the Review as well, you can be satisfied that you understand the material in the skill. Go on to the Preview at the beginning of the next skill. You can continue skipping ahead in this fashion until you score below 80 percent on either a Preview or a Review. At that point, go to the first lesson in the skill and begin work. When you have completed Chapters 1 to 3 with scores averaging 80 percent or better, you are ready to go on to Chapter 4.

You should work on the chapters in Unit II in order. The first chapter will get you started on daily writing activities that will help you improve your writing skills. The second chapter introduces the writing process, and the third chapter reviews that process.

Using the Practice Section

Because there are two units in the instruction section, corresponding to the two parts of the Writing Skills Test, you have several choices about how to use this book. You may complete the instruction section for Unit I and proceed directly to the related Practice Items and Practice Test. You may do the same for Unit II and the related parts of the Practice section. Or, you may wish to complete the Instruction section for both Units I and II before going on to the Practice Section. The choice is up to you.

Taking the Simulated Test

Finally, once you have completed the Instruction and Practice sections, you can take the Simulated Writing Skills Test. This will give you the most accurate assessment of how ready you are to take the actual test.

Try Your Best!

As you study the lessons and complete the activities and tests in this book, you should give it your best effort. In those sections that can be scored, try to maintain at least 80 percent correct as you work through this book. The Progress Charts will help you compare your work with this 80 percent figure. If you maintain 80 percent scores, you are probably working at a level that will allow you to do well on the GED.

What Is the GED?

You are preparing for the GED Tests. The initials GED stand for General Educational Development. You may also have heard the tests referred to as the High School Equivalency Tests. The GED diploma is widely regarded as the equivalent of a high school diploma.

The GED Test is a way for millions of adults in the United States and Canada to get diplomas or certificates without returning to high school. Each year about half a million people take advantage of the opportunity to take the GED tests.

Who Recognizes the GED?

The GED is recognized by employers, unions, and state and federal civil services. Many vocational institutes, colleges, and universities accept students who have obtained a GED. All fifty states and parts of Canada use the GED Test results to issue high school equivalency credentials. However, each state has its own standards for what constitutes a passing grade. For information on the requirements in your state, contact the High School Equivalency Program of the State Department of Education in your state's capital.

What Is Tested on the GED Test?

The material found on the GED is based on the subjects covered in most high schools around the country. Thus you will be learning about the subject areas that you would be most likely to study if you attended four years of high school. However, the focus of the GED is not on content, but on *skills*. You will not have to memorize specific dates, names, and places. For example, whether you recall the date of a battle or the title of a novel is less important than whether you can read and understand a passage on history or literature.

You have already been using many of the thinking skills that will be tested on the GED. For example, many people must do some writing in their lives, and the GED includes a test of writing skills. A lot of people read in their jobs or for pleasure, and reading skills are tested, too. Many people use basic mathematics for such things as figuring out a budget or doubling a recipe, and the GED includes a test of basic math skills.

Instead of testing your memory, the GED tests your ability to get information and apply your thinking to that information.

How Is the GED Structured?

The GED is actually five separate tests. With one exception, the test is composed entirely of multiple choice questions. The one exception is the 200-word essay that you will be required to write as part of the Writing Skills Test.

The chart below describes the structure of the five tests:

Test #	*Test Subject*	*Number of Items*	*Minutes Allowed*
1	Writing Skills Part 1—Multiple Choice Part 2—Essay	 55 1	 75 45
2	Social Studies	64	85
3	Science	66	95
4	Interpreting Literature and the Arts	45	65
5	Mathematics	56	90

Prediction

Introduction

Imagine that you were going to take the GED test today. How do you think you would do? In which areas would you perform best, and in which areas would you have the most trouble? The Predictor Test that follows can help you answer these questions. It is called a Predictor Test because your results can be used to predict where your strengths and your weaknesses lie in relation to the actual Writing Skills Test of the GED.

The Predictor Test is like the actual GED test in many ways. It will check your skills as you apply them to the kinds of items you will find on the real test. The items are like those on the actual test.

How to Take the Predictor Test

Because there are two parts to the actual Writing Skills Test, there are two parts to the Predictor Test. Here are two ways you can take the test:

(1) It may be best to take the Predictor in two sittings. You can complete either part first. After you finish one part of the test, put the test aside and complete the other part at another time.

(2) If you want, you can take the Predictor Test in one sitting. Start with Part I. As soon as you finish Part I, begin Part II.

You may want to time yourself to see how long you take to complete the parts of the test. Part I of the Predictor Test is about half as long as the actual test. If you finish it within 38 minutes, you are right on target. Part II of the Predictor Test is the same length as the actual test. You should try to complete it in about 45 minutes. At this stage, however, you shouldn't worry too much if it takes you longer.

When you are done, check your answers by using the answer key that begins on page 241. Put a check by each item in Part I that you answered correctly. Score your essay according to the instructions in the answer key. You might like to have a teacher or someone else score your essay as well.

How to Use Your Score

At the end of the test, you will find a Performance Analysis Chart. Fill in the chart; it will help you get a general idea about which areas you are more comfortable with, and which give you the most trouble. As you work through Unit I in this book, you will complete several short exercises—Previews and Reviews—that will help you pinpoint your strengths and weaknesses in grammar. Unit II will help you with writing essays.

PREDICTOR TEST
Part I

TIME: *38 minutes*
Directions: *The items in Part I of this test are based on paragraphs that contain numbered sentences. Some of the sentences may contain errors in sentence structure, usage, or mechanics.* ***A few sentences, however, may be correct as written.*** *Read each paragraph and then answer the items that follow it. For each item, choose the answer that would result in the most effective writing of the sentence or sentences. The best answer must be consistent with the meaning and tone of the rest of the paragraph.*

FOR EXAMPLE:

Sentence 1: **Although it may take only two hours to watch the average motion picture takes almost a year to make.**

What correction should be made to this sentence?

(1) replace it with they
(2) change take to have taken
(3) insert a comma after watch
(4) change almost to all most
(5) no change is necessary

The correct answer is **(3)**. In this example, a comma is needed after the clause Although it may take only two hours to watch.

Items 1 to 9 are based on the following paragraph.

(1) People spends a lot of money each year on cold remedies. (2) Many of these products dont really help to prevent or cure colds. (3) In fact, some may even be harmful. (4) Several types of cough medicine contains alcohol and can be habit-forming. (5) The Food and drug Administration reports that mouthwashes can't really fight colds. (6) Gargling with mouthwash may make your sore throat feel better. (7) But salt water probably works just as well. (8) One scientist is named Linus Pauling he believes taking a lot of vitamin C can help prevent the common cold. (9) Other scientists, however, disagree, they say careful research does not support Pauling's claim. (10) In any case, large doses of vitamin C can be harmful to some people. (11) These people include pregnant women the elderly, and people with certain health problems. (12) Maybe the cheapest cold remedies—home remedies, such as tea with lemon and honey—are really the best.

1. Sentence 1: **People spends a lot of money each year on cold remedies.**

What correction should be made to this sentence?

(1) change *spends* to *spend*
(2) change the spelling of *a lot* to *alot*
(3) insert *annually* after *money*
(4) insert a comma after *year*
(5) change *cold* to *Cold*

2. Sentence 2: **Many of these products dont really help to prevent or cure colds.**

What correction should be made to this sentence?

(1) replace *these* with *which*
(2) change the spelling of *dont* to *don't*
(3) change the spelling of *to* to *too*
(4) insert a comma after *prevent*
(5) replace *cure* with *in curing*

3. Sentence 4: **Several types of cough medicine <u>contains alcohol and can be</u> habit-forming.**

Which of the following is the best way to write the underlined portion of this sentence? If you think the original is the best way, choose option (1).

(1) contains alcohol and can be
(2) contains alcohol. And can be
(3) contain alcohol and can be
(4) contain alcohol and were
(5) contained alcohol and can be

4. Sentence 5: **The Food and drug Administration reports that mouthwashes can't really fight colds.**

What correction should be made to this sentence?

(1) change *Food* to *food*
(2) change *drug* to *Drug*
(3) change *reports* to *report*
(4) change the spelling of *can't* to *cant*
(5) no correction is necessary

5. Sentences 6 & 7: **Gargling with mouthwash may make your sore throat feel <u>better. But salt water probably works</u> just as well.**

Which of the following is the best way to write the underlined portions of these sentences? If you think the original is the best way, choose option (1).

(1) better. But salt water probably works
(2) better. But salt water probably worked
(3) better, but salt water probably works
(4) better but salt water probably works
(5) better but, salt water probably works

6. Sentence 8: **One scientist <u>is named Linus Pauling he believes</u> taking a lot of vitamin C can help prevent the common cold.**

Which of the following is the best way to write the underlined portion of this sentence? If you think the original is the best way, choose option (1).

(1) is named Linus Pauling he believes
(2) named Linus Pauling he believes
(3) named Linus Pauling believes
(4) named Linus Pauling, he believes
(5) named Linus Pauling, he believe

7. Sentence 9: **Other scientists, however, disagree, they say careful research does not support Pauling's claim.**

What correction should be made to this sentence?

(1) remove the comma after *scientists*
(2) replace *disagree, they* with *disagree. They*
(3) change the spelling of *careful* to *carefull*
(4) change *Pauling's* to *pauling's*
(5) no correction is necessary

8. Sentence 11: **These people include pregnant <u>women the elderly, and</u> people with certain health problems.**

Which of the following is the best way to write the underlined portion of this sentence? If you think the original is the best way, choose option (1).

(1) women the elderly, and
(2) women the elderly and
(3) women. The elderly and
(4) women, the elderly, and
(5) women; the elderly, and

9. Sentence 12: **Maybe the cheapest cold remedies—home remedies, such as tea with lemon and honey—are really the best.**

If you rewrote sentence 12 beginning with

Maybe home remedies, such as tea with lemon and honey, are not

the next word should be

(1) as
(2) only
(3) the
(4) cheapest
(5) best

Items 10 to 19 are based on the following paragraph.

(1) Many jobs is being created in the fast-food industry. (2) We are beginning to see a change in who fills these openings. (3) The birthrate went down in the 1970s, and there are fewer teenagers to fill counter positions than in the past. (4) We probably found more retired people working at fast-food places in the future. (5) Already, there are more college graduates than there used to be among managers at many fast-food restaurants. (6) The fast-food business has grown, and it has, at the same time, become more complicated to run. (7) Fast-food companies are looking for people which are able to think, speak, read, and write clearly. (8) Today's fast-food managers have many responsibilities, several of these require the use of a computer. (9) Managers have to set sales goals other tasks include figuring how much food has been used and how much wasted. (10) A manager needs good communication skills if when he or she is training new workers. (11) More than ever before, fast-food jobs at all levels went to those with the best thinking and language skills.

10. Sentence 1: **Many jobs is being created in the fast-food industry.**

What correction should be made to this sentence?

(1) change *is* to *was*
(2) change *is* to *are*
(3) change *created* to *create*
(4) insert a comma after *created*
(5) no correction is necessary

11. Sentence 3: **The birthrate went down in the 1970s, and there are fewer teenagers to fill counter positions than in the past.**

If you rewrote sentence 3 beginning with

Because the

the next word should be

(1) birthrate
(2) 1970s
(3) teenagers
(4) counter
(5) past

12. Sentence 4: **We probably found more retired people working at fast-food places in the future.**

Which of the following is the best way to write the underlined portion of this sentence? If you think the original is the best way, choose option (1).

(1) probably found more retired people working
(2) will probably find more retired people working
(3) found more retired people probably working
(4) probably found more retired people, working
(5) probably found more retired people. Working

13. Sentence 5: **Already, there are more college graduates than there used to be among managers at many fast-food restaurants.**

What correction should be made to this sentence?

(1) remove the comma after *Already*
(2) change the spelling of *college* to *collage*
(3) insert a comma after *be*
(4) change *managers* to *Managers*
(5) no correction is necessary

14. Sentence 6: **The fast-food business has grown, and it has, at the same time, become more complicated to run.**

If you rewrote sentence 6 beginning with

As the fast-food business has grown,

the next word should be

(1) and
(2) it
(3) at
(4) the
(5) more

15. Sentence 7: **Fast-food companies are looking for people which are able to think, speak, read, and write clearly.**

Which of the following is the best way to write the underlined portion of this sentence? If you think the original is the best way, choose option (1).

(1) are looking for people which are
(2) were looking for people which are
(3) are looking for people which is
(4) are looking for people who are
(5) are looking for people, which are

16. Sentence 8: **Today's fast-food managers have many responsibilities, several of these require the use of a computer.**

What correction should be made to this sentence?

(1) change *have* to *has*
(2) replace *many* with *a variety of different*
(3) change the spelling of *responsibilities* to *responsabilities*
(4) remove the comma after *responsibilities*
(5) replace the comma after *responsibilities* with a semicolon

17. Sentence 9: **Managers have to set sales goals other tasks include figuring how much food has been used and how much wasted.**

Which of the following is the best way to write the underlined portion of this sentence? If you think the original is the best way, choose option (1).

(1) goals other tasks include
(2) goals, other tasks include
(3) goals and other tasks include
(4) goals. Other tasks include
(5) goals other tasks includes

18. Sentence 10: **A manager needs good communication skills if when he or she is training new workers.**

What correction should be made to this sentence?

(1) change *needs* to *need*
(2) insert a semicolon after *skills*
(3) replace *skills if* with *skills, and if*
(4) remove *if*
(5) replace *he or she* with *they*

19. Sentence 11: **More than ever before, fast-food jobs at all levels went to those with the best thinking and language skills.**

What correction should be made to this sentence?

(1) remove the comma after *before*
(2) insert a comma after *levels*
(3) change *went* to *go*
(4) remove *those with*
(5) change the spelling of *language* to *langauge*

Items 20 to 28 are based on the following paragraph.

(1) People are sending more and more mail, but the U.S. Postal service is hiring fewer and fewer workers. (2) Computers are responsible for the reduced hiring. (3) Fewer people are payed to sort the mail now that zip codes are used. (4) A computer operator types the first three numbers of the zip code. (5) The computer immediately tells the person into which tray he or she should toss the letter. (6) Even computer operators are being replaced, some computers read addresses directly. (7) Computers make delivery more efficient. (8) Computers can also check postal workers' efficiency. (9) It can figure how much mail a carrier or clerk is sorting each minute. (10) Computers even store information about when each carrier leaves the post office and when each is due back. (11) Doing more work at less cost, postal clerks are being replaced by computers. (12) However, when it comes to reading messy writing humans still do as well as or better than computers.

20. Sentence 1: **People are sending more and more mail, but the U.S. Postal service is hiring fewer and fewer workers.**

What correction should be made to this sentence?

(1) remove the comma after *mail*
(2) replace *mail, but* with *mail. But*
(3) change *Postal* to *postal*
(4) change *service* to *Service*
(5) change *is* to *was*

21. Sentence 3: **Fewer people are payed to sort the mail now that zip codes are used.**

What correction should be made to this sentence?

(1) change *are* to *is*
(2) change the spelling of *payed* to *paid*
(3) replace *the mail* with *it*
(4) replace *now* with *because*
(5) change *are used* to *will be used*

22. Sentence 5: **The computer immediately tells the person into which tray he or she should toss the letter.**

What correction should be made to this sentence?

(1) change the spelling of *immediately* to *imediately*
(2) change *tells* to *told*
(3) insert a comma after *person*
(4) replace *he or she* with *they*
(5) no correction is necessary

23. Sentence 6: **Even computer operators are being replaced, some computers read addresses directly.**

What correction should be made to this sentence?

(1) change *are being* to *were*
(2) replace *replaced, some* with *replaced. Some*
(3) remove the comma after *replaced*
(4) insert *who* after *computers*
(5) change the spelling of *addresses* to *adresses*

24. Sentences 7 & 8: **Computers make delivery more efficient. Computers can also check postal workers' efficiency.**

The most effective combination of sentences 7 and 8 would include which of the following groups of words?

(1) They can make delivery
(2) Computers can make it
(3) Not only computers make
(4) and can also check
(5) but also postal workers

25. Sentence 9: **It can figure how much mail a carrier or clerk is sorting each minute.**

Which of the following is the best way to write the underlined portion of this sentence? If you think the original is the best way, choose option (1).

(1) It can figure how much
(2) They can figure how much
(3) It can figure, how much
(4) They can figure, how much
(5) It could figure how much

26. Sentence 10: **Computers even store information about when each carrier leaves the post office and when each is due back.**

Which of the following is the best way to write the underlined portion of this sentence? If you think the original is the best way, choose option (1).

(1) leaves the post office and when each is
(2) left the post office and when each was
(3) leaves the post office and when each was
(4) leave the post office and when each is
(5) left the post office and when each were

27. Sentence 11: **Doing more work at less cost, postal clerks are being replaced by computers.**

Which of the following is the best way to write the underlined portion of this sentence? If you think the original is the best way, choose option (1).

(1) Doing more work at less cost,
(2) Although they do more work at less cost,
(3) Because they do more work at less cost,
(4) Although they do more work, at less cost
(5) Because computers do more work at less cost,

28. Sentence 12: **However, when it comes to reading messy writing humans still do as well as or better than computers.**

What correction should be made to this sentence?

(1) insert a comma after *writing*
(2) change *do* to *done*
(3) replace *as well as* with *as well*
(4) change the spelling of *than* to *then*
(5) no correction is necessary

Answers are on pages 12–13.

Part II

TIME: *45 minutes*

Directions: *This is a test to see how well you can write. In this test, you are asked to write an essay in which you present your opinions about an issue. In preparing your essay, you should take the following steps.*

Step 1. Read all of the information about the topic. Be sure that you understand the topic and that you write about only the assigned topic.

Step 2. Plan your essay before you write.

Step 3. Use scrap paper to make any notes.

Step 4. Write your essay on a separate sheet of paper.

Step 5. Read what you have written. Make sure that your writing is legible.

Step 6. Check your paragraphing, sentence structure, spelling, punctuation, capitalization, and usage; make any changes that will improve your essay.

TOPIC

Credit cards are responsible for many changes in the ways many Americans spend their money. Some of these changes have been for the good, while others have caused problems for consumers.

Write an essay, approximately 200 words long, explaining some of the effects of the credit card. You may describe positive effects, negative effects, or both. Be specific, and use examples to support your view.

When you take the GED test, you will have 45 minutes to write about the topic question you are assigned. Try to write the essay for this test within 45 minutes. Write legibly and use a ballpoint pen so that your writing will be easy to read. Any notes that you make on scrap paper will not be counted as part of your score.

After you complete this essay, you can judge its effectiveness by using the Essay Scoring Guide and Model Essays in the answer key to score your essay. They will be concerned with how clearly you make the main point of your essay, how thoroughly you support your ideas, and how clear and correct your writing is throughout the composition. You will receive no credit for writing about a question other than the one assigned.

Answers are on pages 14–19.

ANSWERS AND EXPLANATIONS FOR THE PREDICTOR TEST
Part I

1. (1) *Usage/Subject-Verb Agreement—Noun-Verb Pairs/Sentence Correction.* A plural subject, *People*, requires a plural verb, *spend*.

2. (2) *Mechanics/Contractions/Sentence Correction.* The contraction, *don't*, is the short form for *do not*. The apostrophe replaces the *o* in *not*.

3. (3) *Usage/Subject-Verb Agreement/Sentence Revision.* The plural subject, *Types*, requires a plural verb, *contain* and *can be*, despite the interrupting phrase, *of cough medicine*.

4. (2) *Mechanics/Capitalization/Sentence Correction.* Capitalize all main words in the proper name of an organization such as the Food and Drug Administration.

5. (3) *Sentence Structure/Sentence Fragment/Sentence Revision.* Connecting words, such as *but*, *and*, and *or*, are not used to begin a sentence.

6. (3) *Sentence Structure/Run-On Sentence/Sentence Revision.* Two complete ideas are incorrectly fused into a run-on sentence. The construction in choice (3) eliminates the run-on by making *scientist* the subject of *believes*.

7. (2) *Sentence Structure/Comma Splice/Sentence Correction.* Do not join two complete ideas with a comma.

8. (4) *Mechanics/Punctuation/Sentence Revision.* Separate items in a series with commas.

9. (2) *Sentence Structure/Parallelism/Construction Shift.* *Maybe home remedies, such as tea with lemon and honey, are not only the cheapest but the best.*

10. (2) *Usage/Subject-Verb Agreement—Noun-Verb Pairs/Sentence Correction.* The plural subject, *jobs*, requires a plural verb, *are*.

11. (1) *Sentence Structure/Subordination/Construction Shift.* *Because the birthrate went down in the 1970s, there are fewer teenagers to fill counter positions than in the past.*

12. (2) *Usage/Verb Tense/Sentence Revision.* Look for clues to tense within the sentence. The word *future* indicates the need for future tense, *will find*.

13. (5) *Mechanics/Spelling/Sentence Correction.* *College*, a frequently misspelled word, is correctly spelled. It is easy to confuse the endings *ege*, *age*, *edge*, *idge*.

14. (2) *Sentence Structure/Subordination/Construction Shift.* *As the fast-food business has grown, it has become more complicated to run.*

15. (4) *Usage/Pronoun Reference—Relative Pronoun/Sentence Revision.* The pronoun *which* refers to things; *who* refers to people.

16. (5) *Sentence Structure/Comma Splice/Sentence Correction.* Two complete ideas are incorrectly joined by a

comma. The error is corrected here by using a semicolon to separate the two ideas.

17. (4) *Sentence Structure/Run-On Sentence/Sentence Revision.* Two complete ideas are incorrectly fused into a run-on sentence. The error is corrected by forming two separate sentences.

18. (4) *Sentence Structure/Subordination/Sentence Correction.* When joining ideas of unequal rank in a sentence, use only one subordinator at a time.

19. (3) *Usage/Verb Tense/Sentence Correction.* Make sure the verb tense is consistent with that used throughout the paragraph. Here, present tense is required.

20. (4) *Mechanics/Capitalization/Sentence Correction.* Capitalize all important words in a proper noun, such as the *U.S. Postal Service.*

21. (2) *Mechanics/Spelling/Sentence Correction.* The past tense of pay is spelled *paid.*

22. (5) *Usage/Pronoun Reference—Agreement with Antecedent/Sentence Correction.* A pronoun should agree in number with the noun it replaces. The pronoun *person* requires *he* or *she.*

23. (2) *Sentence Structure/Comma Splice/Sentence Correction.* Two complete subject-verb structures should not simply be joined by commas. Here, each is made into a complete sentence.

24. (4) *Sentence Structure/Coordination—Combining Sentences/Construction Shift.* *Computers make delivery more efficient and can also check postal workers' efficiency.*

25. (2) *Usage/Pronoun Reference—Agreement with Antecedent/Sentence Revision.* A pronoun should agree in number with the word it replaces. Here, *Computers* should be replaced by *They.*

26. (1) *Usage/Verb Tense/Sentence Revision.* Present tense is consistent with that used throughout the paragraph.

27. (5) *Sentence Structure/Modification—Dangling Modifier/Sentence Revision.* Postal workers are not the ones doing more work at less cost. It is because the computers do more work at less cost that the computers are replacing the postal workers.

28. (1) *Mechanics/Punctuation/Sentence Correction.* Use a comma after the subordinate idea when it comes first in the sentence.

Part II

Introduction to Holistic Scoring

The following GED Essay Scoring Guide provides a general description of the characteristics found in GED essays that are scored by the Holistic Method.

GED ESSAY SCORING GUIDE

Papers will show *some or all* of the following characteristics.

Upper-half papers make clear a definite purpose, pursued with varying degrees of effectiveness. They also have a structure that shows evidence of some deliberate planning. The writer's control of English usage ranges from fairly reliable at 4 to confident and accomplished at 6.

6 Papers scored as a 6 tend to offer sophisticated ideas within an organizational framework that is clear and appropriate for the topic. The supporting statements are particularly effective because of their substance, specificity, or illustrative quality. The writing is vivid and precise, though it may contain an occasional flaw.

5 Papers scored as a 5 are clearly organized with effective support for each of the writer's major points. The writing offers substantive ideas, thought the paper may lack the flair or grace of a 6 paper. The surface features are consistently under control, despite an occasional lapse in usage.

4 Papers scored as a 4 show evidence of the writer's organizational plan. Support, though sufficient, tends to be less extensive or convincing than that found in papers scored as a 5 or 6. The writer generally observes the conventions of accepted English usage. Some errors are usually present, but they are not severe enough to interfere significantly with the writer's main purpose.

Lower-half papers either fail to convey a purpose sufficiently or lack one entirely. Consequently, their structure ranges from rudimentary at 3, to random at 2, to absent at 1. Control of the conventions of English usage tends to follow this same gradient.

3 Papers scored as a 3 usually show some evidence of planning or development. However, the organizaton is often limited to a simple listing or haphazard recitation of ideas about the topic, leaving an impression of insufficiency. The 3 papers often demonstrate repeated weaknesses in accepted English usage and are generally ineffective in accomplishing the writer's purpose.

2 Papers scored as a 2 are characterized by a marked lack of development or inadequate support for ideas. The level of thought apparent in the writing is frequently unsophisticated or superficial, often marked by a listing of unsupported generalizations. Instead of suggesting a clear purpose, these papers often present conflicting purposes. Errors in accepted English usage may seriously interfere with the overall effectiveness of these papers.

1 Papers scored as a 1 leave the impression that the writer has not only *not* accomplished a purpose, but has not made any purpose apparent. The dominant feature of these papers is the lack of control. The writer stumbles both in conveying a clear plan for the paper and in expressing ideas according to the conventions of accepted English usage.

0 The zero score is reserved for papers which are blank, illegible, or written on a topic other than the one assigned.

HOW TO SCORE YOUR ESSAY

The following six essays are designed to be used as models for the scoring of your essay. The essays are presented in order from the essay that deserves the lowest score (1) to the essay that deserves the highest score (6).

To score your essay, first compare your essay with the model essay that received a score of 1. If your essay is better than the 1 essay, compare it with the 2 essay and so on until you are able to decide where your essay fits when compared with the six model essays.

As you score your essay, read the character trait analysis that follows each model essay. This analysis can help you to see how you might have improved your essay in order to have received a higher score.

Model Essay—Holistic Score 1

States the point of view

Listing of unsupported opinions, needs better examples that support the writer's point of view

Credit cards is not good for people to use. Being in debt is not good. Credit cards mean debt debt and more debt. That is not a good thing. You use credit cards and you are spending more money than you have. You are buying things you dont really need. You are wasting money. You are not keeping to your budget. Your heading for trouble. Maybe your even fighting more with your wife or your husband. Not having money hurts the family. Credit cards makes it worse. Because you never know how much you really have. And you think you are getting something for nothing. Its not good for people to think that. You appresiate things more when you work hard for them.

Character Trait Analysis

1. The organization is poor. Paragraphing would help this essay. The reader would be able to follow the ideas more clearly—and the writer might have been able to focus on groups of ideas as well.
2. The point of view is awkwardly stated.
3. The essay is primarily a list of unsupported opinions. Each opinion could have been developed with more supporting explanation. For example, instead of just saying, "You use credit cards and you are spending more money than you have," the writer could have given more detail: *Credit cards are very easy to use. This makes it easy to lose track of how much you are spending. Before you know it, you have spent more than you planned to without realizing it. This cannot happen when you are spending out of a checking account, where you must account for every dollar you spend. Therefore, credit cards make it easy to spend amounts you really can't afford.*
4. The essay should be longer to allow more room to develop ideas.
5. The essay ends without a summary or restatement of the writer's point of view.
6. The errors in punctuation, spelling, and accepted English usage interfere with the writer's purpose.

Model Essay—Holistic Score 2

Point of view is stated

Undeveloped examples do not adequately support the writer's point of view.

Restates the point of view

Undeveloped examples do not adequately support the point of view.

Conclusion is weak.

Credit cards can be a good thing. Also a bad thing. Someone might spend more than they have. Easy to do with a credit card. But if you don't have the money, its nice to buy things. Especially if you really need them. Like something for your children. What if a person needed to buy shoes for their daughter and they didn't have any money but they could do it with a credit card. That would be good. But if the bill came and they couldn't pay? That would be bad. Hard to say. Except you can usually pay a little bit at a time. Probably that work out alright.

I think credit cards can be a good thing if you use them right. Like only for things you really need that don't cost too much money. So's you can pay the bill when it come. People could use credit cards for like children's shoes. But not stereos. Because they might not be able to pay. What I think is that people should be careful with their credit cards. Because if they don't, then there are just more problems with money.

Character Trait Analysis

1. The organization is better than the 1 essay.
2. The point of view is stated immediately.

3. The examples do not support the point of view strongly enough, because they are vague and unspecific. The writer has not explained *why* children's shoes would be an acceptable purchase with a credit card, while a stereo would not. The writer has simply mentioned items that might be bought with a credit card.
4 The conclusion is not clear. The writer has not explained what is meant by "being careful" with credit cards, or what type of "problems with money" might arise.
5. If the essay were longer, there would be more opportunity to develop the examples and to give more detail to support the writer's point of view.
6. There are many serious errors in accepted English usage.

Model Essay—Holistic Score 3

States the point of view

Haphazard listing of ideas about the topic

Credit cards have make a big difference in how people spend money. People can buy things without having the money to pay for them right there. This can be a very good thing. But it can also be a very bad thing. It's a good thing if the person is careful about what he spend. Then credit card mean that the person does not have to wait so long to enjoy his money. He can buy something write away, like television set or radio. Or he can buy present for his children. If he need present for birthday or Christmas, he can buy it. That's a good thing. Credit cards give a person more choices about how to spend his money.

Credit cards can be a bad thing if you are not very very careful about using them too often. If you don't stop and think, you start buying more than you really need. It's so easy to use a credit card, you don't stop and ask yourself, Do I need this? You just go ahead and buy. Then afterwards you are sorry, because you have spent too much. But this does not have to happen if a person is careful. If a person is careful, he can use credit cards to buy thing he would buy anyway, but he would not have to wait so long. Credit cards have change how people spend money, for the good and for the bad.

Restates the point of view

Character Trait Analysis

1. The level of organization is similar to that of the 2 essay. Better paragraphing might have helped the writer focus the ideas more sharply. The writer would have been more aware of how different ideas were grouped in the essay. For example, the first paragraph contains not one, but two ideas: that credit cards have affected how people spend money, and that credit cards can be a good thing if they are used the right way. Making two paragraphs out of the opening paragraph would have helped the writer to identify each of these two ideas, so that each could have been developed more fully in its own paragraph.
2. The examples do not adequately explain the writer's point of view. *Or he can buy present for his children* does not explain how credit cards have "made a big difference in how people spend money." It merely gives an example of something a person can use a credit card for. The example should be more closely tied to the main point of view, with a fuller explanation; for example, *Because credit cards allow more flexibility in spending, they can be used to make purchases that have to be made by a certain date, such as a child's birthday or Christmas present.*
3. The essay contains many errors in subject-verb agreement, such as *he spend*. There are other problems with accepted English usage that interfere with the essay's effectiveness.
4. The essay states its point of view very clearly at the beginning, and restates it clearly at the end.

Model Essay—Holistic Score 4

States the point of view and several reasons why the writer holds it

I think credit cards have changed American consumers' buying habits for the better. Basically, they have given us more flexibility, which means more control over our money. I do temporary work and don't always know how much money I am going to make. Having credit cards means I can pay for some things later, when I have the money. That way I can always pay my rent and my bills on time.

Elaborates on the first reason for the point of view with an abstract example

More flexibility means that you can make better plans for how to use your money. If something is on sale, you can buy it and save the money, if you have a credit card. You can take advantage of the opportunity, even if you don't have the money right then.

Elaborates on the second reason for the point of view with specific examples

Doing temporary work means that my income changes from week to week. But my bills don't change from week to week! I always have to pay my rent, my gas, and my electricity. Of course, I can't use my credit card to pay for those. But I can put other kinds of spending on my credit card. That way, if I have the money at the end of the month, I can pay the bill. If not, I still have at least enough to pay rent and utilities.

Suggests and overcomes counter-evidence; Restates point of view; Summarizes reasons

There are some bad points to credit cards. If people are not careful, they wind up spending way too much. But if you make a budget, decide what will go on the credit card, and what will be paid in cash, you have control over your spending. If they are used right, credit cards give American consumers more control and flexibility over spending, which is a good thing.

Character Trait Analysis

1. The level of organization in this essay is very good.
2. The essay addresses the topic immediately and explains the writer's reasons for choosing the point of view. The point of view is very clearly stated.
3. The supporting examples are better than those in the 3 essay. They are more clear and convincing, and they are more closely tied in to the writer's argument. Notice the use of specific examples in the third paragraph of this essay. The writer ties the examples very clearly to the argument. However, the examples are not as convincing as those used in the 5 and 6 essays. Check those essays for the use of specific examples that better illustrate the writer's point of view.
4. The ideas and the vocabulary in this essay are more sophisticated than those in the 1 through the 3 essays, and the grammar generally conforms to accepted English usage. However, this essay lacks the depth of the 5 and the 6 essays.

Model Essay—Holistic Score 5

Introduces subject and states point of view

Credit cards have had a profound impact on the way people spend money. Using credit cards can have both benefits and disadvantages. Ultimately, it is the judgment of the consumer that tips the scale.

States one reason for point of view, giving supporting details

Using a credit card means maximum flexibility in buying necessities and luxury items. For example, if an item is on sale, the consumer can take advantage of the savings by using a credit card. Using credit cards can also mean that a consumer can make purchases that would otherwise be out of reach. Many people would find it extremely difficult to save up the amounts needed to buy a major appliance or a piece of electronic equipment. With a credit card's monthly payment plan, these purchases become possible to far more people than ever before.

States another reason for point of view, giving supporting details

On the other hand, credit card buyers can accumulate large debts in a very short time. With the increasing number of cards being offered now, it is especially easy to overspend. Many people end up buying items they don't really want or need. The high interest payments on many cards can fool people, too. They end up not only overspending, but stuck with big monthly bills.

Summarizes what has been written, restating the point of view.

As you can see, credit cards have revolutionized people's buying habits. Consumers can buy more goods and services more quickly than ever, using credit cards. Unfortunatley, they can also get into debt more deeply and rapidly than they could before the days of credit cards. Only the consumer's good judgment can insure that the positive side of using credit cards outweighs the negative one.

Character Trait Analysis

1. Both the 4 and the 5 essays have a very good level of organization. This essay's style indicates that the writer has had more practice writing this type of essay. See below.
2. This essay is more interesting to read than the 4 because of the writer's greater command of the language and larger vocabulary. The writer is able to give clear and specific examples and explanations for the opinions stated, and the argument is always clear and easy to follow.
3. The essay flows smoothly and has few problems with usage.
4. Although the examples used in this essay are good, they are not as specific and vivid as those in the 6 essay. Therefore, this essay lacks the impact of the 6 essay.

Model Essay—Holistic Score 6

States the point of view and elaborates on the two sides of the argument

Credit cards have brought the American consumer greater freedom than ever before. But they have also brought greater dangers. Because credit cards have enlarged the choices available to us, they demand that we take greater responsibility for our spending.

First reason for the point of view is given with very specific examples, including convincing details closely tied into argument

One way in which credit cards allow us to spend more responsibly is through the greater flexibility that they offer us. A wise consumer can plan to take advantage of seasonal sales, using credit cards to stock up on linens during the January white sales, or to buy a winter coat during the spring end-of-season sales. Considerable savings can result from this type of planning ahead which might not be possible to someone without the option of credit.

Second reason for the point of view is given; Contrasting argument shows author is aware of opposing views; Again, specific, convincing details used to support argument

Yet credit cards also allow us to spend more irresponsibly. When using their credit cards consumers may tend to forget about the monthly interest payments, which are a big addition to the cost of an item. Using a credit card to pay for a restaurant meal for example, might mean that you are spending several additional dollars, just for the "privilege" of not using cash.

Point of view restated clearly and expanded upon

Freedom always brings with it responsibility. Credit cards have brought both to the American consumer. If we learn to use them wisely, we can enjoy the freedom they bring us. If not, we may find ourselves paying even more heavily than before for irresponsible spending.

Character Trait Analysis

1. The essay shows a high level of organizational ability and a solid command of the English language.
2. The writer has a smooth and confident writing style. This comes from practicing the writing process.

3. The examples that support the writer's point of view are very specific and easy to grasp. The writer ties them in very closely with the argument. Because the examples so clearly show why the argument is right, the writer pulls the reader along. Instead of just saying that "credit cards let you take advantage of sales," the writer mentions the January white sales and the spring end-of-season sales, showing the reader clearly how certain purchases have to be made at certain times to take advantage of sales and their savings.
4. This essay is not perfect. There are some awkward phrases and some errors in punctuation. However, these mistakes are not enough to detract from the overall effectiveness of this essay.

PREDICTOR TEST

Performance Analysis Chart

Part I

Directions: Circle the number of each item that you got correct on the Predictor Test. Count how many items you got correct in each row; count how many items you got correct in each column. Write the amount correct per row and column as the numerator in the fraction in the appropriate "Total Correct" box. (The denominators represent the total number of items in the row or column.) Write the grand total correct over the denominator, **28,** at the lower right corner of the chart. (For example, if you got 24 items correct, write *24* so that the fraction reads *24*/**28.**)

Item Type	*Usage (page 25)*	*Sentence Structure (page 55)*	*Mechanics (page 75)*	TOTAL CORRECT
Construction Shift (page 112)		9, 11, 14, 24		**/4**
Sentence Correction (page 111)	1, 10, 19, 22	7, 16, 18, 23	2, 4, 13, 20, 21, 28	**/14**
Sentence Revision (page 112)	3, 12, 15, 25, 26	5, 6, 17, 27	8	**/10**
TOTAL CORRECT	**/9**	**/12**	**/7**	**/28**

The page numbers in parentheses indicate where in this book you can find the beginning of specific instruction about the areas of grammar and about the types of questions you encountered in the Predictor Test.

Part II

Write your essay's score in the box at the right. ☐

What were some of the strong points of your essay?

What were some of the weak points of your essay?

What improvements do you plan to make when you work on your next essay?

Instruction

Introduction

This section of the book contains lessons with exercises, and activities that can help you learn the things you need to know to pass the Writing Skills Test.

The Instruction section is divided into two units. Unit I, *Writing Skills, Part I: Grammar*, will help you to improve your skills at detecting and correcting errors in written English. Unit II, *Writing Skills, Part II: Essay Writing*, can help you to become more comfortable with writing and will show you a process for writing essays.

The units are divided into chapters which are in turn further divided. There are many exercises, activities, and quizzes, so you will have several opportunities to apply and to test your understanding of the material you study. A Progress Chart at the beginning of each unit will make it easy for you to keep track of your work and record your performance on each lesson.

You may work through these instruction units in a number of ways. Two suggestions follow:

(1) Because Units I and II cover different aspects of writing skills, you can work on both units at the same time. By working on both units at once, you can make advances in your understanding of grammar and editing while, at the same time, learning the composition process.

(2) You can complete all of Unit I before proceeding to Unit II. This method will give you the opportunity to refresh and learn the conventions of English before you begin applying them to your writing.

You do not need to decide which method to follow before you start. Try one and then the other—follow the one (or another method you develop) that is most comfortable to you. You may want to discuss which method would be best with your teacher.

UNIT I

Writing Skills, Part I: Grammar

The lessons in this unit cover the conventions of written English and their application in editing. Chapters 1 to 3 are divided into Skills, which are in turn divided into lessons. Each of the Skills is a topic in usage, sentence structure, or mechanics. The lessons within each skill explore various facets of the topic. The fourth chapter is divided into lessons that cover editing and the format of the items on the GED.

It is best to work through this unit in order: begin with the first chapter and continue through to the test that ends the unit.

Each of the Skills in Chapters 1 to 3 begins with a Preview and ends with a Review. Previews and Reviews are made up of items that test how well you can apply your knowledge of the topic covered in the Skill. Previews allow you to test your present ability. If you get 80 percent of the examples in a Preview correct, you may not need to study the lessons in the Skill. To be sure, do the examples in the Review at the end of the Skill. If you get 80 percent correct again, you may feel comfortable in skipping the lessons in that Skill. If you get fewer than 80 percent of the examples in either the Preview or the Review correct, study all the lessons in the Skill.

Chapter 4 is not divided into Skills. The lessons in Chapter 4 will help you apply the knowledge you gain in Chapters 1 to 3 to editing in the format the GED uses.

You may want to work on Unit II at the same time you are working on this unit. Or, you may prefer to complete this unit before you go on to Unit II. Either way, you should start your work in this unit at the beginning of Chapter 1.

UNIT I PROGRESS CHART

Writing Skills, Part I: Grammar

Directions: Use the following chart to keep track of your work. When you complete a lesson and have checked your answers to the items in the exercise, circle the number of questions you answered correctly. When you complete a Skill Preview, Skill Review, or Chapter Quiz, record your score on the appropriate line. The numbers in color represent scores at a level of 80 percent or better.

Lesson	Page		
		CHAPTER 1: **Usage**	
		Skill 1: Subject-Verb Agreement	
	25	Preview	1 2 3 4 5
1	26	The Basics of Subject-Verb Agreement	1 2 3 4 5 6 7 8 9 10
2	30	Interrupting Phrases	1 2 3 4 5
3	32	Inverted Sentence Structure	1 2 3 4 5
4	33	Expletives	1 2 3 4 5
5	34	Compound Subjects	1 2 3 4 5
	35	Skill 1 Review	1 2 3 4 5 6 7 8 9 10
		Skill 2: Verb Tense	
	36	Preview	1 2 3 4 5
1	36	Verb Forms	1 2 3 4 5 6 7 8 9 10
2	42	Word Clues to Tense in Sentences	1 2 3 4 5
3	43	Word Clues to Tense in Paragraphs	1 2 3 4 5
4	44	Using Tense Consistently	1 2 3 4 5
	45	Skill 2 Review	1 2 3 4 5 6 7 8 9 10
		Skill 3: Pronoun Reference	
	46	Preview	1 2 3 4 5
1	46	Pronouns	1 2 3 4 5
2	48	Avoiding Previous Shifts	1 2 3 4 5
3	49	Relative Pronouns	1 2 3 4 5
4	51	Avoiding Vague Pronoun References	1 2 3 4 5
5	52	Avoiding Ambiguous Pronoun References	1 2 3 4 5
	53	Skill 3 Review	1 2 3 4 5 6 7 8 9 10
	54	Chapter 1 Quiz	1 2 3 4 5 6 7 8 9 10 11 12 13 14 15 16 17 18 19 20
		CHAPTER 2: **Sentence Structure**	
		Skill 1: Complete Sentences	
	55	Preview	1 2 3 4 5
1	56	Eliminating Sentence Fragments	1 2 3 4 5
2	57	Eliminating Run-On Sentences	1 2 3 4 5
3	58	Other Ways of Eliminating Run-On Sentences	1 2 3 4 5 6 7 8 9 10
	60	Skill 1 Review	1 2 3 4 5 6 7 8 9 10
		Skill 2: Coordination and Subordination	
	61	Preview	1 2 3 4 5
1	61	Coordination	1 2 3 4 5
2	64	Subordination	1 2 3 4 5
3	66	Combining Sentences	1 2 3 4 5
	67	Skill 2 Review	1 2 3 4 5 6 7 8 9 10
		Skill 3: Clear Sentences	
	68	Preview	1 2 3 4 5
1	68	Clarity of Thought	1 2 3 4 5
2	70	Proper Modification	1 2 3 4 5
3	72	Parallel Structure	1 2 3 4 5
	73	Skill 3 Review	1 2 3 4 5 6 7 8 9 10
	74	Chapter 2 Quiz	1 2 3 4 5 6 7 8 9 10 11 12 13 14 15 16 17 18 19 20
		CHAPTER 3: **Mechanics**	
		Skill 1: Capitalization	
	75	Preview	1 2 3 4 5
1	76	Proper Nouns and Proper Adjectives	1 2 3 4 5
2	79	Titles of People and Addresses	1 2 3 4 5
3	81	Time, Dates, Seasons, Special Events, and Historical Eras	1 2 3 4 5
	82	Skill 1 Review	1 2 3 4 5 6 7 8 9 10
		Skill 2: Punctuation	
	83	Preview	1 2 3 4 5
1	83	Commas Between Items in a Series	1 2 3 4 5
2	85	Commas in Compound Sentences	1 2 3 4 5
3	86	Commas After Introductory Elements	1 2 3 4 5
4	88	Commas with Sentence Interrupters	1 2 3 4 5
5	89	Avoiding Overuse of Commas	1 2 3 4 5
	91	Skill 2 Review	1 2 3 4 5 6 7 8 9 10
		Skill 3: Spelling	
	91	Preview	1 2 3 4 5
1	92	Basic Spelling Rules	1 2 3 4 5
2	93	Possessives	1 2 3 4 5
3	95	Contractions	1 2 3 4 5
4	97	Homonyms	1 2 3 4 5
5	101	Spelling List	1 2 3 4 5 6 7 8 9 10
	108	Skill 3 Review	1 2 3 4 5 6 7 8 9 10
	108	Chapter 3 Quiz	1 2 3 4 5 6 7 8 9 10 11 12 13 14 15 16 17 18 19 20
		CHAPTER 4: **Editing Paragraphs**	
1	110	The Three Types of Questions on the GED	1 2 3 4 5 6
2	114	The Editing Process	1 2 3 4 5
3	118	Editing for Correct Usage	1 2 3 4 5
4	120	Editing for Correct Sentence Structure	1 2 3 4 5
5	123	Editing for Mechanical Correctness	1 2 3 4 5
6	125	Editing Paragraphs	1 2 3 4 5 6 7 8 9 10
	130	Chapter 4 Quiz	1 2 3 4 5 6 7 8 9 10 11 12 13 14 15 16 17 18 19 20

Chapter

1 Usage

Objective

In this chapter, you will learn to

- Recognize the singular and plural forms of subjects and verbs
- Make subjects and verbs of sentences agree
- Use the correct tenses of verbs
- Check sentences and paragraphs for consistent use of verb tenses
- Use pronouns that agree with the words to which they refer
- Select pronouns that express ideas clearly

Skill 1 Subject–Verb Agreement

Preview

Directions: Edit the following sentences to correct all errors in subject–verb agreement.

1. **Neither Denmark nor Norway have a shoreline on the Mediterranean Sea.**
2. **There is two national anthems played at every All-Star baseball game.**
3. **Into the nearby tunnel rush the frightened prairie dog.**
4. **An American man spend about four hours a year tying his necktie.**
5. **The most popular street name in the United States are Park Street.**

Check your answers. Correct answers are on page 244. If you have at least four answers correct, do the Skill 1 Review on page 35. If you have fewer than four answers correct, study Skill 1 beginning with Lesson 1.

Lesson 1 The Basics of Subject–Verb Agreement

The basic rule for subject–verb agreement is:

A singular subject must use a singular verb.

I *admire* the paintings of Van Gogh.

A plural subject must use a plural verb.

His paintings *include* landscapes, still lifes, and portraits.

You must be able to recognize the singular (one) and plural (more than one) forms of subjects and verbs to determine if a subject agrees with its verb.

Subject

The subject of a sentence tells what the sentence is about. The subject is always a noun or a pronoun. In most cases, a singular noun can be changed to its plural form by adding *-s* or *-es*.

Singular	*Plural*
clock	clocks
tax	taxes
invention	inventions
brush	brushes
menu	menus
lens	lenses

Some nouns, however, have irregular plural forms: the spelling of the noun changes when the noun is made plural.

Singular	*Plural*
woman	women
child	children
leaf	leaves
foot	feet
mouse	mice
goose	geese

If you are unsure of the plural form of a noun, you can use a dictionary to check the spelling.

Verb

The verb shows what the subject is doing, what is happening to the subject, or what the subject is like.

The verb must be singular if the subject of a sentence is *he, she, it,* or a singular noun. The verb must be plural if the subject is *we, you, they,* or a plural noun.

Singular		**Plural**	
Subject	*Verb*	*Subject*	*Verb*
he	runs	we	run
it	has	you	have
city	changes	cities	change
student	answers	students	answer
car	rushes	cars	rush

The pronoun *you* always uses a plural verb.

You look like your older brother.

You are the only customer in the store.

The pronoun *I* usually uses a plural verb.

I agree with the rest of the committee.

I have a meeting this morning.

Although most singular verbs (verbs used with singular subjects: *the athlete swims*) end in *s* or *es*, many verbs have irregular forms. The following sentences illustrate subject–verb agreement for the verb *be*.

I am glad to meet you.

He is a computer programmer.

She is the new supervisor.

It is the largest house.

We are on the same team.

You are the new captain.

They are from the same town.

The sentences below show how the form of the verb changes if the subject changes.

SINGULAR SUBJECT/SINGULAR VERB: The river begins as a small stream.

PLURAL SUBJECT/PLURAL VERB: Many rivers begin as small streams.

Sometimes singular subjects may appear to be plural. Other words may look plural even though they are singular. Follow these rules for subject–verb agreement.

Rule 1: The following *indefinite pronouns* are singular and take a singular verb.

anyone	**everyone**	**someone**	**either**	**one**
anybody	**everybody**	**somebody**	**neither**	**no one**
anything	**everything**	**something**	**another**	**each**

Everyone is anxious to meet the new boss.

Anybody is eligible to apply for the loan.

Rule 2: The following pronouns are plural and take a plural verb.

both **few** **many** **several**

Several were encouraged to continue the discussion.

Many were asked to join the new club.

Rule 3: The following pronouns may be either singular or plural, depending on how they are used in a sentence.

some **most** **part** **any** **all** **none**

Some of the money was spent already.

Some of the windows have screens.

In the first sentence, *some* is singular and takes a singular verb. In the second, *some* refers to more than one thing. It takes a plural verb.

Rule 4: The following nouns can be either singular or plural. When they refer to a group of people or things as one unit, they take a singular verb. When they refer to the individuals within a group, they take a plural verb.

audience	**family**	**orchestra**	**band**
class	**group**	**crowd**	**jury**
			team

The jury was reentering the courtroom. (*acting as one unit*)

The jury were discussing their opinions of the trial. (*acting as individuals within a group*)

Rule 5: The following nouns are singular, although they appear to be plural. As the subject of a sentence, they take a singular verb.

civics	**athletics**	**genetics**	**news**
mumps	**physics**	**politics**	**series**
measles	**United States**	**economics**	**mathematics**

Mathematics has been an important field of study since ancient times.

Mumps is a disease of the salivary glands.

Rule 6: The following nouns do not have singular forms. They are plural in meaning and always take a plural verb.

trousers	**pants**	**jeans**
shears	**scissors**	**pliers**

The pliers are in the toolbox.

My pants are ripped.

NOTE: If the word *pair* precedes the noun, use the singular verb.

The trousers are too long.

The pair of trousers is too long.

When you edit sentences for subject–verb agreement, use this five-step test. After reading a sentence

1. Find the subject by asking whom or what the sentence is about.
2. Determine whether the subject is singular or plural.
3. Locate the verb.
4. Determine whether the verb is singular or plural.
5. If the subject and the verb are both singular or both plural, they agree. If they do not agree, change the verb to agree with the subject.

Use the five-step method to determine the agreement of this sentence.

Microwave ovens cooks with radiation.

Step 1. By asking what the sentence is about, you determine that the subject of the sentence is *ovens*.
Step 2. *Ovens*, which ends in *s*, is plural.
Step 3. *Cooks* is the verb of the sentence.
Step 4. Because *cooks* ends in *s*, it is singular.
Step 5. The plural subject and singular verb do not agree. The verb should be changed so that it agrees with the subject.

Microwave ovens cook with radiation.

Lesson 1 Exercise

Directions: Use the five-step method to determine the agreement of the following sentences. Edit the sentences to correct all errors in subject–verb agreement. Not all of the sentences have errors.

1. The team have lost the last four games.
2. German measles frequently begins with swollen glands.
3. The pair of jeans were in the dryer.
4. No one remembers the original name of the street.
5. Tea leaves needs to be stored in a tight container.
6. A correctly written résumé list your most recent job first.
7. Many experts in the field disagrees with that answer.
8. Both shows the same talent in music.
9. Some of the senators was touring the flood-damaged area.
10. They realizes the importance of a healthy diet.

Answers are on page 244.

Lesson 2 Interrupting Phrases

The verbs in the sentences below do not agree with their subjects. The edited versions, with the changes shown in handwriting, are correct.

Modern pewter, an alloy of tin, antimony and copper, ~~resist~~ resists tarnishing.

The president, accompanied by several staff members, ~~attend~~ attends many public ceremonies.

The subjects and verbs of these sentences are separated by groups of words that give more information about the subject. These groups of words, called phrases, have no subject or verb. Because they break the normal sentence pattern of a subject followed by a verb, they are called *interrupting phrases*.

Notice that in these two sentences, the subjects—*pewter* and *president*—are singular. The corrected verb form in each sentence is also singular. An interrupting phrase that separates the subject and the verb of a sentence does not change the number of the subject.

In the two examples above, the interrupting phrases are set off by commas from the rest of the sentence. Many interrupting phrases are not set off by commas, however.

The increase in costs makes it difficult to keep prices down.

The debate between the candidates reflects sharp differences in opinion.

Words that immediately follow the subject, whether or not they are set off by commas, do not change the number of the subject. The subjects of both of the sentences above are singular. Notice that the verb in each agrees in number with the subject.

Before you use the five-step method given in Lesson 1 for determining subject–verb agreement, cross out all the interrupting phrases in a sentence.

One ~~of the most common eye problems~~ are

nearsightedness.

When the interrupting phrase is crossed out, it is easier to locate the subject and the verb. The subject of the sentence is *one*. The verb, therefore, must be changed to *is* to agree in number with the subject.

Lesson 2 Exercise

Directions: Edit the following sentences to correct all errors in subject–verb agreement. First cross out the interrupting phrases. Then use the five-step agreement test described in Lesson 1. Not all of the sentences have errors.

1. Broiling, as well as poaching, is a healthy alternative to frying foods.
2. Requirements for a driver's license varies from state to state.
3. Successful dieting, according to nutritionists, demand patience and determination.
4. One of the best salt subsitutes are lemon juice.
5. Foods with a high moisture content, such as lettuce, does not freeze well.

Answers are on page 244.

Lesson 3 Inverted Sentence Structure

In most sentences, the subject comes before the verb. In some sentences, however, the subject comes after the verb. Such sentences have *inverted sentence structure.*

A sentence with inverted sentence structure may begin with a prepositional phrase. The sentence below, which has inverted structure and begins with a prepositional phrase, is incorrect as written. The edited version, with the change shown in handwriting, is correct.

`In tropical seas ~~live~~ lives a variety of native animals.`

To find the subject of an inverted sentence that begins with a prepositional phrase, cross out the prepositional phrase first. That will make it easier to identify whom or what the sentence is about. In the sentence above, the subject is *variety*—a singular noun that therefore requires a singular verb.

Sentences that ask questions often have inverted structure. The edited version of the question below shows correct subject-verb agreement.

`~~Are~~ Is the delivery date of the computers acceptable?`

If a question has inverted sentence structure, change the question into a statement. Rephrased as a statement, the edited question above reads:

The delivery date of the computers is acceptable.

Then cross out any phrases that separate the subject from the verb.

`The delivery date ~~of the computers~~ is acceptable.`

Note that the verb, *is,* agrees with the subject, *date.*

Lesson 3 Exercise

Directions: Edit the following sentences to correct all errors in subject–verb agreement. Where necessary, put sentences in subject–verb order and cross out interrupting phrases. Not all of the sentences have errors.

1. At the bottom of the contract were the space for their signatures.
2. During the winter most heating bills increase dramatically.
3. Does eggs boiled with vinegar resist cracking?
4. In the shuttle sits the astronauts.
5. Is the sun's rays as hot in the afternoon as in the morning?

Answers are on page 244.

Lesson 4 Expletives

Read the following sentences. Notice how the sentences have been edited to correct errors in subject–verb agreement.

`There ~~is~~ are desert regions in the northern and western parts of China.`

`There ~~are~~ is a national marble tournament held each year in the United States.`

`Here ~~are~~ is the set of blueprints for the new office building.`

Each of these sentences begins with the word *here* or *there*. These words are called *expletives* when they begin a sentence such as the ones above. Because expletives come directly before the verb, they may appear to be the subjects of the sentences. An expletive, however, is never the subject of a sentence.

The subject of the first sentence above is *regions*. Because *regions* is a plural noun, a plural verb, *are*, is required. The subject of the second sentence, *tournament*, needs the singular verb *is*. In the third sentence, the subject is *set*, a singular noun that therefore requires a singular verb, *is*.

To determine subject–verb agreement in a sentence that begins with an expletive, use the five-step agreement test given in Lesson 1. Then, after you cross out any interrupting phrases, cross out the expletive.

Lesson 4 Exercise

Directions: Edit the following sentences to correct all errors in subject–verb agreement. Cross out interrupting phrases and expletives, where necessary. Not all of the sentences have errors.

1. There are at least 300 people in the audience.
2. Here are the map of the Hawaiian Islands.
3. There is many ancient myths that explain forces in nature.
4. Here come the winner of the Boston Marathon.
5. There is 11 players on each team in field hockey.

Answers are on page 244.

Lesson 5 Compound Subjects

Read the sentences below. Notice how they have been edited to correct subject–verb agreement.

Swimming and jogging ~~is~~ are forms of aerobic exercise.

Neither Bolivia nor Paraguay ~~are~~ is north of the equator.

Either direct pressure or cold compresses ~~is~~ are used to stop a nosebleed.

Many sentences have more than one subject. In such cases, the sentence has a *compound subject*. The separate subjects in a compound subject may be connected by single connective words, such as *and, or,* or *nor*, or by paired connective words, such as *either . . . or, neither . . . nor, both . . . and*, or *not only . . . but also*.

When paired connective words are used in a compound subject, these rules must be followed to determine whether the verb used should be singular or plural.

Rule 1: When two subjects are joined by *or, nor, neither . . . nor, either . . . or*, or *not only . . . but also*, the verb agrees in number with the subject that is closer to the verb.

Neither the coach nor the players have discussed the next game.

BUT

Neither the players nor the coach has discussed the next game.

The two subjects in both of these sentences are *coach* and *players*. In the first sentence, the subject, *players*, is closest to the verb. Because *players* is plural, the verb used, *have*, is also plural. In the second sentence, the singular *coach* is closer to the verb, requiring the use of the singular verb, *has*.

Rule 2: When two subjects are joined by *and* or *both . . . and*, they usually take plural verbs. It does not matter if one subject is plural and one is singular. The connective *and* combines them to make a plural subject.

Both the teacher and the students were ready for summer vacation.

Both the students and the teacher were ready for summer vacation.

NOTE: If the words of a compound subject refer to the same person, place, or thing, the verb is singular.

My accountant and business partner is a cautious investor.

Lesson 5 Exercise

Directions: Edit the following sentences to correct all errors in subject–verb agreement. Not all of the sentences have errors.

1. Not only carbon but also diamonds are used in industry.
2. Either gravel or crushed rock combine with cement to form concrete.
3. The Rocky Mountains and the Andes is part of the same mountain chain.
4. Both a blanket and warm clothing is recommended when traveling in the winter.
5. Neither creams nor lotions is effective in the prevention of wrinkles.

Answers are on page 244.

Skill 1 Review

Directions: Edit the following sentences to correct all errors in subject–verb agreement. Not all of the sentences have errors.

1. Everyone need a passport to travel in a foreign country.
2. Neither an ostrich nor a penguin are able to fly.
3. There is more than 800,000 kinds of insects.
4. One of the most common diseases in the world are malaria.
5. Both Robert De Niro and Dustin Hoffman has won Academy Awards.
6. Are a group of lions called a *herd* or a *pride*?
7. On the Bonneville Salt Flats in Utah are an automobile racecourse.
8. The whale shark, the largest fish in the world, weigh twice as much as an elephant.
9. You seem interested in many different kinds of music.
10. In cold climates, a caterpillar take two or three years to reach the butterfly stage.

Check your answers. Correct answers are on pages 244–245. If you have at least eight answers correct, go on to Skill 2. If you have fewer than eight answers correct, study Skill 1 beginning with Lesson 1.

Skill 2 Verb Tense

Preview

Directions: Edit the following sentences to correct all errors in verb tense. Not all of the sentences have errors.

1. **The Julian calendar is developed in 46 B.C. by Julius Caesar.**
2. **The diameter of the moon is about 2,160 miles, and its surface area was 14,650,000 square miles.**
3. **Richard Byrd spent many years exploring Antarctica.**
4. **Beethoven had wrote nine symphonies before his death in 1827.**
5. **Tomorrow we learn about Sir John A. Macdonald, the first prime minister of Canada.**

Check your answers. Correct answers are on page 245. If you have at least four answers correct, do the Skill 2 Review on page 45. If you have fewer than four answers correct, study Skill 2 beginning with Lesson 1.

Lesson 1 Verb Forms

Every complete sentence has a verb. A verb expresses an action or a state of being. The verbs in the following sentences are underlined.

> The bicycle rider <u>travels</u> at an average speed of ten miles per hour.
>
> Some jobs in industry <u>will become</u> obsolete in the future.
>
> Millions of years ago, glaciers <u>covered</u> parts of North America.
>
> A land bridge <u>had connected</u> Asia and North America.

Some verbs, as in the first and third sentences above, consist of only one word. Many verb forms contain more than one word, as in the second and fourth sentences above. When two or more words act as a single verb, those words are called a *verb phrase*.

Verb phrases consist of one or more *helping verbs* followed by a main verb. In the second example sentence above, *will* is the helping verb. *Become* is the main verb. In the fourth example sentence, the helping verb, *had*, is followed by the main verb, *connected*.

Many helping verbs are forms of the verb *to be* (*am, are, was, were,* for example). Forms of the verb *to do* (*do, does, did*) and *to have* (*have, has, had*) are also common helping verbs. Other helping verbs include

can	will	shall	may	must
could	would	should	might	

Words such as *not, never, usually, always,* and so forth may interrupt a verb phrase. Remember that these words are not considered to be part of the verb phrase.

You should never look directly at the sun.

The effect of the sun can be deceptive.

Categories of Verbs

You need to be able to identify the verb in a sentence to determine if it has been used correctly. The two categories of verbs are *action verbs* and *linking verbs.*

An action verb shows either physical or mental action.

Ancient Egyptians developed a complex system of irrigation.

Some scientists think the universe may someday shrink.

A linking verb connects the subject of a sentence with a word or a phrase that renames or describes the subject.

The capital of Norway is Oslo.

The pioneers were adventurous and brave.

Forms of the verb *to be* are often used as linking verbs, as in the sentences above. Other verbs that can be used as linking verbs include

appear	feel	remain	smell	stay
become	look	seem	sound	taste

Verb Tense

What do you notice about each of the verbs in the following sentences?

The pilot looks at the instrument panel.

The pilot looked at the instrument panel.

The pilot will look at the instrument panel.

The *form* of the verb used in each sentence—*look*—changed to express a different meaning. These various forms are called *tenses.* The tense of a verb shows the time of the action described. In the first sentence, the action takes place in the present; in the second sentence, the action took place in the past; in the third sentence, the action will take place in the future.

A verb in the present tense can also express something that is generally true or a current state of affairs.

GENERAL TRUTH: Tornadoes move quickly.

CURRENT STATE: The city lacks adequate transportation services.

Chart 1 explains the uses and forms of the three basic tenses.

Chart 1 The Three Basic Tenses

Tense	Meaning	Form	Examples
Present	Something is happening now, or is true now, or is generally true.	Adds *-s* or *-es* when used with singular nouns or with *he, she,* or *it.*	The plane descends. It lands.
		No ending when used with plural nouns or with *I, you, we, they.*	The planes descend. They land.
Past	Something happened in the past.	Adds *-d* or *-ed* to present tense.	The plane descends./ The plane descended. We arrive./ We arrived.
Future	Something will happen.	Adds a helping verb, *will* or *shall,* to the present tense.	The passengers will arrive. I shall arrive.

Principal Parts of Regular Verbs

Every verb has three principal parts—the *present,* the *past,* and the *past participle.* The principal parts are used to form the different tenses of verbs.

Present	*Past*	*Past Participle*
need	needed	needed
agree	agreed	agreed
join	joined	joined
vanish	vanished	vanished
desire	desired	desired

In the examples above, both the past and the past participle forms are the same. These verbs are called *regular verbs*. The past and past participle forms of regular verbs are formed by adding *-d* or *-ed* to the present tense form.

If the helping verb *have* is used in a verb phrase, the main verb is always a past participle form.

The committee members have agreed to postpone the meeting.

Some species of animals have vanished entirely.

The weather has changed suddenly.

Principal Parts of Irregular Verbs

Verbs known as *irregular verbs* use endings other than *-d* or *-ed* to form the past and the past participle. Compare the present and past participle forms of the verbs in the pairs of sentences below.

The wind shakes the leaves of the tree.

The wind shook the leaves of the tree.

The noise grows louder.

The noise grew louder.

Chart 2 is a list of commonly used verbs that have irregular past and past participle forms.

Chart 2 Irregular Verbs

Present (*Now I . . .*)	Past (*Yesterday I . . .*)	Past Participle (*Often, I have . . .*) (*Often, I had . . .*) (*Often, he/she has . . .*)
am, is, are	was, were	been
become	became	become
begin	began	begun
bite	bit	bitten
blow	blew	blown
break	broke	broken
bring	brought	brought
built	built	built
burst	burst	burst
buy	bought	bought
choose	chose	chosen
come	came	come

Chart 2 Irregular Verbs

Present *(Now I . . .)*	Past *(Yesterday I . . .)*	Past Participle *(Often, I have . . .)* *(Often, I had . . .)* *(Often, he/she has . . .)*
dive	dived *or* dove	dived
do	did	done
draw	drew	drawn
drink	drank	drunk
drive	drove	driven
eat	ate	eaten
fall	fell	fallen
fly	flew	flown
forget	forgot	forgotten
freeze	froze	frozen
get	got	got *or* gotten
give	gave	given
go	went	gone
grow	grew	grown
hide	hid	hidden
know	knew	known
lay (put)	laid	laid
leave	left	left
lie (recline)	lay	lain
raise (lift)	raised	raised
ride	rode	ridden
ring	rang	rung
rise (go up)	rose	risen
run	ran	run
say	said	said
see	saw	seen
set (put)	set	set
shake	shook	shaken
shrink	shrank *or* shrunk	shrunk *or* shrunken
sing	sang	sung
sink	sank *or* sunk	sunk
sit	sat	sat
speak	spoke	spoken
spend	spent	spent
spring	sprang *or* sprung	sprung
stand	stood	stood
steal	stole	stolen
swim	swam	swum
take	took	taken
teach	taught	taught
tear	tore	torn
throw	threw	thrown
wake	woke *or* waked	waked *or* woken
wear	wore	worn
write	wrote	written

Lesson 1 Exercise

Directions: Complete the following sentences by adding the verb in the tense indicated in parentheses.

1. The Supreme Court ____________ each term on the first Monday in October. (**begin,** *present tense*)
2. Chester Gould ____________ the popular cartoon "Dick Tracy" for many years. (**draw,** *past tense*)
3. The Nile catfish ____________ upside down. (**swim,** *present tense*)
4. Most tornadoes ____________ in the central section of the country. (**occur,** *past tense*)
5. Germany ____________ its treaty with the Soviet Union in 1941. (**break,** *past tense*)

Complete the following sentences by adding the past participle of the verb given in parentheses.

6. Birds have ____________ their nests with many different materials. (**build**)
7. Scientists have ____________ experiments to determine the mineral composition of the moon. (**do**)
8. The president of the company had ____________ that the hiring freeze was temporary. (**say**)
9. Native Americans had ____________ the colonists how to grow corn. (**teach**)
10. Many people have ____________ to their representatives about the proposed law. (**write**)

Answers are on page 245.

Lesson 2 Word Clues to Tense in Sentences

Many sentences contain words that answer the question *When?* These words tell when something is occurring, has occurred, or will occur. Here are some examples of words that indicate the time of an event.

Present	*Past*	*Future*
today	yesterday	tomorrow
now	recently	later
at the moment	last Friday	next month

You can use these kinds of words as clues to help you determine if the tense of a verb is correct. For example, read the following sentence.

Currently, there were more cars in Los Angeles than people.

Currently tells you that the action is taking place now. However, *were* is in the past tense. To correctly edit the sentence, change the tense of the verb to match the clue word or words given in the sentence.

Currently, there <u>are</u> more cars in Los Angeles than people.

Also look for words that give you time references.

The world population in the year 6000 B.C. was approximately 5 million people.

The words "in the year 6000 B.C." tell you that the action is in the past. Therefore, the past tense verb *was* is correct.

Occasionally, a word that usually indicates the present may be used in a sentence that concerns an event in the future.

Today, he will buy his first car.

Today in this sentence means "later today." Therefore, the use of the future tense verb is correct.

Lesson 2 Exercise

Directions: Edit these sentences to correct all errors in verb tense. Not all of the sentences have errors.

1. The first depression in the United States happens at the end of the Revolutionary War.
2. Right now, we imported more goods than we exported.

3. During the next decade, new kinds of heart surgery are developed.
4. Recently historians learned that the Egyptians invented the sailboat.
5. The last survivor of the *Mayflower* is John Alden.

Answers are on page 245.

Lesson 3 Word Clues to Tense in Paragraphs

When you take the GED Test, you will be asked to read paragraphs. In order to complete some of the questions at the end of each paragraph, you will need to determine whether the action of the paragraph is in the present, the past, or the future. Then you will be able to determine if a particular sentence is written in the correct tense.

Tenses should be used consistently throughout a paragraph. Read the paragraph below and notice the verb tenses used.

> (1) Lizards are reptiles that range in size from a few inches to ten feet long. (2) Because lizards are cold blooded, most of them live in the tropics and other areas with warm climates. (3) When the temperature became too warm, they moved to the shade or buried themselves under the sand. (4) Lizards defend themselves in a variety of interesting ways. (5) The Australian frilled lizard frightened its enemies by unfolding the large frill that encircled its head.

This paragraph provides a general description of lizards and therefore should be written in the present tense. The first two sentences are written in the present tense, but the third sentence describes the behavior of lizards in the past tense. The fifth sentence also incorrectly shifts to the past tense to describe the behavior of the Australian frilled lizard. It is difficult to follow the meaning of a paragraph when tenses are not used consistently.

Here is the correctly edited paragraph. Notice that the present tense is consistently used.

> (1) Lizards are reptiles that range in size from a few inches to ten feet long. (2) Because lizards are cold blooded, most of them live in the tropics and other areas with warm climates. (3) When the temperature becomes too warm, they move to the shade or bury themselves under the sand. (4) Lizards defend themselves in a variety of interesting ways. (5) The Australian frilled lizard frightens its enemies by unfolding the large frill that encircles its head.

Lesson 3 Exercise

Directions: The following paragraph uses verb tenses inconsistently. Rewrite the paragraph in the *proper tense*. Not all of the sentences will have to be changed.

Joseph Priestley, an eighteenth-century chemist, made several discoveries through his mistakes. For example, he invents seltzer quite by accident. While performing an experiment, he added gas to water. Priestley was amazed at the new taste that results from the combination. As he studied a certain type of tree sap, some of the substance dropped onto a piece of paper. He notices the sap makes pencil marks disappear from the paper. This leads to the development of what we now call the *eraser*.

Answers are on page 245.

Lesson 4 Using Tenses Consistently

Some sentences have more than one verb. Read the following sentences. Which one uses verb tenses consistently?

1. Many people are not athletic, but they enjoyed watching sports events.
2. Thousands of visitors go to national parks each year and will enjoy hiking and camping.
3. People looked for shelter as the lightning storm began.

The verb in the first part of sentence 1—*are*—is a clue that can help you determine if the verb in the second part of the sentence is in the correct tense. *Are* is a present tense verb, but the verb in the second part of the sentence—*enjoyed*—is a past tense verb. Verb tenses, therefore, have not been used consistently in sentence 1. Sentence 2 is also incorrect because the action shifts from the present (*go*) to the future (*will enjoy*). Sentence 3 describes a sequence of events that took place in the past. Both verbs—*looked* and *began*—are past tense verbs. Sentence 3, therefore, is correct.

Lesson 4 Exercise

Directions: Edit the following sentences for correct sequence of tenses. Underline the correct verb form from the pair given in parentheses.

1. The light from a laser is very powerful and (**travels, traveled**) in one direction.

2. The deepest lake in the world is Lake Baikal in Siberia, as it (**measures, measured**) almost a mile deep in some places.
3. A gorilla sleeps about 14 hours a day, whereas an elephant (**sleeps, slept**) about 2 hours.
4. Earth is closer to the sun in December than it (**is, was**) in July.
5. The person who said "If you can't stand the heat, get out of the kitchen" (**is, was**) Harry Truman.

Answers are on page 245.

Skill 2 Review

Directions: Edit the following sentences to correct all errors in verb usage. Not all of the sentences have errors.

1. The Puritans think soap and water were bad for one's health.
2. The first American to fly in space was Alan Shepard, and he flies for a total of 15 minutes.
3. In 1804, Lewis and Clark begin their expedition to the Northwest.
4. Yesterday the president will discuss the new tax bill with several of his advisors.
5. Charles F. Carlson invented the photocopy machine, although he had difficulty finding financial support.
6. So far, how many people have successfully swimmed across the English Channel?
7. The words "Mankind must put an end to war or war will put an end to mankind" were speaked by John Kennedy.
8. *Lochner v. New York* was a Supreme Court case that gives employees and employers the right to decide hours and wages without government interference.
9. In 1930, Sinclair Lewis became the first American author who wins the Nobel prize for literature.
10. Many people believed food production will be unable to keep up with population growth.

Check your answers. Correct answers are on pages 245–246. If you have at least eight answers correct, go on to Skill 3. If you have fewer than eight answers correct, study Skill 2 beginning with Lesson 1.

Skill 3 Pronoun Reference

Preview

Directions: Edit the following sentences to correct all errors in pronoun reference. Not all of the sentences have errors.

1. **The cornea is the only part of the human body who has no blood supply.**
2. **Either pepper or salt can improve the taste of food when it is used in moderation.**
3. **We benefit from studying history because it helps you learn from past mistakes.**
4. **An angler fish can swallow food twice their own size.**
5. **After a new traffic light was installed at the intersection, it was safer.**

Check your answers. Correct answers are on page 246. If you have at least four answers correct, do the Skill 3 Review on page 53. If you have fewer than four answers correct, study Skill 3 beginning with Lesson 1.

Lesson 1 Pronouns Agreement with Antecedent

Nouns name people, places, or things. Pronouns are words that refer to nouns or to other pronouns in sentences. Read the following two sentences. Which one sounds better?

> When Captain William Driver raised the American flag over Captain William Driver's ship in 1831, Captain William Driver exclaimed, "I name thee 'Old Glory'!"
>
> When Captain William Driver raised the American flag over his ship in 1831, he exclaimed, "I name thee 'Old Glory'!"

The first sentence sounds awkward because the noun *Captain William Driver* is repeated so often. The second sentence has exactly the same meaning as the first, but it uses pronouns to eliminate repetition of the noun.

A pronoun, then, is a word that can be used in place of a noun. Chart 3 lists singular and plural pronouns that you will need to know for the GED Test.

Chart 3 Singular and Plural Pronouns

	Singular	Plural
Personal pronouns	I, you, he, she, it, me, him, her	we, you, they, us, them
Reflexive pronouns	myself, yourself, himself, herself, itself	ourselves, yourselves, themselves
Possessive pronouns	my, mine, your, yours, his, her, its	our, ours, your, yours, their, theirs
Demonstrative pronouns	this, that	these, those
Indefinite pronouns	anyone, anybody, everybody, no one, nobody, each, one, someone, somebody, either, neither, a person	others, few, both, several, many

Read the sentence below. To what does the word *their* refer?

The Stamp Act was repealed after nine colonies expressed their opposition to taxation without representation.

In this sentence the word *their* refers to the noun *colonies*. The word that a pronoun replaces or refers to is called its *antecedent*. A pronoun must agree with its antecedent in number.

Rule 1: A singular antecedent requires a singular pronoun.

Eleanor Roosevelt wrote a newspaper column during her husband's presidency.

Rule 2: A plural antecedent requires a plural pronoun.

Both Virginia and Maryland gave up some of their land to form the capital of the United States, Washington, D.C.

Rule 3: When a pronoun is separated from its antecedent by a phrase, the pronoun agrees with the antecedent.

The Declaration of Independence, one of the most famous documents in American history, was signed in 1776.

Rule 4: A singular pronoun is used to refer to two or more singular antecedents that are joined by *or*.

A food store or a clothing store can please its customers by providing efficient service.

Rule 5: A plural pronoun is used to refer to two or more antecedents that are joined by *and*.

Frank and Marjorie saved most of their money to buy a new car.

Rule 6: When two antecedents are joined by *neither . . . nor* or *either . . . or*, the pronoun agrees with the closer antecedent.

Neither Truman nor Cleveland attended college before he became president.

Neither Truman nor several other presidents attended college before they became president.

Lesson 1 Exercise

Directions: Edit the following sentences to correct all errors in pronoun–antecedent agreement. Not all of the sentences have errors.

1. Many individuals had to learn their lessons the hard way.
2. A new cosmetic or a drug must be tested before they can be sold to the public.
3. People with a good sense of humor should be able to laugh at himself.
4. Neither the salespeople nor the manager knew he would be laid off.
5. The kangaroo and the opossum carry its young in a pouch.

Answers are on page 246.

Lesson 2 Avoiding Pronoun Shifts

Pronouns must agree in number with their antecedents. They also must agree in person. *Person* refers to the difference between the *person speaking* (first person), the *person spoken to* (second person), and the *person or thing being spoken about* (third person).

If we do not limit salt intake in the diet, your chance of getting heart disease increases.

This sentence is confusing because it shifts from the first person (*we*) to the second person (*you*). There are two ways this sentence could be correctly edited.

If we do not limit salt intake in the diet, our chance of getting heart disease increases.

OR

If you do not limit salt intake in the diet, your chance of getting heart disease increases.

Avoid confusing shifts in person by deciding which person is appropriate to the meaning of the sentence and then using that person consistently throughout the sentence.

The three types of personal pronouns are in Chart 4.

Chart 4 **Personal Pronouns**	
First-person pronouns	I, me, my, mine, we, us, our, ours
Second-person pronouns	you, your, yours
Third-person pronouns	he, him, his, she, her, hers, it, its, they, them, theirs

Lesson 2 Exercise

Directions: Edit the following sentences to correct all errors in pronoun shift. Not all of the sentences have errors.

1. I exercise daily because physical exercise helps you maintain good health.
2. Whenever you buy merchandise, you should find out the return policy of the store.
3. When we are nervous, your pulse may quicken.
4. It is important for us to understand the new tax law before filing your tax returns.
5. People are more likely to be injured at home than if he is riding in a car.

Answers are on page 246.

Lesson 3 Relative Pronouns

Find the pronoun in the following sentence.

> The Leaning Tower of Pisa, which leans 17 feet to the right, has a foundation only 10 feet deep.

If you chose *which*, you were correct. The word *which* is used as a relative pronoun. A *relative pronoun* introduces a group of words that modify a noun or a pronoun. In the example above, *which leans 17 feet to the right* modifies or refers to *Leaning Tower of Pisa*. *Leaning Tower of Pisa* is the antecedent of the relative pronoun *which*.

The following words are used as relative pronouns.

which that who whom

A common error in the use of pronouns is choosing an incorrect relative pronoun. To choose the correct relative pronoun, remember the following.

***Who* and *whom* refer to people or animals.**

***Which* refers to animals, places, or things.**

***That* refers to people, animals, places, or things.**

Blackbird, who was a chief of the Omaha Indian tribe, was buried sitting on his horse.

A dog that is trained to guide the blind cannot tell the difference between a red and a green light.

Himalayan cats, which are a cross between Siamese and Persian cats, are a rare breed.

To choose correctly between *who* and *whom*, substitute a personal pronoun for the relative pronoun in the sentence.

Benjamin Franklin, (**who, whom**) was one of the signers of the Declaration of Independence, was also a talented inventor.

To decide whether the correct relative pronoun is *who* or *whom*, think: *He was* one of the signers of the Declaration of Independence. If *I, we, he, she,* or *they* can be substituted for the relative pronoun, then the correct relative pronoun is *who*.

The only president (**who, whom**) Congress impeached was Andrew Johnson.

To decide whether the correct relative pronoun is *who* or *whom*, think: *Congress impeached him*. If *us, me, him, her,* or *them* can be substituted for the relative pronoun, then the correct pronoun is *whom*.

The word *what* is sometimes used incorrectly as a relative pronoun.

INCORRECT: *The books what I enjoy most are science fiction.*

CORRECT: *The books that I enjoy most are science fiction.*

Lesson 3 Exercise

Directions: Edit the following sentences to correct all errors in relative pronoun usage. Not all of the sentences have errors.

1. Only people which are registered blood donors may duel in Uruguay.

2. The elephant is the only animal that has four knees.
3. Ants and humans are the only two animal species what wage war on their own kind.
4. The state who uses the phrase "Land of Lincoln" on its license plates is Illinois.
5. The first American astronaut whom orbited Earth was John Glenn.

Answers are on page 246.

Lesson 4 Avoiding Vague Pronoun References

In order for the meaning of a sentence to be clear, a pronoun must have a clear antecedent.

Read the following sentences.

UNCLEAR: The workers walked off the job, which is why there is a backlog of orders.

CLEAR: There is a backlog of orders because the workers walked off the job.

In the first sentence above, the relative pronoun *which* is used. There is no clear antecedent for *which* in the sentence, however. The clearly written version of the sentence eliminates the vague pronoun reference by eliminating the pronoun *which*.

The example below shows you how vague pronoun references can be eliminated by replacing a pronoun with a noun.

UNCLEAR: You should buy your ticket early because they are always crowded during holidays.

CLEAR: You should buy your ticket early because the airlines are always crowded during holidays.

In the first version of the sentence, the pronoun *they* does not have a clear antecedent. If the writer's subject is airline tickets, then the meaning of the sentence can be clarified by using a noun—*airlines*—instead of the pronoun *they*.

Lesson 4 Exercise

Directions: Edit the following sentences to correct all errors in vague pronoun reference. More than one answer may be correct if you need to substitute a noun for a pronoun.

1. The machinist did not wear safety goggles, which was against the company's policy.
2. On last night's weather forecast, they said there was an 80 percent chance of rain.
3. Helium contracts the vocal cords, which causes the pitch of the voice to rise.
4. It says that ten inches of snow equals one inch of rain.
5. They predict that during the next decade the price of housing will triple.

Answers are on page 246.

Lesson 5 Avoiding Ambiguous Pronoun References

You have seen that a pronoun depends on other words for its meaning. In the last lesson, you studied examples of sentences that were unclear because they included pronouns that did not have specific antecedents. Sometimes, a writer uses a pronoun that may refer to more than one word in the sentence, making the pronoun reference ambiguous.

Read the following sentence.

UNCLEAR: The New York Mets and the Boston Red Sox were tied after the sixth game, but they finally won the last game.

Did you understand this sentence? Who won the game—the Mets or the Red Sox? Because the pronoun, *they*, might refer to either team, the meaning of the sentence is not clear. Read the edited version below.

CLEAR: The New York Mets and the Boston Red Sox were tied after the sixth game, but the Mets finally won the last game.

On the GED Test, you will need to look for ambiguous pronoun references. If a sentence is unclear because a pronoun may refer to more than one noun, reword the sentence to eliminate the ambiguous pronoun.

UNCLEAR: The staff told the Board of Directors that they could not attend today's meeting.

CLEAR: The staff told the Board of Directors, "We cannot attend today's meeting."

OR

The Board of Directors was told that the staff could not attend today's meeting.

Lesson 5 Exercise

Directions: Edit the following sentences to correct all errors in ambiguous pronoun reference. There may be more than one way to edit each sentence.

1. Because the discussion leader and the secretary were responsible for the minutes of the meeting, he was told to take accurate notes.
2. When she returned from vacation, the supervisor gave the employee additional responsibilities.
3. The student asked the teacher if she could change the assignment.
4. If a child has an allergic reaction to a certain food, throw it away.
5. Mike told Randy that he was the starting pitcher for tomorrow's game.

Answers are on pages 246–247.

Skill 3 Review

Directions: Edit the following sentences to correct all errors in pronoun usage. Not all of the sentences have errors.

1. Amethysts are purple stones, which may be caused by impurities such as iron or manganese.
2. A mosquito cannot beat their wings in temperatures below 60 degrees.
3. A human being which is at rest breathes about 16 times per minute.
4. The president told the adviser that she should cancel the press conference.
5. Anyone that uses the metric system is using a mathematical system developed by the French.
6. Frank Lloyd Wright was an architect whom designed houses with low, horizontal shapes.
7. Animals that live in cold climates have smaller ears than its cousins in warmer climates.
8. The legends what are told about King Arthur may be based on historical facts.
9. Neither potato chips nor candy bars give us the nutrition you need to stay healthy.
10. After World War II, the housing supply could not keep up with the demand because it grew so rapidly.

Check your answers. Correct answers are on page 247. If you have at least eight answers correct, go on to the Chapter 1 Quiz. If you have fewer than eight answers correct, study Skill 3 again beginning with Lesson 1.

Chapter 1 Quiz

Directions: Edit the following sentences to correct all errors in usage: subject–verb agreement, verb tense, and pronoun reference. No sentence has more than one error, although not all of the sentences have errors.

1. They say that at one time ketchup was sold as a medicine in the United States.
2. Dinosaurs live on Earth for 100 million years.
3. The people which live in Hawaii tend to live about four years longer than Americans who live in other states.
4. There is a logical reason why most grandfather clocks lose time in warm weather.
5. The candidate whom was elected won by a large majority.
6. Do everyone understand the directions?
7. In ancient Greece, a woman counted her age from the date on which you were married.
8. Mark Spitz had broke many Olympic swimming records.
9. In 1864, Travelers Insurance Company will issue the first insurance policy for two cents.
10. Ann and Linda told the staff that they would no longer need to work on Saturdays.
11. The band rehearses three times a week before their performances.
12. The Liberty Bell is made of bronze and weighed over a ton.
13. The storm has shook the leaves from the tree.
14. Were the tour of the art museums interesting?
15. Many elephants are killed because its tusks are considered valuable.
16. Spiders has been found on the top of Mt. Everest.
17. Neither the book nor the movie were successful.
18. As early as 700 A.D., fingerprints are taken for identification purposes.
19. Both civics and economics is listed as required courses in many schools.
20. Injections for measles is being given free at the clinic.

Answers are on page 247.

Chapter

2 Sentence Structure

Objective

In this chapter, you will learn to

- Write complete sentences
- Correct faulty sentence structure
- Combine sentences
- Express ideas clearly

Skill 1 Complete Sentences

Preview

Directions: Edit the following items to correct all errors in complete sentence structure. Not all of the items have errors.

1. **There are 206 bones in the human body the thigh bone is the longest.**
2. **The total shown on the receipt.**
3. **The United States government owns 365,482 acres of land in Alaska, and this land accounts for about 96 percent of the state.**
4. **Sat in front of the television for five hours.**
5. **This dish can be heated in a microwave oven, it will not crack.**

Check your answers. Correct answers are on pages 247–248. If you have at least four answers correct, do the Skill 1 Review on page 60. If you have fewer than four answers correct, study Skill 1 beginning with Lesson 1.

Lesson 1 Eliminating Sentence Fragments

People usually write because they want to communicate an idea, a fact, or a feeling. To communicate clearly, a sentence must have a subject and a verb. It also must express a complete thought.

Each of the following items is missing some necessary piece of information.

1. All the boxes on this shelf. (*What is being said about all the boxes?*)
2. Traded in his camera for a better one. (*Who traded in his camera?*)
3. When the president signed the bill into law. (*What happened when the president signed the bill?*)

Items 1 to 3 are called *sentence fragments.* Item 1 is missing a verb. To correct the error in item 1, add a verb and any other words that are needed to complete the thought.

All of the boxes belong on this shelf.

OR

All of the boxes on this shelf are dusty.

Item 2 needs a subject in order to express a complete thought.

Stan Mulroy traded in his camera for a better one.

Item 3 has both a subject (*president*) and a verb (*signed*), but it does not express a complete thought. To correct this type of sentence-fragment error, add words to make the meaning clear.

When the president signed the bill into law, he thanked Congress for passing the bill.

OR

Reporters were present when the president signed the bill into law.

Notice that there may be many ways of correcting a sentence-fragment error.

Lesson 1 Exercise

Directions: Edit the following items to correct all sentence-fragment errors. Not all of the items have errors.

1. Some cash registers are actually computers.

2. Even though I missed my usual train.

3. Stood and cheered the home team's victory.
4. The treasurer of the Hikers' Club.
5. Tomatoes that are grown in hothouses.

Answers are on page 248.

Lesson 2 Eliminating Run-on Sentences

Sometimes two complete ideas are incorrectly written as if they were one idea. Read the following example:

The sun was very hot we decided to sit in the shade.

There are two complete thoughts—that the sun was very hot and that we decided to sit in the shade. When two or more complete thoughts are joined without any punctuation, a *run-on sentence* results. One way to correct this type of error is to write each complete idea as a separate sentence.

The sun was very hot. We decided to sit in the shade.

Notice that a period ends the first sentence and that the second sentence begins with a capital letter.

A common error in sentence structure is to write two complete ideas and separate them with only a comma. The result is also a run-on sentence; for example:

Milk is a good source of calcium, nonfat milk is also low in calories.

This type of run-on sentence is called a *comma splice*. Again, the error can be corrected by writing two separate sentences.

Milk is a good source of calcium. Nonfat milk is also low in calories.

Sentences with Compound Verbs

To decide if a sentence is a run-on, identify each *complete* thought. For example, the following sentence expresses only one complete thought, and this is not a run-on:

Mr. Sherman wrote a letter to his cousin and sent it by Air Mail.

The second part of this sentence (*sent it by Air Mail*) is not a complete idea. Notice that the sentence has two verbs, *wrote* and *sent*, but only one subject, *Mr. Sherman*. Two verbs that have the same subject in a sentence are called *compound verbs*.

Lesson 2 Exercise

Directions: Edit the following items to correct all run-on sentences. Not all of the items have errors.

1. Woodrow Wilson was our 28th president he was the only president who had a Ph.D. degree.
2. The Nineteenth Amendment to the Constitution gave women the right to vote, it was adopted in 1920.
3. Congress established the first U.S. mint it was located in Philadelphia.
4. This supermarket carries a good selection of foods and has weekly sales.
5. Pizza was first made by Roman soldiers they used olive oil, cheese, and crackers.

Answers are on page 248.

Lesson 3 Other Ways of Eliminating Run-on Sentences

Run-on sentences, including comma splices, can be corrected by writing them as two separate sentences. The following are some additional ways of editing a run-on sentence.

1. **Use a comma and a connecting word after the first complete idea.** Connecting words that may be used with a comma are *and, but, or, nor, for,* and *yet.* Choose a connecting word that expresses the relationship between ideas. For example, in the following run-on sentence, there is a relationship of choice between the two main ideas:

   I might use my bonus to buy a color television I might deposit the money in my savings account.

   The connecting word *or* expresses choice. A comma and *or* should be placed after the first idea.

   I might use my bonus to buy a color television, <u>or</u> I might deposit the money in my savings account.

2. **Use a semicolon after the first complete idea.**

   Mrs. Ortiz did not fly to Philadelphia, she went by train.

   This comma splice can be corrected by changing the comma after *Philadelphia* to a semicolon.

   Mrs. Ortiz did not fly to Philadelphia; she went by train.

3. **Use a semicolon and a connecting word after the first complete idea.** Certain connecting words can be used with a semicolon to show the relationship between ideas.

Mrs. Ortiz did not fly to Philadelphia; instead, she went by train.

The word *instead* contrasts the second idea with the first. When a connecting word is used with a semicolon, the word must be followed by a comma.

The connecting words that may be used with a semicolon are not the same words that may be used with a comma. The following are some words and phrases that may be used after a semicolon.

as a result	furthermore	instead	otherwise
besides	however	likewise	still
consequently	in addition	moreover	therefore
for example	in fact	nevertheless	thus

Compound Sentences

The edited sentences in this lesson are examples of compound sentences. A *compound sentence* is a sentence that expresses two or more complete thoughts. The complete thoughts may be joined in any of the ways shown in this lesson.

Read the following sentences. Which ones are compound sentences? Are any of the sentences punctuated incorrectly?

1. Breeds of dogs are organized into groups; for example, there are 23 breeds of terriers.

2. Kabuki theater developed in Japan during the 1600s, and is still very popular today.

3. Detergents have many uses, yet they can harm the skin and eyes.

Sentences 1 and 3 are compound sentences and are correct as written. Sentence 2 is not a compound sentence. Although sentence 2 has compound verbs (*developed* and *is*), it does not express two complete ideas. The comma should be removed from this sentence.

Kabuki theater developed in Japan during the 1600s and is still very popular today.

Lesson 3 Exercise

Directions: Edit the following items to correct all run-on sentences. Use any of the methods described in this lesson or in Lesson 2. Not all of the items have errors.

1. Egyptians made candy over 4,000 years ago, they used dates and honey.
2. England and France fought the longest war it lasted from 1337 to 1453 and was called the Hundred Years' War.
3. The first black American to become a Supreme Court justice was Thurgood Marshall he was appointed in 1967 by President Lyndon Johnson.
4. A deer's antlers fall off every winter and grow back in the summer.
5. This apartment needs some repairs, however, the rent is reasonable.
6. The United States is the world's largest producer of cheese, France is second.
7. The country with the largest number of doctors is not America, nor is it Japan.
8. The first government employee strike was the Boston police strike it happened in 1919.
9. Pluto takes 248 years to complete one orbit around the sun, many comets orbit beyond Pluto.
10. Pretzels were invented by a French monk, they shaped the dough to represent arms folded in prayer.

Answers are on page 248.

Skill 1 Review

Directions: Edit the following items to correct all errors in complete sentence structure. Not all of the items have errors.

1. The world's oldest computer is located in Great Britain, it was built in 1949.
2. The salt-water crocodile weighs approximately 1,100 pounds, and grows to more than 12 feet long.
3. Until the downpour stopped.
4. Wilt Chamberlain holds the record for scoring the most points in a basketball game he scored 100 points in a game against the New York Knicks.
5. Added thinner to the can of paint.
6. William Taft was the 27th president of the United States; furthermore he served as chief justice of the Supreme Court.

7. The wildest ball game I have ever seen.

8. The first subway was built in London; however, the first subway in America was built in Boston.

9. The Grand Coulee Dam is the largest concrete dam in the United States; and it is located on the Columbia River.

10. The first woman to be a member of a president's cabinet was Frances Perkins, Roosevelt appointed her secretary of labor in 1933.

Check your answers. Correct answers are on page 248. If you have at least eight answers correct, go on to Skill 2. If you have fewer than eight answers correct, study Skill 1 beginning with Lesson 1.

Skill 2 Coordination and Subordination

Preview

Directions: Edit these sentences to correct all errors in coordination and subordination. Not all of the sentences have errors.

1. **When the Depression occurred in 1931 Nevada legalized gambling.**
2. **James Ritty invented the cash register because when he wanted to keep a record of the sales in his restaurant.**
3. **The first electronic computer was developed in 1945, and I am taking a programming course this fall.**
4. **William Henry Harrison was president of the United States for only 31 days; as a result, he died of pneumonia in 1841.**
5. **Although their first flight took place in 1903, the Wright brothers did not receive public recognition for their "flying machine" until 1908.**

Check your answers. Correct answers are on page 248. If you have at least four answers correct, do the Skill 2 Review on page 67. If you have fewer than four answers correct, study Skill 2 beginning with Lesson 1.

Lesson 1 Coordination

A compound sentence expresses two or more complete ideas that are of equal importance. If a comma is used after the first complete idea, a connecting word, such as *and,* must be used. If a semicolon follows the first complete idea, a special connecting word or phrase (such as *meanwhile* or *on the other hand*) is sometimes used.

The words used to connect the ideas in a compound sentence are called *coordinators*. Chart 1 lists some coordinators that are often used. Notice that coordinators can show the relationship between the ideas in a sentence.

Chart 1 Coordinators

Meaning of Coordinator	Coordinators Used with a Comma	Coordinators Used with a Semicolon
Adds one idea to another	and	also, besides, furthermore, in addition, likewise, moreover
Contrasts one idea with another	but, yet	however, instead, nevertheless, on the contrary, on the other hand, still
Shows time or order	and then	afterward, later, meanwhile, next, then
Shows a result or a conclusion	and so, so	accordingly, as a result, consequently, hence, therefore, thus
Shows a reason or an example	for	for example, for instance, indeed, in fact, that is
Expresses choice between ideas	nor, or	either . . . or neither . . . nor, otherwise

Several things are important to keep in mind in writing or editing compound sentences.

1. If a coordinator is used, it should be chosen to express the relationship between ideas. In the following sentence, the coordinator has a meaning of contrast, but the ideas are not really in contrast with each other.

   The worst earthquake in history occurred in 1556 in China; on the other hand, over 800,000 people died.

   A correct coordinator would be *as a result* or *in fact.*

   The worst earthquake in history occurred in 1556 in China; as a result, over 800,000 people died.

2. Ideas that are not related should not be joined in a compound sentence. Is the following a correct compound sentence?

The movie that has grossed the most money is *Gone with the Wind,* and I'm going to see *Ordinary People* tonight.

Because the ideas are not closely related, they should be separate sentences. It is also possible to change the second idea to one that has some connection with the first, as in the following revision.

The movie that has grossed the most money is *Gone with the Wind,* and it was based on the best-selling novel by Margaret Mitchell.

3. A sentence should not contain so many ideas that it becomes confusing.

For many years the Empire State Building was the tallest building in the world; later, the World Trade Center in New York became the tallest; however, the Sears Tower in Chicago is now the tallest, for it stands at 1,451 feet and has 109 stories; in addition, the Sears Tower has 16,000 windows and 103 elevators.

This sentence should be divided into several shorter sentences, so that the ideas and the connections between them can be readily understood.

For many years the Empire State Building was the tallest building in the world; later, the World Trade Center in New York became the tallest. Now, however, the Sears Tower in Chicago is the tallest, for it stands at 1,451 feet and has 109 stories. In addition, the Sears Tower has 16,000 windows and 103 elevators.

Lesson 1 Exercise

Directions: Edit the following sentences to correct all errors in sentence coordination. Not all of the sentences have errors.

1. Irving Berlin wrote "White Christmas," the most popular song ever recorded; however, over 100 million copies have been sold.

2. The Great Wall of China is 1,684 miles long; on the other hand, it is the longest wall in the world.

3. O'Hare Airport in Chicago is the busiest in the world, and my aunt is a flight attendant.

4. The largest prison in the world is Kharkov Prison in Russia; in fact, it can hold 40,000 prisoners.

5. Jon Fitch designed the first steamboat, and it looked like a canoe but had steam-driven paddles; moreover, he also built a boat that had paddle wheels on the side, but he had difficulty finding people to back him financially, so his designs failed to be successful.

Answers are on pages 248–249.

Lesson 2 Subordination

Ideas of equal importance can be combined in a compound sentence. Sometimes, though, you may want to combine ideas while showing that one idea is more important than the other. To do this, change the wording of the sentence by making one idea of lesser importance, or subordinating it.

> The Dallas–Fort Worth Airport covers more than 18,000 acres, and it is the largest airport in the world.
>
> Because the Dallas–Fort Worth Airport covers more than 18,000 acres, it is the largest airport in the world.

The word *Because* makes the first idea subordinate, or of lesser importance than the second idea. The subordinate idea becomes a sentence fragment; the more important idea remains a complete thought. This complete thought is called the *main idea* of the sentence.

The subordinate idea may also appear second in a sentence.

> In 1867, Congress was called the Billion Dollar Congress because it passed a budget of over one billion dollars.

Following is a list of the most common words used to connect ideas of unequal rank in a sentence. These words are called *subordinators.*

after	because	unless
although	before	until
as	even though	when
as if	if	whenever
as long as	in order that	whereas
as soon as	so that	wherever
as though	though	while

There are four rules to remember about using subordinators.

1. The two sentence ideas must have something in common.

INCORRECT: Unless we could get good seats, we were surprised at the price of tickets.

CORRECT: Unless we could get good seats, we did not want to see the show.

2. One idea will be stated in a sentence fragment, and one idea will be a complete sentence.

COORDINATED IDEAS: Lungfish have lungs and breathe air, but they also have gills.

SUBORDINATED IDEAS: Although lungfish have lungs and breathe air, they also have gills.

NOTE: The coordinator (*but*) is dropped when the subordinator (*Although*) is used.

3. If the subordinate idea comes first in the sentence, it is followed by a comma.

INCORRECT: When goldfish are kept in a dark room they lose their color.

CORRECT: When goldfish are kept in a dark room, they lose their color.

4. Only one subordinator should be used at a time.

INCORRECT: Because even though he is a talented professional golfer, Sam Snead never won the U.S. Open.

CORRECT: Even though he is a talented professional golfer, Sam Snead never won the U.S. Open.

The ideas in this sentence are related by contrast, not by cause and effect. Thus, *even though* is an appropriate subordinator.

Lesson 2 Exercise

Directions: Edit the following sentences to correct all subordination errors. Not all of the sentences have errors.

1. As long as you don't overdo it, jogging is a healthful activity.
2. Even though some mushrooms are poisonous, but others can be eaten safely.
3. After when the stock market crashed in 1929, many people refused to put their money in banks.
4. When Shakespeare wrote his historical plays he sometimes altered the truth to fit his story lines.
5. Pollution will continue to be a major problem in many of our cities until people begin to read more.

Answers are on page 249.

Lesson 3 Combining Sentences

Sometimes a sentence repeats words that were used in an earlier sentence. It is often possible to improve a paragraph by combining such sentences into one. Coordinators such as *and*, *or*, and *but* can be used for this purpose.

Liver is a good source of vitamin A.
Butter is a good source of vitamin A.

To avoid repeating the words *is a good source of vitamin A*, the sentences can be combined.

Liver and butter are good sources of vitamin A.

Notice that the compound subject, *liver and butter*, requires a plural verb, *are*.

Other parts of sentences besides subjects can be combined to eliminate needless repetitions.

Miss Rodgers may buy a station wagon.
Miss Rodgers may buy a van.

COMBINED: Miss Rodgers may buy a station wagon or a van.

There is a vaccine against measles.
There is a vaccine against mumps.

COMBINED: There are vaccines against measles and mumps.

Notice that some words may have to be made plural in the combined sentence.

The paired coordinators *either . . . or* and *neither . . . nor* can also be used to combine sentences. Other changes in wording may be necessary when these coordinators are used.

A salad would be good for dinner.
A casserole would be good for dinner.

COMBINED: Either a salad or a casserole would be good for dinner.

Hilary did not attend the meeting.
Wiley did not attend the meeting.

COMBINED: Neither Hilary nor Wiley attended the meeting.

Sentences found by combining in these ways are not compound sentences. They do not need commas unless the combined sentence lists a series of three or more items, as in the following example.

Liver and butter are good sources of vitamin A.
Milk is a good source of vitamin A.

COMBINED: Liver, butter, and milk are good sources of vitamin A.

Lesson 3 Exercise

Directions: Edit the following pairs of sentences to make them less repetitious. Combine sentences in any of the ways used in this lesson.

1. Seneca Lake is in western New York State. Cayuga Lake is in western New York State.
2. Mr. Wittenberg did not enjoy the concert. Mr. Bush did not enjoy the concert.
3. You can buy that book in a hardcover edition. You can buy that book in paperback.
4. Roberta is making a skirt. Roberta is making a blazer.
5. Eliot fixed the faucet with a wrench. Eliot fixed the faucet with a screwdriver.

Answers are on page 249.

Skill 2 Review

Directions: Edit these sentences to correct all errors in coordination and subordination. Not all of the sentences have errors.

1. Before its building was completed the United Nations met at Lake Success in New York.
2. Ursa Major is one name of that constellation; therefore, it is also called the Big Dipper.
3. As soon as when you are well, you can leave the hospital.
4. Whenever a new contract is being negotiated, and tension among employees increases.
5. The highest golf course in the world is in Peru, so the lowest course is in Death Valley, California.
6. It is possible to solve the Rubik's Cube puzzle; nevertheless, the record for mastering the solution is 22.95 seconds.
7. Jeanette Rankin was the first woman to be elected to Congress, but I voted for Reagan in the last election.
8. Aristotle believed the heart was the body's center of intelligence, however, we now know the brain is.
9. Whenever it is possible, turn off unnecessary lights to help conserve energy.
10. Microwave ovens are very popular; in fact, estimates show that by 1990 three-quarters of American households will own one of these ovens; accordingly, food manufacturers are developing new lines of frozen microwave products for people who want quick, easy meals; for example, single-serving pizzas are a new item.

Check your answers. Correct answers are on page 249. If you have at least eight answers correct, go on to Skill 3. If you have fewer than eight answers correct, study Skill 2 beginning with Lesson 1.

Skill 3 Clear Sentences

Preview

Directions: Edit these sentences to correct all errors in clarity. Not all of the sentences have errors.

1. **Because he is so loyal, Al continues to remain my best friend.**
2. **Good reading skills will help you to enjoy literature and to learn more about our world.**
3. **With joyful happiness Ms. Fischer gladly accepted the promotion.**
4. **Flown from sunrise to sunset, the White House displays the U.S. flag every day.**
5. **Huffing and puffing, the house was blown down.**

Check your answers. Correct answers are on page 249. If you have at least four answers correct, do the Skill 3 Review on page 73. If you have fewer than four answers correct, study Skill 3 beginning with Lesson 1.

Lesson 1 Clarity of Thought

A sentence may be free of grammatical errors but still not be understandable. Such a sentence lacks clarity, or clearness.

> I ate nachos before I rode the roller coaster, which made me sick to my stomach.

Is the meaning of this sentence clear? *What* made me sick to my stomach? The nachos? Or the roller coaster? Or both? It is difficult to tell by the wording of the sentence.

Unclear writing can result from any of the following problems.

1. **Unclear use of pronouns.** Pronouns must clearly refer to their antecedents. If the reader cannot tell to whom or to what a pronoun refers, the meaning will not be clear. Reword the sentence to make it understandable.

UNCLEAR: A rabbit's natural dwelling has a special name; they call it a warren.

CLEAR: A rabbit's natural dwelling has a special name; biologists call it a warren.

OR

A rabbit's natural dwelling is called a warren.

UNCLEAR: Mike told John to clean up his messy desk.

CLEAR: Because John's desk was messy, Mike told him to clean it up.

To correct an unclear pronoun reference, decide what the antecedent of the pronoun is. Then reword the sentence in any way that allows the reader to understand what is being said.

2. **Unclear choice of words.** Whenever possible, a sentence should express an idea in clear, simple words. Long words and complicated sentences do not necessarily help to make an idea understandable. In fact, they may confuse the reader.

UNCLEAR: I abhor nutriment that savors of acidity.

CLEAR: I dislike food that has an acid taste.

UNCLEAR: The employee reconciled himself to a remuneration reduction in order to obviate his termination.

CLEAR: The employee took a pay cut to prevent losing his job.

3. **Use of unnecessary words.** If a writer uses more words than are needed to express an idea, the result is called *wordiness.* This problem can be caused by unclear word choice, as the examples above show. Avoid unnecessary repetition and overuse of words by simply getting to the point.

WORDY: You shiver on account of the fact that your body is attempting to try to increase heat within the body.

CLEAR: You shiver because your body is trying to create heat within itself.

Most wordy sentences are long; however, a short sentence can also be wordy.

WORDY: The soldiers advanced forward.

CLEAR: The soldiers advanced.

Because *advance* means "move forward," it is unnecessary to write *advanced forward.*

Lesson 1 Exercise

Directions: Edit the following sentences to correct all errors in clarity. Not all of the sentences have errors.

1. At last we finally had all the boxes packed and sealed.
2. The supervisor told the employee that she was being promoted.
3. The singer spoke with the drummer before they went on stage.
4. I have commenced to inscribe an autobiography of myself.
5. Last year we spent a week in Florida, which was very nice.

Answers are on page 249.

Lesson 2 Proper Modification

The meaning of a sentence can also be unclear if its parts are not in logical order or if a needed part is missing.

Hoping and praying, the plane landed safely after all.

Containing 12,000 words and 40,000 definitions, Noah Webster compiled the first English language dictionary.

In both sentences, the meaning is uncertain. The first sentence seems to say that the plane is hoping and praying, which does not make sense. The second sentence seems to state that Noah Webster contains 12,000 words and 40,000 definitions. Neither sentence expresses the writer's meaning well.

The following versions have been edited to state clearly what the writer means.

1. Hoping and praying, we saw the plane land safely after all.
2. Noah Webster compiled the first English language dictionary, which contained 12,000 words and 40,000 definitions.

A *modifier* is a word or phrase that explains or describes another word in a sentence. In sentence 1, *hoping* and *praying* are modifiers that describe *we*. In sentence 2, the words *which contained 12,000 words and 40,000 definitions* explain, or modify, *dictionary*. A modifier should be placed near the word it modifies.

Two errors often result from incorrect use of modifiers.

1. **Dangling modifiers.** A modifier must clearly and logically explain another word in the sentence. If there is no word that can logically be modified, the result is a *dangling modifier*. That is, the modifier cannot "attach" its meaning to another word to express a clear meaning.

   Exhausted after a long day, a hot bath sounded good.

   This sentence seems to be saying that the bath was exhausted. However, it is not logical for *exhausted* to modify *bath*. The sentence can be corrected by introducing a word that *exhausted* can modify:

   Exhausted after a long day, I thought a hot bath sounded good.

   Sometimes it is possible to reword the dangling modifier as a separate idea introduced by a subordinator.

   Because I was exhausted after a long day, a hot bath sounded good.

2. **Misplaced modifiers.** A modifier should be placed as close as possible to the word it describes. If the modifier is too far from this word, the sentence becomes confusing. The result is called a *misplaced modifier*.

   Lake Victoria is located in Africa, which is 270 feet deep.
   (*This sentence seems to say that Africa is 270 feet deep.*)

   To correct this sentence, rearrange the words. Place the misplaced modifier as close as possible to the word it modifies.

   Lake Victoria, which is 270 feet deep, is located in Africa.
   (*This sentence states that Lake Victoria is 270 feet deep.*)

Lesson 2 Exercise

Directions: Edit the following sentences to correct all modification errors. Not all of the sentences have errors.

1. Running into the end zone, the winning touchdown was scored.
2. Wishing to become an expert chess player, Ernest practices every day.
3. A rainbow from an airplane can be seen as a complete circle.
4. Michelangelo painted the ceiling of the Sistine Chapel on his back.
5. The detective watched the suspect's house wearing a disguise.

Answers are on pages 249–250.

Lesson 3 Parallel Structure

The following sentence tells about a person's interests.

Art's hobbies are hiking, sketching, and gardening.

Notice the form of the words that name Art's hobbies: each is the *-ing* form of a verb. Because all of the activities are being mentioned as a person's hobbies, they all play similar roles in the sentence. Ideas that have similar roles in a sentence should be worded with similar, or parallel, structures.

Do the following sentences have parallel structure? Decide whether or not related ideas are worded in similar ways.

We are driving to Milwaukee, to Chicago, and Detroit.

In this sentence, the places where we are driving are not listed in the same form. Two ideas begin with the word *to,* but the third does not. Parallel structure requires the word *to* before *Detroit,* as well.

We are driving to Milwaukee, to Chicago, and to Detroit.

Alexander Graham Bell was a painter, a teacher, and he invented things.

In this sentence, two nouns describe Alexander Graham Bell; however, the third idea uses a verb, *invented.* To give the sentence parallel structure, change the words *he invented things* to a noun.

Alexander Graham Bell was a painter, a teacher, and an inventor.

Use this method when you look for errors in parallel structure:

1. See if the sentence includes a listing. The connecting words *and, or, nor,* or *but also* are often used in listings.
2. Decide if all items in the listing have been written in the same form.
3. If there is an error in parallel structure, select one form and use it consistently throughout the listing.

Lesson 3 Exercise

Directions: Edit the following sentences to correct all errors in parallel structure. Not all of the sentences have errors.

1. A U.S. senator must be at least 30 years old, be a U.S. citizen for a minimum of 9 years, and to live in the state in which he or she seeks election.

2. Activities that strengthen the heart muscle include swimming, jogging, and to ride a bike.
3. I enjoy sports that are challenging, fast-paced, and don't need expensive equipment.
4. Is the birthstone of those born in July a ruby, a sapphire, or the diamond?
5. The American Hospital Association believes that every patient has a right to be treated with dignity and to be given an explanation of the bill.

Answers are on page 250.

Skill 3 Review

Directions: Edit the following sentences to correct all errors in clarity. Not all of the sentences have errors.

1. It is a good idea to plan ahead for the future.
2. In the eventuality of an inundation situation, decamp from your habitation instantaneously.
3. So that I would learn to play the piano well, my teacher told me often to practice.
4. While working with the computer, the telephone rang.
5. She enjoyed singing and dancing more than to act.
6. The human body has over 600 muscles; it accounts for 40 percent of the body's weight.
7. The feathers of an archer's bow are called vanes.
8. The doctor explained the patient's symptoms, diagnosis, and what treatment would be used.
9. Discovered in 1789, the German scientist Martin Klaproth developed several uses for uranium.
10. Excited and anxious, the birthday gifts were quickly unwrapped.

Check your answers. Correct answers are on page 250. If you have at least eight answers correct, go on to the Chapter 2 Quiz. If you have fewer than eight answers correct, study Skill 3 beginning with Lesson 1.

Chapter 2 Quiz

Directions: Edit these sentences to correct all errors in sentence structure: incomplete or run-on sentences, improper coordination and subordination, and unclear sentences. No sentence has more than one error, although not all of the sentences have errors.

1. Taking place in New Orleans, I visited the World's Fair.

2. Davy Crockett was an early American folk hero he eventually became a U.S. congressman.

3. In the International Morse Code, the S.O.S. signal consists of three dots, three dashes, and then you use three more dots.

4. The volleyball and the basketball were invented in Massachusetts in the 1800s, volleyball is a popular team sport.

5. My father is a loyal football fan, but he thinks they are paid too much.

6. The house next door to ours.

7. Built in Springfield, Massachusetts, my family and I visited the Basketball Hall of Fame.

8. The monetary unit of China is the yuan, the monetary unit of Japan is the yen.

9. In an angry rage, the enraged driver shouted furiously.

10. Disney World is the largest amusement park in the world it is located in Orlando, Florida.

11. Riding in the car, the fan belt broke.

12. The dentist who crowned Sam's tooth.

13. After Spiro Agnew resigned, Gerald Ford became Vice President in 1974.

14. The stories of Edgar Allan Poe are unusual, exciting, and they have suspense.

15. An astronaut is an American space traveler a cosmonaut is a Russian space traveler.

16. Stephen Crane wrote *The Red Badge of Courage;* instead, he died of tuberculosis at age 28.

17. Having studied for many hours, the test was easy.

18. While when Lincoln was president, the first paper money was issued in the United States.

19. Although Mrs. Rossi does not usually go to movies.

20. The human body contains several chemical elements, these include carbon, hydrogen, nitrogen, and oxygen.

Answers are on page 250.

Chapter

3 Mechanics

Objective

In this chapter, you will learn to

- capitalize appropriate words within a sentence
- use commas properly in different kinds of sentences
- use apostrophes to form possessive words and contractions
- recognize the differences between closely related words
- improve your spelling using several suggested techniques

Skill 1 Capitalization

Preview

Directions: Edit the following sentences to correct all errors in capitalization. Not all of the sentences have errors.

1. There are 26 letters in the english alphabet.
2. Dorothy's aunt in *The Wizard of Oz* was named aunt Em.
3. The Baltimore Orioles belong to the Eastern Division of the American League.
4. During the American Revolution, the Battle of Bunker Hill really was fought on Breed's Hill.
5. Fred and Wilma Flintstone live at 39 stone canyon way.

Check your answers. Correct answers are on pages 250–251, If you have at least four answers correct, do the Skill 1 Review on page 82. If you have fewer than four answers correct, study Skill 1 beginning with Lesson 1.

Lesson 1 Proper Nouns and Proper Adjectives

A word is "capitalized" if it begins with a capital letter. The first word of a sentence is always capitalized to show that it is the beginning of a sentence. Other words in a sentence may also be capitalized, as illustrated in the following sentence.

> Niagara Falls, a famous landmark located between the United States and Canada, recedes about 2½ feet each year.

All of the underlined words in this sentence are nouns. Some of these nouns are capitalized, whereas, others are not.

Rule 1: A noun that does not name a specific person, place, or thing is called a *common noun.* Do not capitalize a common noun.

Rule 2: A noun that names a specific person, place, or thing is called a *proper noun.* Capitalize all proper nouns.

Chart 1 gives examples of common and proper nouns.

Chart 1 Common and Proper Nouns

Category	Common Noun	Proper Noun
People	generals	George C. Marshall Omar Bradley
	presidents	Ronald Reagan Gerald Ford
	actresses/actors	Jane Fonda Bill Cosby
	races of people	Afro-American Caucasian (Note: Do not capitalize color distinction: *blacks, whites*)
	nationalities of people	Mexican Japanese
	languages of people	Spanish English
	religions of people	Lutheran Catholic
Places	states	Minnesota Oregon
	countries	Germany Brazil

Chart 1 Common and Proper Nouns

Category	Common Noun	Proper Noun
	cities	Atlanta London
	continents	South America Asia
	islands	Hawaiian Islands Greenland
	bodies of water	Lake Michigan Mississippi River
	mountains	Atlas Mountains Alps
	sections of the country	the West the Midwest (Note: Do not capitalize these words when they indicate direction: *We were traveling west.*)
Things	awards	Emmy Award Pulitzer Prize
	buildings	White House Sears Tower
	clubs, organizations, and associations	Chicago Bears American Dental Association
	government departments and agencies	Senate Defense Department
	businesses and companies	American Airlines International Business Machines (Note: Capitalize abbreviations: *IBM*)
	boats, trains, airplanes, and spacecraft	*Concorde* *U.S.S. Arizona*
	newspapers and magazines	*Chicago Tribune* *Time*
	movies, books, television shows, plays, and songs	*The Scarlet Letter* *Romancing the Stone* (Note: Only the first, the last, and other important words are capitalized in a title.)

A proper noun may have more than one word, as shown by some of the examples in Chart 1. Capitalize all the words naming a particular thing, place, or person.

NOTE: Words such as *of* are not capitalized, unless they are the first word of the proper noun.

Of Mice and Men (*novel*)

Strait of Magellen (*body of water*)

The Sound of Music (*movie title*)

In addition to proper nouns, certain kinds of adjectives should always be capitalized. An adjective is a word that describes, or modifies, a noun or pronoun.

Rule 3: When an adjective is formed from a proper noun, it is called a *proper adjective*. Always capitalize a proper adjective.

Proper Noun	**Proper Adjective**
Africa	**African tribe**
China	**Chinese acrobats**
the South	**Southern hospitality**
Greece	**Greek mythology**

NOTE: The proper adjective is capitalized but not the common noun that it modifies.

Leif Ericson was the first European explorer to reach mainland North America.

Lesson 1 Exercise

Directions: Edit the following sentences to correct all capitalization errors. Not all of the sentences have errors.

1. The Mediterranean Sea is part of the atlantic ocean.
2. Louisa May Alcott is the American author of *Little Women*.
3. The presidential medal of freedom was established in 1963.
4. In 1865 a Steamboat explosion on the Mississippi River killed 1,653 people.
5. Using his research ship *Calypso*, Jacques Cousteau explored the oceans.

Answers are on page 251.

Lesson 2 Titles of People and Addresses

A person's name is always capitalized because it is a proper noun. Sometimes titles of people are also capitalized.

Rule 1: Capitalize the title of a person when it is used as part of the person's name.

A famous book about raising children was written by Doctor Benjamin Spock.

Do not capitalize a title if it is not used as part of a person's name. (For exceptions, see the note following Rule 3.)

The doctor who wrote a famous book about raising children was Benjamin Spock.

NOTE: Capitalize the first letter of an abbreviation that stands for a title.

Dr. Wells Mrs. Finley
Mr. Paulson Ms. White

Rule 2: Capitalize words such as *aunt*, *uncle*, *mother*, and *father* only when they are used as part of a person's name.

We borrowed Uncle Ray's fishing equipment for the weekend.

Do not capitalize titles indicating family relationships when they are not part of a person's name.

Our uncle has an expensive collection of rods and reels.

NOTE: Capitalize these titles when they are used in place of a person's name.

We thought Mother would enjoy breakfast in bed this morning.

Rule 3: Civil titles and offices usually are not capitalized.

Franklin D. Roosevelt, president of the United States
the president of the United States
the president
the presidency

NOTE: Titles immediately following a person's name are capitalized when they are used in business letters or in formal lists, such as acknowledgments and lists of contributors. A title used alone, in place of a person's name, may be capitalized in formal introductions or in direct address.

The Animal Rescue League wishes to acknowledge the generous support of the following contributors:

John Jones President of Jones Corporation

Molly Brown, Executive Director of the Pet Protection Society

Ladies and gentlemen, I am honored to introduce the President of the United States.

Mr. President, I have a question about your foreign policy.

Because proper names of places are capitalized and because an address is a specific part of a place, the words that make up an address are capitalized.

Rule 4: The names of streets and highways (and their abbreviations) in a specific address are capitalized.

Common Noun	**Proper Noun**
street	**Madison St.**
freeway	**Marquette Fwy.**
avenue	**Greenfield Ave.**
road	**Barker Rd.**

The president lives on Pennsylvania Avenue in Washington, D.C.

The street was closed for repairs.

NOTE: Also capitalize the words *north, south, east,* and *west* when used before a street number or name.

The package was sent to 3972 West 55 Street.

Lesson 2 Exercise

Directions: Edit the following sentences to correct all capitalization errors. Not all of the sentences have errors.

1. The first woman to be appointed to the Supreme Court was justice Sandra Day O'Connor.
2. Carnegie Hall is located at Seventh avenue and fifty-seventh Street in New York City.

3. My doctor received his medical degree from Harvard Medical School.
4. While he was President, Herbert Hoover gave all of his paychecks to charity.
5. Our new offices are located at 5310 south 27 Street.

Answers are on page 251.

Lesson 3 Time, Dates, Seasons, Special Events, and Historical Eras

Rule 1: Use small capital letters for the abbreviations A.D. and B.C. in reference to a specific date. Also use small capital letters for the abbreviations A.M. and P.M., which show the time of day.

In A.D. 600 the Arabs used coffee beans as a medicine.

The first American satellite lifted off the launchpad at 1:44 P.M. on December 6, 1957.

Rule 2: Capitalize the months of the year, the days of the week, holidays, and special events.

Memorial Day is celebrated on the last Monday in May.

Many communities hold special programs during Fire Prevention Week.

NOTE: The names of the seasons are not capitalized.

A winter vacation is a good way to renew your energy.

There is nothing imaginary about spring fever.

Rule 3: Capitalize the names of historical periods and events.

The Renaissance produced a revival of art, literature, and learning in Europe.

During World War I the United States and Russia were allies.

NOTE: A numerical designation of a historical period is not capitalized.

Two of the most tumultuous decades in the twentieth century were the twenties and the sixties.

Lesson 3 Exercise

Directions: Edit the following sentences to correct all capitalization errors. Not all of the sentences have errors.

1. The word "monday," referring to the second day of the week, was taken from an Old English word that meant "moon's day."
2. The first day of Winter is usually on December 21.
3. Socrates, the famous Greek philosopher, died in 399 B.C., but his ideas had a major influence on the philosophers of the christian era.
4. Babe Ruth Day was held on april 27, 1947, at Yankee Stadium.
5. Charles Dickens was one of the most popular novelists of the nineteenth century.

Answers are on page 251.

Skill 1 Review

Directions: Edit the following sentences to correct all capitalization errors. Not all of the sentences have errors.

1. Cary Grant never won an academy award.
2. Cleopatra, an egyptian queen born in 69 B.C., married her brother.
3. Peter O'Toole starred in the 1962 movie *Lawrence Of Arabia*.
4. Old Kent Road and Park Lane are two of the squares in the british version of Monopoly.
5. Thanksgiving Day was designated as a national holiday by President Abraham Lincoln.
6. Where are you going for your vacation this Summer?
7. The Tokyo World Lanes Bowling Center in japan has 252 lanes.
8. Sherlock Holmes' landlady was mrs. Hudson.
9. The *Apollo 11* landed on the moon at 4:17 p.m. on July 20, 1969.
10. Lucas Santomee was the first known Black doctor in the United States.

Check your answers. Correct answers are on page 251. If you have at least eight answers correct, go on to Skill 2. If you have fewer then eight answers correct, study Skill 1 again. Then go on to Skill 2.

Skill 2 Punctuation

Preview

Directions: Edit the following sentences to correct all errors in comma punctuation. Not all of the sentences have errors.

1. **The first passengers to ride in a hot-air balloon were, a duck, a sheep, and a rooster.**
2. **The Statue of Liberty has special meaning to the United States for, it was a gift from France.**
3. **Because it didn't fade purple was the ancient color of royalty.**
4. **Memphis, a city in Tennessee, was also an ancient city in Egypt.**
5. **Laser beams are the brightest, artificial, light sources.**

Check your answers. Correct answers are on page 251. If you have at least four answers correct, do the Skill 2 Review on page 91. If you have fewer than four answers correct, study Skill 2 beginning with Lesson 1.

Lesson 1 Commas Between Items in a Series

A *series* is a number of similar things arranged one after another. Many sentences include words or phrases in a series.

Whale oil is used to make shampoos cosmetics and waxes.

The underlined words are similar because they all name things that contain whale oil. When these items follow one another, commas are used to separate them. Here is the correctly punctuated sentence.

Whale oil is used to make shampoos, cosmetics, and waxes.

Rule 1: Use commas to separate three or more items in a series.

Because dogs and cats like garlic, it is added to most canned pet food.

(Because only two items are listed [*dogs and cats*], commas are not used.)

If you lived in a town named "Warren," you might live in Ohio, Pennsylvania, Illinois, Texas, or Arizona.

(Commas are used in this sentence because more than three items [*Ohio, Pennsylvania, Illinois, Texas, or Arizona*] are listed.)

Notice that commas are not placed before the first item or after the last item in a series.

INCORRECT: Lasers can, perform surgery, split gems, and scan prices, at grocery checkout counters.
CORRECT: Lasers can perform surgery, split gems, and scan prices at grocery checkout counters.

NOTE: When pairs of words are listed in a series, each pair of words is treated as one item.

For dinner, the cafeteria offered bread and butter, soup and salad, macaroni and cheese, pork and beans, apples and oranges, and cake and ice cream.

Rule 2: When all the items in a series are joined by a connecting word such as and, or, or nor, do not use commas.

Was Neptune or Mars or Zeus the Roman god of the sea?

Thin people are more sensitive to the weather because they have less calcium and vitamins and water in their bodies.

Rule 3: When two or more adjectives modify the same noun, use a comma after each adjective except the last one just before the noun.

Yesterday was a cold, damp, windy day.

NOTE: If one of the adjectives in a series modifies another adjective in the series, the two adjectives are not separated by a comma.

A pale red glow was the last we saw of the sun.

In example above, *pale* is an adjective that modifies the adjective *red*.

Lesson 1 Exercise

Directions: Edit the following sentences to correct all punctuation errors. Not all of the sentences have errors.

1. *Sputnik* 5, a Russian satellite, orbited the earth with two dogs, and six mice aboard.
2. The tired, weary, and hungry, travelers could not find a motel room.
3. The background color of a flag is called the "field," or "ground."
4. Presidents Washington, Lincoln, Adams, and Monroe were descendants of England's King Edward I.
5. The five basic swimming strokes are, the crawl, the backstroke, the breaststroke, the butterfly, and the sidestroke.

Answers are in page 251.

Lesson 2 Commas in Compound Sentences

Two sentences that express related ideas can be joined to form a *compound sentence.*

SENTENCE 1: *Every state has an official state bird.*

SENTENCE 2: *New Mexico's state bird is the road runner.*

COMPOUND SENTENCE: *Every state has an official state bird, and New Mexico's is the road runner.*

In the last example, the word *and* is used to join the two separate sentences. Each part of the compound sentence also expresses a complete thought.

Words that join two sentences to form a compound sentence are called *coordinators. And, but, or, nor, for,* and *yet* can be used as coordinators.

Punctuate a compound sentence by using a comma before the coordinator.

In 1816 the first glued postage stamp was issued, and it pictured Queen Victoria.

In the United States, 1816 is known as "the year there was no summer," for it had one of the coldest summers on record.

NOTE: If the two complete ideas that are expressed in a compound sentence are very short, you may omit the comma.

She passed English but she flunked geometry.

She talked and he listened.

Lesson 2 Exercise

Directions: Edit the following sentences to correct all punctuation errors. Not all of the sentences have errors.

1. Charles Dodgson wrote *Alice's Adventures in Wonderland* but he used the pen name Lewis Carroll.
2. Scientists count the number of times fish cough, for, it helps scientists determine the amount of water pollution.
3. June is known as the month of romance and marriage yet, it also has one of the highest crime rates.
4. I worked, and he played.
5. The word *slavery* does not appear in the U.S. Constitution, nor does the word *slave* appear.

Answers are on page 251.

Lesson 3 Commas After Introductory Elements

The following sentences begin with a word, or a group of words, that introduces the sentences but is *not* part of the main idea. These words are called *introductory elements*.

Yes, a bank can provide the current exchange rate of a nation's currency.

In space travel terms, "burnout" is the point where a rocket in flight has used up its fuel.

Because temperatures of $-127°$ F have been recorded there, Vostok in Antarctica is called "the coldest place in the world."

Introductory elements usually are followed by a comma. The following rules illustrate the kinds of introductory elements that require a comma after them.

Rule 1: Words such as *well, yes, no, why, still, oh, however, therefore, consequently, besides, yet,* and *nevertheless* that appear at the beginning of a sentence are followed by a comma.

Yes, it is possible to make oil from sawdust.

Oh, I didn't know that some plants can eat insects.

Therefore, some dolphins can jump higher than over 20 feet above the water.

However, the "lead" in a pencil is really "graphite."

Rule 2: Whan a writer uses *direct address,* he or she addresses remarks directly to a person or to a group of people. Names or expressions used in direct address are always followed by a comma.

Ladies and gentlemen, here is tonight's speaker.

Gary, did you reserve a room for Friday night?

Rule 3: Many introductory elements are followed by a comma.

Wanting to win the race, the runner ran faster

As a matter of interest to those of us who like to put off things until tomorrow, National Procrastination Week is the first week in March.

NOTE: If the introductory phrase is short and does not have a verb, the comma may be omitted, unless the sentence would be misread without it.

In 1849 Walter Hunt invented the safety pin.

In the past, age was respected.

In the first example above, a comma is not needed after *In 1849*. In the second example, a comma is needed after *In the past,* so that the word *past* is not misread as an adjective modifying the noun *age*.

Rule 4: Some sentences express two ideas: a main idea and a subordinate idea. A *subordinate idea* is a sentence fragment—it does not express a complete thought. When a subordinate idea appears at the beginning of the sentence, it is followed by a comma.

Because he saw a need, Walter Hunt invented the safety pin.

Before milk bottles were invented, customers had to provide their own containers for milk.

Lesson 3 Exercise

Directions: Edit the following sentences to correct all punctuation errors. Not all of the sentences have errors.

1. When it started in 1860 the Pony Express mail service took ten days to deliver a letter from Missouri to California.
2. Consequently a leap year has 366 days.
3. Gentlemen our program is ready to begin.
4. No I did not know that there is a town in Arizona called Bumble Bee.
5. In 1962 John Glenn became the first American to orbit the earth.

Answers are on page 252.

Lesson 4 Commas with Sentence Interrupters

Words other than adjectives sometimes are used to explain or describe nouns and pronouns in a sentence.

> The Marianas Trench, the lowest spot on the ocean floor, measures 36,200 feet below sea level.

The phrase, the lowest spot on the ocean floor, describes the proper noun, *Mariana Trench*. The phrase is not essential to the meaning of the sentence, but it *provides additional information* about the noun that is the subject of the sentence. Phrases that "interrupt" a sentence in this way are set off by commas from the rest of the sentence.

If the interrupting phrase is omitted, the sentence still can express a complete idea.

> The Marianas Trench measures 36,200 feet below sea level.

If a word or phrase that describes a noun in a sentence is essential to the meaning of the sentence, it is not set off by commas.

> The novel *Jaws* was made into a movie.
>
> My cousin Mary celebrated her birthday yesterday.

The title of the novel, *Jaws*, is needed to make the meaning of the first sentence clear. Without it, you would not know which novel was made into a movie. Similarly, the meaning of the second sentence would not be clear without the name *Mary*, which tells *which* cousin celebrated her birthday.

The main idea of a sentence may be interrupted also by an expression that simply adds a "pause" to the sentence.

> The White House, incidentally, has 132 rooms.

The word *incidentally* does not add information to the main idea of the sentence.

The following are some common expressions that are used as sentence interrupters.

I believe	on the contrary	after all
I think	on the other hand	by the way
I hope	incidentally	of course
I know	in my opinion	for example
I am sure	nevertheless	however

> Many people, I am sure, take the course at night.
>
> Your book, by the way, is selling very well.

Like other interrupters that are not essential to the main idea of the sentence, these expressions are set off by commas from the rest of the sentence.

NOTE: These expressions are only interrupters when they are not part of the main idea of the sentence. In the following sentence, *I know* is the subject and verb of the sentence, therefore, commas should not be used.

I know that chemicals inside a firefly's body make it glow.

Lesson 4 Exercise

Directions: Edit the following sentences to correct all punctuation errors. Not all of the sentences have errors.

1. Baseball was introduced to Japan by Horace Wilson an American teacher.
2. A flashlight fish, of course has lights beneath each eye that blink on and off.
3. I believe, that the Otis Elevator Company is the world's largest manufacturer of elevators.
4. The disease "neuritis" is characterized by pain and muscle tenderness.
5. The Greater Antilles a group of islands in the West Indies, includes the islands of Cuba, Jamaica, and Puerto Rico.

Answers are on page 252.

Lesson 5 Avoiding Overuse of Commas

The comma is the most frequently misused punctuation mark. Many writers use commas unnecessarily or incorrectly. Lessons 1 through 4 presented several ways to use commas to punctuate elements in sentences. This lesson will explain when not to use commas and will review the rules you learned in the previous lessons.

Chart 2 illustrates the most frequently made mistakes involving commas. Compare the underscored portions of the correct and incorrect sample sentences as you read each pair of sentences.

Chart 2 Frequent Comma Errors

Rule	Incorrect	Correct
Do not use a comma between the subject and verb of a sentence.	The speed of a computer, is measured in billionths of a second called nanoseconds.	The speed of a computer is measured in billionths of a second called nanoseconds.
Do not use commas with compound subjects or verbs	Robert E. Peary, and his team reached the North Pole in 1909. The first U.S. oil gusher blew in 1901, and sent oil 200 feet into the air.	Robert E. Peary and his team reached the North Pole in 1909. The first U.S. oil gusher blew in 1901 and sent oil 200 feet into the air.
Do not use a comma between two complete sentences that are not joined by a coordinator.*	John Philip Sousa was a famous bandmaster of the U.S. Marine Band, he wrote "The Washington Post March."	John Philip Sousa was a famous bandmaster of the U.S. Marine Band and he wrote "The Washington Post March."
Do not use a comma after a coordinator that joins two complete sentences.	The United States possesses a large energy resource for, it has about one-third of the world's coal deposits.	The United States possesses a large energy resource, for it has about one-third of the world's coal deposits.
Do not use a comma before the first item or before the last item in a series. Also, do not use a comma after the last item in a series.	Biology is the branch of science that studies the, history, physical characteristics, and habits of plants and animals. Two eggs, three cups of flour, one cup of sugar, and a teaspoon of baking soda, were needed for the recipe.	Biology is the branch of science that studies the history, physical characteristics, and habits of plants and animals. Two eggs, three cups of flour, one cup of sugar, and a teaspoon of baking soda were needed for the recipe.
Do not use a comma to separate an adjective from the noun it describes, or modifies.	A bassoon is a woodwind instrument with a long, curved, mouthpiece.	A bassoon is a woodwind instrument with a long, curved mouthpiece.

*NOTE: If the two sentences are not joined by a coordinator, *Marine Band* should be followed by a period.

Lesson 5 Exercise

Directions: Edit the following sentences to correct all punctuation errors. Not all of the sentences have errors.

1. In 1920 Elmer Smith of the Cleveland Indians, hit the first grand-slam home run in a World Series game.
2. Dave DeBusschere played basketball for the New York Knicks, and pitched for the Chicago White Sox.
3. While playing water polo, one team wears white caps, the opposing team wears blue caps.
4. In ancient Rome, one year was 10 months long, and September had 29 days.
5. Bruce Jenner, Bill Toomey, and Rafer Johnson, were all Olympic decathlon winners.

Answers are on page 252.

Skill 2 Review

Directions: Edit the following sentences to correct all punctuation errors. Not all of the sentences have errors.

1. Both the Bering Sea, and the Coral Sea are in the Pacific Ocean.
2. An owl can turn its head 270 degrees but, it cannot move its eyes.
3. In Thailand people give presents on their own birthdays rather than receive them.
4. The first, automobile, license plates were required by the state of New York.
5. More dinosaur bones have been found in Canada for example than in any other place in the world.
6. The music for the song, "On Wisconsin," originally was written for the University of Minnesota.
7. Nevertheless a lizard that loses its tail can grow a new one.
8. John is it true that more than 60,000 bees can live in a single hive?
9. The first space shuttle flight took place in 1981, and, John Young was the commander.
10. One hot dog, or one ounce of cheese, or one chicken drumstick provides seven grams of protein.

Check your answers. Correct answers are on page 252. If you have at least eight answers correct, go on to Skill 3. If you have fewer than eight answers correct, study Skill 2 again. Then go on to Skill 3.

Skill 3 Spelling

Preview

Directions: Edit the following sentences to correct all errors in spelling. Not all of the sentences have errors.

1. **Most of Earths physical changes are so gradual that we do not notice them.**
2. **Only two city council members thought it was alright to raise parking fees.**
3. **Beside teaching, Larry enjoys coaching basketball.**
4. **There were several mispelled words in the letter.**
5. **Millions of animals are so small that you'd have to use a microscope to see them.**

Check your answers. Correct answers are on page 252. If you have at least four answers correct, do the Skill 3 Review on page 108. If you have fewer than four answers correct, study Skill 3 beginning with Lesson 1.

Lesson 1 Basic Spelling Rules

It is often difficult to figure out the spelling of a word in English by listening to the way it is pronounced. However, some basic spelling rules can be used when changing the form of a word, such as changing a singular noun to a plural noun or a present-tense verb to a past-tense verb.

Noun Forms

Rule 1: In general, plural nouns are formed by adding *s* or *es* to the singular form. The *-es* ending is used with nouns that end in *s*, *x*, *ch*, or *sh*.

bench/benches box/boxes crash/crashes

Rule 2: Singular nouns that end in *y* preceded by a consonant are pluralized by replacing the *y* with *i* and adding *es*.

mystery/mysteries party/parties

NOTE: Nouns that end in *y* preceded by a vowel usually form their plurals by the addition of *s*.

key/keys pulley/pulleys

Rule 3: Some nouns are the same in the singular and the plural form.

sheep/sheep deer/deer fish/fish

Rule 4: Many singular nouns that end in *f* are pluralized by changing the *f* to *v* and adding *es*.

shelf/shelves leaf/leaves

The plural of many nouns ending in *fe* are formed by changing the *f* to *v* and adding *s*.

knife/knives life/lives

Verb Forms

Rule 5: To form the *-ing* tense of a verb that ends in *e*, drop the final *e*.

wave/waving decide/deciding precede/preceding

Rule 6: Many one-syllable verbs that end in a single consonant require doubling of the consonant in the past tense and in the *-ing* tense.

wrap/wrapped/wrapping pet/petted/petting
fit/fitted/fitting plot/plotted/plotting
strum/strummed/strumming

NOTE: This rule applies to words that contain short vowel sounds, as illustrated in the above examples.

Lesson 1 Exercise

Directions: Edit the following sentences to correct all errors in spelling. Not all of the sentences have errors.

1. Recent discoverys in medicine have changed the way people live.
2. In many citys, trolleys once ran along main streets.
3. The train was delayed for several hours before arriving at the station.
4. The candidates runing for office appeared to have similar views.
5. Many families are prepareing their children for school by helping them learn to read.

Answers are on page 252.

Lesson 2 Possessives

In this lesson, you will learn how to use an *apostrophe* ('), the punctuation mark that is used to show possession or ownership.

A rainbow is made up of raindrops that reflect the sun's rays.

Weather forecasters' predictions have become more accurate because of improved forecasting equipment.

The underlined words in the above sentences are called possessive nouns. They show that something belongs to something or someone else.

Follow the rules below when using apostrophes to form possessive nouns.

Rule 1: If a noun is singular, add an apostrophe and the letter *s* to form the possessive.

Singular Noun	Singular Possessive
catcher	catcher's mitt
driver	driver's license
actress	actress's role

NOTE: If a singular noun ends in *s*, the possessive is formed in the same way—by adding an apostrophe and the letter *s* to the noun. (See the last example given above.)

Rule 2: If a noun is plural and ends in *s*, add only the apostrophe after the *s* to form the possessive.

Plural Noun	Possessive Noun
buses	buses' routes
boys	boys' club
workers	workers' wages

Rule 3: If the noun is plural and does not end in *s*, add an apostrophe and the letter *s* to form the possessive.

Plural Noun	Possessive Noun
people	people's choice
men	men's suits
mice	mice's tails

Pronouns that show possession or ownership are called *possessive pronouns.* Notice the spelling of the underlined possessive pronouns in the sentence below.

Is this <u>your</u> sweater or <u>mine</u>?

The following is a list of possessive pronouns.

my	his	our
mine	her	ours
your	hers	their
yours	its	theirs

Rule 4: Do not use an apostrophe with a possessive pronoun. The possessive pronouns *its* and *your* are frequently misspelled. Remember that if pronouns contain an apostrophe, they are contractions, not possessive pronouns. (For more information on contractions, see Lesson 3.)

A camel stores fat in <u>its</u> hump. <u>It's</u> possible for a deep sea clam to live more than 100 years.

The thickness of the vocal cords determines the pitch of <u>your</u> voice.

Be sure to see the Great Sandy Desert when <u>you're</u> in Australia.

In the above examples, *its* and *your* are possessive pronouns, and *It's* and *you're* are contractions.

Lesson 2 Exercise

Directions: Edit the following sentences to correct all errors in the spelling of possessive nouns and pronouns. Not all of the sentences have errors.

1. The only flag on the moon is our's.
2. American's spend over $1 billion on gum each year.

3. In 1897 girls' bicycles cost about $29.00 each.

4. The anaconda, the world's largest snake, squeezes it's prey to death and swallows it whole.

5. Beethovens' music teacher criticized him for not having musical talent.

Answers are on pages 252–253.

Lesson 3 Contractions

A *contraction* is a word formed by combining two words into one and omitting one or more letters. An apostrophe is used to show where the letter or letters have been omitted in forming a contraction.

Are not Saturn and Uranus the two planets that have rings?

Aren't Saturn and Uranus the two planets that have rings?

Do not hide under a tree during a thunderstorm.

Don't hide under a tree during a thunderstorm.

Chart 3 lists frequently used contractions and the words that form them.

Chart 3	**Contractions and the Words That Form Them**				
is not	isn't	cannot	can't	could have	could've
are not	aren't	could not	couldn't	should have	should've
was not	wasn't	should not	shouldn't	must have	must've
		do not	don't		
		does not	doesn't		
he is	he's	she is	she's	it is	it's
he has	he's	she has	she's	it has	it's
he will	he'll	she will	she'll	it will	it'll
he would	he'd	she would	she'd	it would	it'd
you are	you're	we are	we're	they are	they're
you have	you've	we have	we've	they have	they've
you would	you'd	we would	we'd	they would	they'd
you will	you'll	we will	we'll	they will	they'll
I am	I'm	who is	who's		
I have	I've	let us	let's		
I will	I'll	of the clock	o'clock		
I would	I'd

NOTE: When using contractions, be careful not to confuse them with possessive pronouns.

CONTRACTION: It's estimated that the average American uses the telephone 940 times a year.

POSSESSIVE PRONOUN: Because of its agility, an antelope can outrun a horse.

POSSESSIVE PRONOUN: Spiders do not get caught in their own webs.

CONTRACTION: Cinnamon sticks are a unique spice, for they're rolls of bark from a tree.

CONTRACTION: When you eat cauliflower, you're actually eating undeveloped flower blossoms.

POSSESSIVE PRONOUN: Eating fish can lower your chance of getting heart disease.

NOTE: When you use contractions, do not put the apostrophe in the wrong place. Remember that the apostrophe in a contraction always replaces the missing letter or letters.

INCORRECT: *Was'nt Aristotle the first person to believe the earth was round?*

CORRECT: *Wasn't Aristotle the first person to believe the earth was round?*

Lesson 3 Exercise

Directions: Edit the following sentences to correct all errors in contractions. Not all of the sentences have errors.

1. A person cant jump higher than a horse.
2. Their more telephones in the Pentagon than there are employees.
3. Although it drinks huge amounts of water, a camel does'nt sweat.
4. Its a fact that light travels about 186,000 miles per second.
5. Isn't a seven-sided figure called a heptagon?

Answers are on page 253.

Lesson 4 Homonyms

Many words in the English language are pronounced the same way but are spelled differently and have different meanings. These words are called *homonyms*.

In writing, using the wrong homonym is considered a spelling error.

INCORRECT: Are you already to go?

CORRECT: Are you all ready to go?

In this example the word *already* means *previously*. This would not make sense in the sentence. The correct homonym is *all ready*, meaning *everyone ready* or *completely ready*.

Do not confuse the meaning of a sentence by choosing the wrong homonym. The following list of paired words contains homonyms that are frequently confused. Study the list carefully.

1. **a lot** very much (two words)
   allot to allow

   A lot of people don't like to eat liver.

   Each month I allot $50 for entertainment.

2. **already** previously
   all ready completely ready; everyone ready

   He had already seen that movie.

   They are all ready to sign the contract.

3. **all right** entirely correct
   alright no such word. Do not use.

   It is all right to borrow my car.

4. **altar** a table or stand in a church
   alter to change

   The candles were burning on the altar.

   We had to alter our vacation plans.

5. **altogether** completely or entirely
   all together everyone or everything in the same place

   She wasn't altogether unhappy with the job.

   The family was all together for the holidays.

6. **born** brought forth by birth
borne carried

He was born in October.

The hockey player has borne many injuries.

7. **bored** not interested
board a piece of wood; a group of people who set policy

I was bored with the conversation.

He drove a nail into the board.

The board will meet next Tuesday.

8. **brake** device used to stop a machine
break to fracture or shatter

The engineer pulled the brake to stop the train.

Did you break the window?

9. **Capitol** the name of a building in Washington, D.C.
capital a city that is the official seat of government in a state

The lobby in the Capitol is being repaired.

The capital of California is Sacramento.

10. **coarse** rough
course part of a meal; subject studied in school; path or route

The wallpaper had a coarse feel to it.

We were served salad for the first course.

My math course is difficult but challenging.

We looked for a straight course home.

11. **complement** something that completes something else
compliment a flattering remark

Fresh spices can complement any dish.

How well can you take a compliment?

12. **council**—a group of people that gives advice or makes decisions
counsel—to give advice

The council elected a new president.

The teacher tried to counsel the disruptive student.

13. **dessert**—the final course of a meal
desert—to leave; a dry region

For health reasons, eat fresh fruit for dessert.

Don't desert me now!

The desert has many unusual kinds of plants.

14. **herd**—a group of cattle
heard—the past tense of the verb hear

The herd ran toward the river.

I heard the violinist practicing.

15. **lead**—a metal; graphite in a pencil
led—the past tense of the verb lead

Lead is a very heavy metal.

I broke the lead in this pencil.

The lost hunters were led to safety.

16. **miner**—a worker in a mine
minor—of little importance; under legal age

The miner wore a hard hat for protection.

After a few minor repairs, my car was as good as new.

A child is protected by laws because he or she is a minor.

17. **passed** the past tense of the verb pass
past time that has gone by; beyond in position

Yesterday I passed my driver's test.

The team has not won many games in the past.

He walked past me without saying a word.

18. **peace** the absence of war or strife
piece a part of something

He longed for some peace and quiet.

She offered her guests a second piece of cake.

19. **plain** clear; ordinary; an expanse of level land
plane a tool; an airplane

She made her reasons for retiring very plain.

The house was decorated with plain furniture.

Cattle grazed on the open plain.

We used a plane to smooth the door's edge.

The plane landed on the runway.

20. **principal** head of a school; the most important, main
principle a basic law or rule of action

The principal enjoyed talking to the students.

The principal character died at the end of the play.

The experiment demonstrated the scientific principle.

21. **role** a part in a play
roll to move by turning over and over; a list of names; a round piece of bread

Who played the role of the butler?

The children liked to roll down the steep hill.

The teacher called the roll at the beginning of class.

I like to eat a roll with my soup.

22. **sight** vision; range of vision; spectacle
site a piece of land or location

He valued his sight more than his hearing.

There wasn't a gas station in sight.

The parade was quite a sight.

We looked for a quiet site for our picnic.

23. **stationery** writing paper
stationary in a fixed position

Karen bought another box of stationery.

The desks in the classroom were stationary.

24. **there** in that place; expletive
their possessive pronoun

We are to wait for the bus over there.

Their dog has run away.

25. **to** indicates direction
too also; excessive
two the number 2

I'm anxious to ride in your new car.

Do you like to eat cold pizza, too?

I was too excited to sleep.

Lunch costs two dollars in the cafeteria.

26. **waist** a part of the body
waste to squander; unused material

She wore a leather belt around her waist.

Be careful not to waste food.

A current problem is the disposal of toxic waste.

27. **weak** not strong
week period of seven days

I felt weak after the surgery.

I'll call you next week.

28. **weather** the climate
whether if

The weather in Florida is usually warm.

I didn't know whether or not you heard the telephone ring.

29. **who's** contraction meaning who is or who has
whose possessive pronoun showing ownership

Who's the best pitcher in the major leagues?

I'm not sure whose idea it was.

Lesson 4 Exercise

Directions: Edit the following sentences to correct all homonym errors. Not all of the sentences have errors. Some sentences may have more than one error.

1. It is alright to smile when you receive a complement.
2. In the passed, I have always eaten dessert because I enjoy sweets a lot.
3. Whose car were you driving when you had that minor accident?
4. Next weak the counsel will decide what coarse of action to take.
5. Don't waist stationery because it is to expensive.

Answers are on page 253.

Lesson 5 Spelling List

Good spellers are made, not born. That means that practice is necessary if you want to become a better speller. The following are several ways you can eliminate spelling errors from your writing.

1. **Refer to your dictionary as you write.** Do not guess at the spelling of a word. If you are unsure of the spelling of a word, look it up. To do this, you must first decide how you think the word should be spelled. If the word does not appear in the dictionary according to your initial spelling, try a different spelling. Continue to do this until you find the right word.
2. **Proofread and edit your writing.** When you have finished writing, check your work for errors in capitalization, punctuation, and spelling. Read line by line, looking at each word separately. Concentrate on misused homonyms, troublesome words, incorrect contractions and possessive words, and wrong letters.
3. **Record the errors you make frequently.** Make a special spelling notebook. Divide a page into two columns. In the first column, record the error and underline the letters that were incorrect. In the second column, write the correct spelling of the word. In addition to your dictionary, use this notebook as a reference source when you write.
4. **Learn the spelling rules and devise memory tricks.** Study the spelling rules in this lesson carefully. Remember, however, that most spelling rules have exceptions. It helps to learn these exceptions by devising "memory tricks" for those words that you spell incorrectly most often. These words should also be recorded in your spelling notebook.

   For example, let's say that you have difficulty remembering the spelling of the word *beleive*. When you locate this word in a dictionary, you will find its correct spelling is *believe*. To help you remember to write the *i* before the *e* you might say

   Eve couldn't believe her luck.

   You have taken the word apart, found that it has a word within a word, and devised a memory trick to remember the spelling of this word.
5. As you learn to spell words, use this method:

   See it
   Say it
   Try it

   To use this method, follow these steps.

   1. Picture the word in your mind.
   2. Say the word slowly, dividing it into its syllables (parts). Say it several times.

      su-per-in-ten-dent

   3. Write the word without looking at a list or a dictionary. Check to make sure you have written the word correctly. Then write it several more times.

Study Chart 4, a list of frequently misspelled words. These words, and forms of these words, should be reviewed as part of your preparation for the GED Writing Skills Test.

Chart 4 The Master List of Frequently Misspelled Words

a lot	among	awful	ceiling
ability	amount	awkward	cemetery
absence	analysis	bachelor	cereal
absent	analyze	balance	certain
across	angel	balloon	changeable
abundance	angle	bargain	characteristic
accept	annual	basic	charity
acceptable	another	beautiful	chief
accident	answer	because	choose
accommodate	antiseptic	become	chose
accompanied	anxious	before	cigarette
accomplish	apologize	beginning	circumstance
accumulation	apparatus	being	congratulate
accuse	apparent	believe	citizen
accustomed	appear	benefit	clothes
ache	appearance	benefited	clothing
achieve	appetite	between	coarse
achievement	application	bicycle	coffee
acknowledge	apply	board	collect
acquaintance	appreciate	bored	college
acquainted	appreciation	borrow	column
acquire	approach	bottle	comedy
across	appropriate	bottom	comfortable
address	approval	boundary	commitment
addressed	approve	brake	committed
adequate	approximate	breadth	committee
advantage	argue	breath	communicate
advantageous	arguing	breathe	company
advertise	argument	brilliant	comparative
advertisement	arouse	building	compel
advice	arrange	bulletin	competent
advisable	arrangement	bureau	competition
advise	article	burial	compliment
aerial	artificial	buried	conceal
affect	ascend	bury	conceit
affectionate	assistance	bushes	conceivable
again	assistant	business	conceive
against	associate	cafeteria	concentration
aggravate	association	calculator	conception
aggressive	attempt	calendar	condition
agree	attendance	campaign	conference
aisle	attention	capital	confident
all right	audience	capitol	conquer
almost	August	captain	conscience
already	author	career	conscientious
although	automobile	careful	conscious
altogether	autumn	careless	consequence
always	auxiliary	carriage	consequently
amateur	available	carrying	considerable
American	avenue	category	consistency

Chart 4 The Master List of Frequently Misspelled Words (continued)

consistent	develop	endeavor	frequent
continual	development	engineer	friend
continuous	device	English	frightening
controlled	dictator	enormous	fundamental
controversy	died	enough	further
convenience	difference	entrance	gallon
convenient	different	envelope	garden
conversation	dilemma	environment	gardener
corporal	dinner	equipment	general
corroborate	direction	equipped	genius
council	disappear	especially	government
counsel	disappoint	essential	governor
counselor	disappointment	evening	grammar
courage	disapproval	evident	grateful
courageous	disapprove	exaggerate	great
course	disastrous	exaggeration	grievance
courteous	discipline	examine	grievous
courtesy	discover	exceed	grocery
criticism	discriminate	excellent	guarantee
criticize	disease	except	guess
crystal	dissatisfied	exceptional	guidance
curiosity	dissection	exercise	half
cylinder	dissipate	exhausted	hammer
daily	distance	exhaustion	handkerchief
daughter	distinction	exhilaration	happiness
daybreak	division	existence	healthy
death	doctor	exorbitant	heard
deceive	dollar	expense	heavy
December	doubt	experience	height
deception	dozen	experiment	heroes
decide	earnest	explanation	heroine
decision	easy	extreme	hideous
decisive	ecstasy	facility	himself
deed	ecstatic	factory	hoarse
definite	education	familiar	holiday
delicious	effect	fascinate	hopeless
dependent	efficiency	fascinating	hospital
deposit	efficient	fatigue	humorous
derelict	eight	February	hurried
descend	either	financial	hurrying
descent	eligibility	financier	ignorance
describe	eligible	flourish	imaginary
description	eliminate	forcibly	imbecile
desert	embarrass	forehead	imitation
desirable	embarrassment	foreign	immediately
despair	emergency	formal	immigrant
desperate	emphasis	former	incidental
dessert	emphasize	fortunate	increase
destruction	enclosure	fourteen	independence
determine	encouraging	fourth	independent

Chart 4 The Master List of Frequently Misspelled Words (continued)

indispensable	light	neighbor	perfect
inevitable	lightning	neither	perform
influence	likelihood	newspaper	performance
influential	likely	newsstand	perhaps
initiate	literal	nickel	period
innocence	literature	niece	permanence
inoculate	livelihood	noticeable	permanent
inquiry	loaf	obedient	perpendicular
insistent	loneliness	obstacle	perseverance
instead	loose	occasion	persevere
instinct	lose	occasional	persistent
integrity	losing	occur	personal
intellectual	loyal	occurred	personality
intelligence	loyalty	occurrence	personnel
intercede	magazine	ocean	persuade
interest	maintenance	o'clock	persuasion
interfere	maneuver	offer	pertain
interference	marriage	often	picture
interpreted	married	omission	piece
interrupt	marry	omit	plain
invitation	match	once	playwright
irrelevant	material	operate	pleasant
irresistible	mathematics	opinion	please
irritable	measure	opportune	pleasure
island	medicine	opportunity	pocket
its	million	optimist	poison
it's	miniature	optimistic	policeman
itself	minimum	origin	political
January	miracle	original	population
jealous	miscellaneous	oscillate	portrayal
journal	mischief	ought	positive
judgment	mischievous	ounce	possess
kindergarten	misspelled	overcoat	possession
kitchen	mistake	paid	possessive
knew	momentous	pamphlet	possible
knock	monkey	panicky	post office
know	monotonous	parallel	potatoes
knowledge	moral	parallelism	practical
labor	morale	particular	prairie
laboratory	mortgage	partner	precede
laid	mountain	pastime	preceding
language	mournful	patience	precise
later	muscle	peace	predictable
latter	mysterious	peaceable	prefer
laugh	mystery	pear	preference
leisure	narrative	peculiar	preferential
length	natural	pencil	preferred
lesson	necessary	people	prejudice
library	needle	perceive	preparation
license	negligence	perception	prepare

Chart 4 The Master List of Frequently Misspelled Words (continued)

prescription	remedy	soldier	toward
presence	renovate	solemn	tragedy
president	repeat	sophomore	transferred
prevalent	repetition	soul	treasury
primitive	representative	source	tremendous
principal	requirements	souvenir	tries
principle	resemblance	special	truly
privilege	resistance	specified	twelfth
probably	resource	specimen	twelve
procedure	respectability	speech	tyranny
proceed	responsibility	stationary	undoubtedly
produce	restaurant	stationery	United States
professional	rhythm	statue	university
professor	rhythmical	stockings	unnecessary
profitable	ridiculous	stomach	unusual
prominent	right	straight	useful
promise	role	strength	usual
pronounce	roll	strenuous	vacuum
pronunciation	roommate	stretch	valley
propeller	sandwich	striking	valuable
prophecy	Saturday	studying	variety
prophet	scarcely	substantial	vegetable
prospect	scene	succeed	vein
psychology	schedule	successful	vengeance
pursue	science	sudden	versatile
pursuit	scientific	superintendent	vicinity
quality	scissors	suppress	vicious
quantity	season	surely	view
quarreling	secretary	surprise	village
quart	seize	suspense	villain
quarter	seminar	sweat	visitor
quiet	sense	sweet	voice
quite	separate	syllable	volume
raise	service	symmetrical	waist
realistic	several	sympathy	weak
realize	severely	synonym	wear
reason	shepherd	technical	weather
rebellion	sheriff	telegram	Wednesday
recede	shining	telephone	week
receipt	shoulder	temperament	weigh
receive	shriek	temperature	weird
recipe	siege	tenant	whether
recognize	sight	tendency	which
recommend	signal	therefore	while
recuperate	significance	thorough	whole
referred	significant	through	wholly
rehearsal	similar	title	whose
reign	similarity	together	wretched
relevant	sincerely	tomorrow	
relieve	site	tongue	

Lesson 5 Exercise

Directions: In each set of words, one or more words are misspelled. Circle the misspelled words and write the correct spelling of each word in the exercise.

1. abundance alright
adress antiseptic

2. ascend benefitted
auxilary breadth

3. calender committment
cheif conscientious

4. coroborate deceive
critisism dependant

5. dissappoint exersice
entrence exhileration

6. Febuary freind
financier government

7. grammer imaginary
hankerchief manuever

8. newstand ommission
occassion parallel

9. perserverance rhythm
representative shephard

10. syllable vacuumm
unecessary wierd

Answers are on page 253.

Skill 3 Review

Directions: Edit the following sentences to correct all spelling errors. Not all of the sentences have errors.

1. The flea can jump a distance that is 130 times the height of it's body.
2. Many lives were lost in the war for independance from England.
3. The Caterpillar Club is an organization who's members have used parachutes to save their lives.
4. Every effort was made to accommodate the new principal.
5. Orbiting whether satellites take pictures of cloud formations that surround the earth.
6. Solar energy is an efficeint way to use the sun's energy.
7. More people are buying frozen convenience foods than they ever have before.
8. Honey bee's wings beat over 250 times a second.
9. The developement of the Popsicle is credited to an 11-year-old boy.
10. Did'nt you know that silver is made from the mineral cinnabar?

Check your answers. Correct answers are on page 253. If you have at least eight answers correct, go on to the Chapter 3 Quiz. If you have fewer than eight answers correct, study Skill 3 again. Then go on to the Chapter 3 Quiz.

Chapter 3 Quiz

Directions: Edit the following sentences to correct all errors in mechanics: capitalization, punctuation, and spelling. No sentence has more than one error. Not all of the sentences have errors.

1. If you put a pat of butter on top of cooking liquid, itll keep the liquid from boiling over.
2. The Lincoln Memorial is patterned after an ancient greek temple.
3. When the North Pole tips toward the sun summer occurs in the Northern Hemisphere.
4. A hurricane, a typhoon, and a cyclone, refer to the same kind of storm.

5. Pike's Peak, a famous tourist attraction in colorado, stands 14,110 feet high.

6. At the age of 26, general George Custer fought in the Civil War.

7. President Kennedys two pet cats were named Kitten and Tom.

8. Evergreens are trees that keep their leaves all winter.

9. During the middle ages, Europeans thought garlic would frighten away vampires.

10. Pong, the first coin-operated video game was introduced in 1972.

11. Birds that live in high places are, condors, eagles, and hawks.

12. The Lombardi Trophy is the prize given to the winning Team of the Super Bowl.

13. The U.S. Battleship *Oregon* was built very close to the dimensions of Noah's Ark.

14. The Atacama Desert by the way, is located in South America.

15. In a librarys' Dewey Decimal Classification System, rare books can be found under the number 090.

16. Our universe contains billions of galaxies and, the nearest to our own is two billion light-years away.

17. Neither Bolivia nor Paraguay borders on either the Atlantic, or Pacific oceans.

18. Yes the Hawaiian Islands are actually the tops of an underwater mountain range.

19. Begining in 1943, income tax was withheld from workers' paychecks.

20. Their are more than 20,000 kinds of fish, but we eat very few of them.

Answers are on pages 253–254.

Chapter 4

Editing Paragraphs

Objective

In this chapter you will learn about

- The three types of questions on Part 1 of the GED Writing Skills Test: Sentence-Correction Items, Sentence-Revision Items, and Construction-Shift Items
- The editing process, including the 5-R method of editing
- Editing for correct usage
- Editing for correct sentence structure
- Editing for mechanical correctness
- Editing paragraphs

Lesson 1 The Three Types of Questions on the GED Writing Skills Test

Chapters 1 to 3 dealt with the kinds of errors that are found most often in writing. You used this knowledge to find errors in individual sentences. In this chapter you will practice finding these errors in sentences within paragraphs.

On the GED Test, you will read paragraphs to find various kinds of errors, but you will not be told what specific type of error to find. This chapter will teach you about the actual types of multiple-choice test items that are used on the Writing Skills section of the GED Test. It will also help you learn how to apply techniques to find usage, mechanical, and sentence structure errors in sentences within paragraphs.

To successfully complete the Writing Skills section of the GED Test, you will have to know how to proofread effectively. *Proofreading* is the skill of recognizing and correcting errors within sentences. The GED Test will require that you do four basic tasks:

1. Read paragraphs.
2. Proofread sentences.
3. Evaluate suggested answers.
4. Select answers that illustrate effective writing.

As you read a paragraph, you will see that each sentence is numbered. These numbers correspond to multiple-choice test items that follow each paragraph. For example, a test item might look like this:

(1) Have you ever wondered how a magician succeeds at the trick of sawing a woman in half? (2) The illusion really involves two women. (3) One is already hidden in the table. (4) She climbs into the box through a trap-door in the table and sticks her feet out of the end of the box. (5) The other woman draws her knees up to her chin. (6) An empty space results, and its here that the magician begins to saw the box in half.

Sentence 6: **An empty space results, and its here that the magician begins to saw the box in half.**

What correction should be made to this sentence?

(1) change *results* to *result*
(2) remove the comma after *results*
(3) change *its* to *it's*
(4) insert a comma after *begins*
(5) change *half* to *halve*

The sentence to be corrected is repeated in the item. The five suggested alternatives (or answers) will follow. They will be presented in the order in which they occur in the sentence. These alternatives may suggest different kinds of changes: spelling, capitalization, punctuation, verb tense, subject-verb agreement, pronoun reference, and sentence structure.

Remember, however, that there is only one possible error in each sentence. That means that only one answer can be correct in any test item. Look at the sample paragraph and test item again. Which answer would you choose to correct sentence 6? If you chose alternative 3, you were correct, because the original sentence has a contraction error.

The Three Types of Test Items

There are three types of multiple-choice items on the Writing Skills Test. Each type will test your knowledge of sentence structure, usage, and mechanics.

Approximately 50 percent of the questions will be *sentence-correction items*. These items will test your knowledge of sentence structure, usage, spelling, punctuation, and capitalization. This type of test item will repeat a sentence from the paragraph and ask what correction is needed.

Sentence 3: **Most prosessed foods are high in salt, and some are high in sugar.**

What correction should be made to this sentence?

(1) change the spelling of *prosessed* to *processed*
(2) change *are* to *is*
(3) remove the comma after *salt*
(4) insert a comma after *and*
(5) no correction is necessary

After you read the sentence, review each alternative carefully. In this example, alternative (1) is the correct choice. In several of this type of test item, the fifth alternative will be *no correction is necessary*, as it is in this example. This will sometimes be the correct choice.

The second type of question will be *sentence-revision items*, which test your knowledge of sentence structure, usage, and punctuation. In these items, part of the sentence will be underlined. This underlined portion may or may not contain an error. These items also will have five alternatives. The first alternative will be the same as the original sentence. The other alternatives will suggest possible changes.

Sentence 1: **The purchase of videocassette recorders, a popular form of electronic entertainment has exceeded expected sales levels.**

Which of the following is the best way to write the underlined portion of this sentence? If you think the original is the best way, choose option (1).

(1) entertainment has exceeded
(2) entertainment. Has exceeded
(3) entertainment, has exceeded
(4) entertainment; has exceeded
(5) entertainment has exceeded,

Which answer would you choose? The word *entertainment* is at the end of a sentence-interrupting phrase, which should end with a comma. Alternative (3) is the correct choice.

Construction-shift items are the third type of test item. They will also test your knowledge of sentence structure, usage, and mechanics. You will not, however, be looking for the same kinds of errors as you did in sentence-revision and sentence-correction items. Instead, you will be asked to change a sentence that may be awkward or unclear. In each item, you will be shown how the sentence might be changed.

Sentences 8 & 9: **Bob is going on vacation. His cousin is going, too.**

If you rewrote sentences 8 and 9 beginning with Bob and his cousin, the next word would be

(1) doesn't
(2) is
(3) are
(4) isn't
(5) aren't

You will need to decide which alternative suggests the best way to write the sentence without changing its meaning. In the example, one element of each sentence has been combined in the new sentence. A verb form is needed to agree with the new plural subject. Alternative (5) would be incorrect because it changes the meaning of the original sentence. Alternative (3) is the correct choice.

Check your understanding of the three types of multiple-choice questions. If you have difficulty finding errors in these sentences, you may need to review Chapters 1 to 3. Remember, however, that some items may not have an error.

Lesson 1 Exercise

Directions: Read the following sentences. They contain errors in sentence structure, usage, and mechanics. No sentence contains more than one error. Answer the questions that follow by circling the number of the one best answer for each question.

1. Sentence 1: **The U.S. Air Force use planes equipped with radar to determine the position of a hurricane.**

   What correction should be made to this sentence?

   (1) change *use* to *uses*
   (2) change the spelling of *equipped* to *equipted.*
   (3) insert a comma after *radar*
   (4) replace *to* with *two*
   (5) no correction is necessary

2. Sentence 2: **In 1925, a committee was appointed to decide who was to be pictured on the United States currency it decided that the presidents should be pictured.**

   Which of the following is the best way to write the underlined portion of this sentence? If you think the original is the best way, choose option (1).

   (1) currency it decided
   (2) currency, it decided
   (3) currency. It was decided
   (4) currency and it decided
   (5) currency and, it decided

3. Sentence 3: **With the use of a radar gun, teams have determined that "Goose" Gossage can throw a baseball 98 miles an hour.**

   What correction should be made to this sentence?

   (1) remove the comma after gun
   (2) change *have* to *has*
   (3) change *can* to *will*
   (4) change *throw* to *through*
   (5) no correction is necessary

4. Sentence 4: **Ernest Hemingway a notable American author, received the Nobel Prize for Literature in 1954.**

   What correction should be made to this sentence?

   (1) insert a comma after *Hemingway*
   (2) change the spelling of *notable* to *noteable*
   (3) change *American* to *american*
   (4) remove the comma after *author*
   (5) change the spelling of *received* to *recieved*

5. Sentences 5 & 6: **Neal enjoyed being with people. He went to the movies alone.**

If you rewrote sentences 5 and 6 beginning with Neil enjoyed being with people, the next word would be

(1) because
(2) sometimes
(3) but
(4) it
(5) with

Answers are on page 254.

Lesson 2 The Editing Process

Proofreading for errors in written material can help produce more effective writing. In addition to checking for usage and mechanical errors, it is important to check for correct meaning and word choice. The application of these skills is called *editing*.

The word *edit* can be thought of as a description of the combination of these skills. When you edit, you

- Evaluate written material
- Delete errors
- Increase understanding
- Transmit effectively written material

As you read and edit each sentence, ask yourself these questions.

Is it correct? Look for capitalization, punctuation, grammar, and spelling errors. Apply all of your proofreading skills.

Is it complete? Look for errors in sentence structure. Each sentence must be well written and must express a complete thought.

Is it clear? Proper word choice is necessary to make a sentence easy to understand.

Is it consistent? The ideas in a sentence should be logical. Check to make sure the sentence and its usage are uniform in the expression of ideas.

Following a process will help you work through each multiple-choice item on the GED Test. This process will help you to concentrate on the content of each question.

This lesson will teach you a process for using your proofreading and editing skills to identify usage, sentence structure, and mechanics errors in paragraphs. It is called the 5-R method of editing.

The 5-R Method of Editing

The 5-R method of editing is an effective process for answering items on the GED Test. In this method you will

Read Reflect Revise Reread Record

To use this method, complete each step in this order.

Step 1 Read Read the paragraph for its meaning and its writing style.

Step 2 Reflect Read through the paragraph, underlining errors that you can recognize. Ask yourself: Is it correct? complete? clear?

Step 3 Revise Read the first item and its alternatives. Decide which alternative identifies and corrects the error.

Step 4 Reread Read the revised sentence with the selected correction. If you are satisfied with the answer, you are ready to go on to the next step. If you are not satisfied with the answer, go back to Step 3.

Step 5 Record Mark the number of the alternative that you have chosen. Then, move on to the next item.

Use the steps in the 5-R method with the following paragraph.

(1) Rick Barry has always been a top scorer in his basketball career. (2) His ability was aparent even in high school, when more than 30 colleges offered him basketball scholarships. (3) After he became a leading scorer for the University of Miami he was chosen to play for the San Francisco Warriors. (4) He averaged more than 25 points a game and was named Rookie of the Year in 1965. (5) The next year he scored 40 points in the All-Star game. (6) He was named the game's Most Valuable Player.

1. Sentence 2: **His ability was aparent even in high school, when more than 30 colleges offered him basketball scholarships.**

   What correction should be made to this sentence?

   (1) change *was* to *were*
   (2) change the spelling of *aparent* to *apparent*
   (3) insert a comma after *aparent*
   (4) replace *when* with *where*
   (5) no correction is necessary

2. Sentence 3: **After he became a leading scorer for the University of Miami he was chosen to play for the San Francisco Warriors.**

   Which of the following is the best way to write the underlined portion of this sentence? If you think the original is the best way, choose option (1).

   (1) Miami he was chosen
   (2) Miami. He was chosen
   (3) Miami, he was chosen
   (4) Miami, because he was chosen
   (5) Miami and he was chosen

3. Sentences 5 & 6: **The next year he scored 40 points in the All-Star game. He was named the game's Most Valuable Player.**

The most effective combination of sentences 5 and 6 would begin with which word?

(1) Whenever
(2) Although
(3) On the other hand
(4) Because
(5) However

The correct answer for item 1 is alternative (2). This sentence-correction item has a spelling error. The correct answer for item 2 is alternative (3). This sentence-revision item points out a punctuation error. The correct answer for item 3 is alternative (4), as shown in a construction-shift item.

As you practice the 5-R method, you will gain confidence in using it. Eventually, you will not need to write down every response in each step. You should be able to answer an item by just thinking about it.

Lesson 2 Exercise

Directions: Read the following paragraph. It contains errors in usage, sentence structure, and mechanics. No sentence contains more than one error. Use the 5-R method of editing to work through the first three items and to record your responses at each step. Your final answer should be written on the line for Step 5.

Items 1 to 5 are based on the following paragraph.

(1) Did you know that salt is added to canned vegetables, soups, ice cream, cheeses, frozen dinners, pizza, crackers and cereals? (2) In fact, salt are in almost every convenience food on grocery store shelves. (3) Eating too many of these foods can be dangerous your health may suffer. (4) Excessive salt intake can lead to high blood pressure. (5) In fact, one in every five Americans had high blood pressure. (6) Studies have shown that patients with hypertension can be treated successfully. (7) They can control the amount of salt they eat.

1. Sentence 1: **Did you know that salt is added to canned vegetables, soups, ice cream, cheese, frozen dinners, <u>pizza, crackers and cereals?</u>**

Which of the following is the best way to write the underlined portion of this sentence? If you think the original is the best way, choose option (1).

(1) pizza, crackers and cereals?
(2) pizza crackers and cereals?
(3) pizza, crackers and, cereals?
(4) pizza, crackers, and, cereals?
(5) pizza, crackers, and cereals?

Step 1. Read: ____________ **Step 2.** Reflect: ____________
Step 3. Revise: ____________ **Step 4.** Reread: ____________
Step 5. Record: ____________

2. Sentence 2: **In fact, salt are in almost every convenience food on grocery store shelves.**

(1) replace *In* with *As*
(2) remove the comma after *fact*
(3) change *are* to *is*
(4) change the spelling of *convenience* to *convenence*
(5) insert a comma after *food*

Step 1. Read: ____________ **Step 2.** Reflect: ____________
Step 3. Revise: ____________ **Step 4.** Reread: ____________
Step 5. Record: ____________

3. Sentence 3: **Eating too many of these foods can be dangerous your health may suffer.** What correction should be made to this sentence?

(1) replace *too* with *to*
(2) insert a comma after *foods*
(3) change *can be* to *was*
(4) insert a semicolon after *dangerous*
(5) no correction is necessary

Step 1. Read: ____________ **Step 2.** Reflect: ____________
Step 3. Revise: ____________ **Step 4.** Reread: ____________
Step 5. Record: ____________

Directions: For the next two items, do not write any response to the steps. Simply check each step after you have completed thinking about it. Circle the correct answer within the test item itself.

4. Sentence 5: **In fact, one in every five Americans had high blood pressure.**

Which of the following is the best way to write the underlined portion of this sentence? If you think the original is the best way, choose option (1).

(1) Americans had high
(2) Americans, had high
(3) americans has high
(4) Americans has, high
(5) Americans has high

Step 1. ____________ **Step 2.** ____________
Step 3. ____________ **Step 4.** ____________
Step 5. ____________

5. Sentences 6 & 7: **Studies have shown that patients with hypertension can be treated successfully. They can control the amount of salt they eat.**

The most effective combination of sentences 6 and 7 would include

(1) treated successfully, to control
(2) treated successfully by controlling
(3) treated successfully and controlling
(4) treated successfully during controlling
(5) treated successfully controlling

Step 1. ____________ **Step 2.** ____________
Step 3. ____________ **Step 4.** ____________
Step 5. ____________

Answers are on page 254.

Lesson 3 Editing for Correct Usage

Your knowledge of usage will be tested in about 35 percent of the questions on Part I of the GED Writing Skills Test. All three types of questions that were discussed in Lesson 1 will be used. To answer usage questions effectively, you need to organize your thinking in two ways.

First, use these two steps from the 5-R method of editing.

1. *Read* the paragraph.
2. *Reflect* by looking for and underlining errors in usage.

Second, as you *reflect*, ask yourself these questions.

1. *Do the subjects agree with the verbs?*

INCORRECT: One of the letters have been received.
CORRECT: One of the letters had been received.

2. *Are the verbs in the correct tense?*

INCORRECT: I had wrote to him two weeks ago.
CORRECT: I had written to him two weeks ago.

3. *Are the pronouns used correctly and clearly?*

INCORRECT: Him and her were assigned to the same project.
CORRECT: He and she were assigned to the same project.

Read the following paragraph. *Read* and *reflect*, and then apply the three usage questions listed above.

> (1) Married women is entering the labor force because of economic need. (2) Nearly three million working women have husbands who are not worked. (3) Inflation has caused families to rely on a second income to maintain its standard of living.

You should have found one subject that did not agree with its verb (sentence 1: *women/is*), one verb that was not in the correct tense (sentence 2: *not worked*), and one pronoun that was not used correctly (sentence 3:

its). If you had difficulty finding these errors, you may need to review Chapter 1 before doing the exercise for this lesson.

Lesson 3 Exercise

Directions: Read the following paragraph. As you read, ask yourself the three basic questions that are used when editing for usage. No sentence contains more than one error. Use the 5-R method of editing as you work through each question.

Items 1 to 5 are based on the following paragraph.

(1) The first microwave oven produced for home use was introduced in 1945. (2) Since then, the use of these ovens is increased because of the speed with which they cook food. (3) Food in these ovens is cooked by friction. (4) Short radio waves, called microwaves, travels through a metal tube that scatters the waves throughout the oven. (5) They bounce off the oven's wall and enter the food. (6) They cause the food's molecules to vibrate. (7) The resulting motion produce heat, which, in turn, cooks the food. (8) These waves can pass through glass, cardboard, or china. (9) Therefore, containers made of these materials are safe to used in this type of oven.

1. Sentence 2: **Since then, the use of these ovens is increased because of the speed with which they cook food.**

   What correction should be made to this sentence?

   (1) change *then* to *than*
   (2) change *is* to *have*
   (3) change *is* to *has*
   (4) insert a comma after *because*
   (5) change *they* to *it*

2. Sentence 4: **Short radio waves, called microwaves, travels through a metal tube that scatters the waves throughout the oven.**

   Which of the following is the best way to write the underlined portion of this sentence? If you think the original is the best way, choose option (1).

   (1) waves, called microwaves, travels
   (2) waves called microwaves, travels
   (3) waves called microwaves travel
   (4) waves called microwaves travels
   (5) waves, called microwaves, travel

3. Sentences 5 & 6: **They bounce off the oven's walls and enter the food. They cause the food's molecules to vibrate.**

   The most effective combination of sentences 5 and 6 would include which of the following groups of words?

   (1) enter the food, causing
   (2) enter the food, and causes
   (3) enter the food, causes
   (4) enter the food, in fact causing
   (5) enter the food, but cause

4. Sentence 7: **The resulting motion produce heat, which, in turn, cooks the food.**

What correction should be made to this sentence?

(1) insert a comma after *motion*
(2) change *produce* to *produces*
(3) remove the comma after *which*
(4) change *cooks* to *cook*
(5) no correction is necessary

5. Sentence 9: **Therefore, containers made of these materials are safe to used in this type of oven.**

What correction should be made to this sentence?

(1) remove the comma after *Therefore*
(2) change *these materials* to *this material*
(3) insert a comma after *materials*
(4) change the spelling of *safe* to *saif*
(5) change *used* to *use*

Answers are on page 254.

Lesson 4 Editing for Correct Sentence Structure

Your knowledge of sentence structure will be tested in about 35 percent of the questions on Part I of the GED Writing Skills Test. All three types of questions discussed in Lesson 1 will be used.

To effectively answer these questions, you will need to organize your thinking in two ways.

First, follow the *Read* and *Reflect* steps of the 5-R method of editing. Then ask yourself these questions.

1. **Do all groups of words that have a subject and a verb express a complete thought?**

INCORRECT: Wooden ducks.
CORRECT: Mark enjoys carving wooden ducks.

2. **Are all compound sentences written in proper form?**

INCORRECT: Last Tuesday John went to the doctor, he went to the dentist.
CORRECT: Last Tuesday John went to the doctor and he went to the dentist.

3. **Are the sentences clearly written, logically organized, and consistent in form?**

INCORRECT: The dog chased the cat barking noisily up the tree.
CORRECT: Barking noisily, the dog chased the cat up the tree.

Read the following paragraph. As you *read* and *reflect*, apply the sentence-structure questions that are listed above.

(1) Video games have become a big business. (2) Over 14 million game consoles have been installed in U.S. homes, over 75 million game cartridges have been sold. (3) Each year, over $5 billion is spent playing video machines in video arcades. (4) Why are people intent on spending so much money on these games? (5) Video games provide a source of stimulation, a temporary escape from the real world, and broke up the feeling of boredom. (6) Because as long as people feel this need to add excitement to their lives, they will continue to spend money on this form of entertainment.

You should have found one comma-splice sentence (sentence 2), one sentence that lacked parallel structure (sentence 5), and one sentence that had a subordination error (sentence 6). If you had difficulty finding these errors, you may need to review Chapter 2 before doing the exercise for this lesson.

Lesson 4 Exercise

Directions: Read the following paragraph. As you read, ask yourself the three basic questions that are used when editing for sentence structure. No sentence contains more than one error. Use the 5-R method of editing as you work through each question.

Items 1 to 5 are based on the following paragraph.

(1) Everyone at some time faces the task of looking for a job. (2) However, job seekers often limit themselves. (3) They only look in the want-ad section of the newspaper. (4) Even while this will give you a start, it's not the only source to use. (5) Some people have actually run their own ads. (6) They list their skills, the type of work they are seeking, and telling their phone number. (7) Another good idea is to check library bulletin boards they frequently display job listings. (8) A third idea is to choose a field of employment that interests you, locate employers in the Yellow Pages of the telephone book, and call a few, asking if they need additional help. (9) Last, such job sources don't overlook as school alumni associations, employment agencies, and government personnel offices.

1. Sentences 2 & 3: **However, job seekers often limit themselves. They only look in the want-ad section of the newspaper.**

The most effective combination of sentences 2 and 3 would include which of the following groups of words?

(1) themselves, besides they only look
(2) themselves, but they only look
(3) themselves by only looking
(4) themselves, afterward looking
(5) themselves whether looking

2. Sentence 4: **Even while this will give you a start, it's not the only source to use.**

   What correction should be made to this sentence?

   (1) remove *Even*
   (2) insert a comma after *while*
   (3) remove the comma after *start*
   (4) change *it's* to *its*
   (5) no correction is necessary

3. Sentence 6: **They list their skills, the type of work they are seeking, and telling their phone number.**

   Which of the following is the best way to write the underlined portion of this sentence? If you think the original is the best way, choose option (1).

   (1) seeking, and telling their phone number.
   (2) seeking and telling their phone number.
   (3) seek, and tell their phone number.
   (4) seek and their phone number.
   (5) seeking, and their phone number.

4. Sentence 7: **Another good idea is to check library bulletin boards they frequently display job listings.**

   Which of the following is the best way to write the underlined portion of this sentence? If you think the original is the best way, choose option (1).

   (1) boards they frequently display
   (2) boards who frequently display
   (3) boards; they frequently display
   (4) boards, employers frequently display
   (5) boards, who frequently display

5. Sentence 9: **Last, such job sources don't overlook as school alumni associations, employment agencies, and government personnel offices.**

   Which of the following is the best way to write the underlined portion of this sentence? If you think the original is the best way, choose option (1).

   (1) such job sources don't overlook
   (2) such sources do not overlook
   (3) overlook such sources
   (4) don't overlook such job sources
   (5) don't overlook, such job sources

Answers are on page 254.

Lesson 5 Editing for Mechanical Correctness

Your knowledge of mechanics will be tested in about 30 percent of the questions on Part I of the GED Writing Skills Test. Once again, all three types of questions that were discussed in Lesson 1 will be used.

To answer these questions effectively, you will need to organize your thinking in two ways.

First, follow the first two steps in the 5-R method of editing.

1. *Read* the paragraph.
2. *Reflect* by looking for mechanical errors.

Second, as you *reflect*, ask yourself these three questions.

1. Are all the appropriate words capitalized correctly?

INCORRECT: The white house is on pennsylvania avenue in washington, d.c.

CORRECT: The White House is on Pennsylvania Avenue in Washington, D.C.

2. Are all words and sentences punctuated correctly?

INCORRECT: Diane likes jazz country and heavy metal music.

CORRECT: Diane likes jazz, country, and heavy metal music.

3. Are all words spelled correctly?

INCORRECT: The pilot announced that our flight was on scedule.

CORRECT: The pilot announced that our flight was on schedule.

Read the following paragraph. As you read and reflect, apply the mechanics questions listed above.

(1) Using a rocket-powered airplane, captain Charles E. Yeager was the first person to break the sound barrier. (2) Because of the speed of the airplane a sonic boom was created. (3) This sound is nothing more than a shock wave, which is caused by differences in air pressure. (4) The sonic boom has been an important part of the further development of supersonic plains.

You should have found one capitalization error (sentence 1), one punctuation error (sentence 2), and one spelling error (sentence 4). If you had difficulty finding these errors, you may need to review Chapter 3 before doing the exercise for this lesson.

Lesson 5 Exercise

Directions: Read the following paragraph. As you read, ask yourself the three basic questons that are used when editing for mechanical errors. No sentence contains more than one error. Use the 5-R method of editing as you work through each question.

Items 1 to 5 are based on the following paragraph.

(1) Television networks rely upon ratings to determine the popularity of they're shows. (2) The A.C. Nielsen company is one of the most important firms that provides this sevice. (3) The Nielsen service includes over 1,200 homes across the United States. (4) On the basis of Census Bureau figures, certain households are selected as representitive of certain locations. (5) An audimeter, a machine that measures all TV set usage is placed in these homes. (6) It records when a TV set is turned on and the length of time each channel is used. (7) The audimeter is connected to a special phone line that retrieves the stored information. (8) This information is then processed by the companys computer, and within a few hours the ratings are ready for publication.

1. Sentence 1: **Television networks rely upon ratings to determine the popularity of they're shows.**

   What correction should be made to this sentence?

   (1) change *rely* to *relies*
   (2) insert a comma after *ratings*
   (3) replace *to* with *too*
   (4) change *they're* to *their*
   (5) no correction is necessary

2. Sentence 2: **The A.C. Nielsen company is one of the most important firms that provides this service.**

   What correction should be made to this sentence?

   (1) change *company* to *Company*
   (2) insert a comma after *most*
   (3) replace *that* with *whom*
   (4) change *provides* to *provide*
   (5) change the spelling of *service* to *servise*

3. Sentence 4: **On the basis of Census Bureau figures, certain households are selected as representitive of certain locations.**

   What correction should be made to this sentence?

   (1) remove the comma after *figures*
   (2) change *are* to *is*
   (3) insert a comma after *selected*
   (4) change the spelling of *representitive* to *representative*
   (5) no correction is necessary

4. Sentence 5: **An audimeter, a machine that measures all TV set usage is placed in these homes.**

Which of the following is the best way to write the underlined portion of this sentence? If you think the original is the best way, choose option (1).

(1) usage is placed
(2) usage; is placed
(3) ,usage is placed
(4) usage, is placed
(5) usage is placed,

5. Sentence 8: **This information is then processed by the companys computer, and within a few hours the ratings are ready for publication.**

Which of the following is the best way to write the underlined portion of this sentence? If you think the original is the best way, choose option (1).

(1) companys computer, and
(2) companys computer and
(3) companys computer and,
(4) company's computer and
(5) company's computer, and

Answers are on page 254.

Lesson 6 Editing Paragraphs

In this chapter, you have learned how to organize your thinking. You have learned about

- The three types of questions on Part I of the GED Writing Skills Test
- The 5-R method of editing paragraphs
- Questions to ask yourself when applying your knowledge of usage, sentence structure, and mechanics

This lesson will show you how to edit paragraphs that contain all types of errors. Continue using the 5-R method of editing and ask yourself the three groups of content questions. Chart 1 will help you review the process.

Chart 1 The 5-R Method of Editing

5-R Step	That Means:
Read	Read the paragraph for meaning and organization.
Reflect	Locate possible errors by asking the three groups of content questions. **Usage** 1. Do the subjects agree with the verbs? 2. Are the verbs in the correct tense? 3. Are the pronouns used correctly and clearly? **Sentence Structure** 1. Do all groups of words that have a subject and a verb express a complete thought? 2. Are all compound sentences written in proper form? 3. Are the sentences written clearly, organized logically, and consistent in form? **Mechanics** 1. Are all appropriate words capitalized correctly? 2. Are all words and sentences punctuated correctly? 3. Are all words spelled correctly?
Revise	Choose the correct alternative.
Reread	Check your selection.
Record	Mark your answer.

Remember these points when answering any questions on the GED Writing Skills Test.

Four Points to Remember

1. You will not be told the kinds of errors that will appear in a paragraph.
2. The alternatives to an item will suggest possible errors.
3. There will be only one kind of error in each sentence.
4. Not all sentences have errors. In some items, your choice will show that the sentence is correct.

Lesson 6 Exercise

Directions: Read the following paragraph. Using the knowledge and methods that you have learned in this book, answer the items that follow.

Items 1 to 10 are based on the following paragraph.

(1) Our society has become increasengly obsessed with height. (2) Recent studies have showed that our stature may influence the jobs we get and the salaries we earn. (3) The *Wall Street Journal* reported the results of a study done by David Kurtz a marketing professor. (4) His study revealed that when 140 job recruiters had to make a choice between two equally qualified applicants, the applicant who was over 6 feet tall was hired more often than the applicant who's height was significantly under 6 feet tall. (5) In fact, 72 percent of the recruiters hired the taller person. (6) Since taller people also began with higher starting salaries and received larger salary increases. (7) There is an explanation for height being given so much consideration; it is much easier to assess than a person's ability or motivation. (8) However though, these results have been interpreted as a possible source of prejudice and employment discrimination. (9) Whatever the interpretation, height have been an important factor in employment decisions. (10) *U.S. News and World Report* have said that height bias is ". . . a reality most must face at one time or another in their working lives."

1. Sentence 1: **Our society has become increasengly obsessed with height.**

   What correction should be made to this sentence?

   (1) change *our* to *our'*
   (2) change *has* to *have*
   (3) change the spelling of *increasengly* to *increasingly*
   (4) insert a comma after *increasengly*
   (5) no correction is necessary

2. Sentence 2: **Recent studies have showed that our stature may influence the jobs we get and the salaries we earn.**

   What correction should be made to this sentence?

   (1) change the spelling of *studies* to *studys*
   (2) change *have showed* to *have shown*
   (3) insert a comma after *showed*
   (4) insert a comma after *get*
   (5) change *salaries* to *salary's*

3. Sentence 3: **The *Wall Street Journal* reported the results of a study done by David Kurtz a marketing professor.**

Which of the following is the best way to write the underlined portion of this sentence? If you think the original is the best way, choose option (1).

(1) by David Kurtz
(2) by David Kurtz.
(3) by, David Kurtz
(4) by David Kurtz,
(5) by, David Kurtz,

4. Sentence 4: **His study revealed that when 140 job recruiters had to make a choice between two equally qualified applicants, the applicant who was over 6 feet tall was hired more often than the applicant who's height was significantly under 6 feet tall.**

What correction should be made to this sentence?

(1) insert a comma after *that*
(2) change *between* to *among*
(3) change the spelling of *applicants* to *aplicants*
(4) remove the comma after *applicants*
(5) change *who's* to *whose*

5. Sentence 5: **In fact, 72 percent of the recruiters hired the taller person.**

Which of the following is the best way to write the underlined portion of this sentence? If you think the original is the best way, choose option (1).

(1) recruiters hired
(2) recruiters, hired
(3) recruiters hired,
(4) recruiters who hired
(5) recruiters who hired,

6. Sentence 6: **Since taller people also began with higher starting salaries and received larger salary increases.**

What correction should be made to this sentence?

(1) remove *Since*
(2) insert a comma after *began*
(3) insert a comma after *and*
(4) change the spelling of *received* to *recieved*
(5) no correction is necessary

7. Sentence 7: **There is an explanation for height being given so much consideration; it is much easier to assess than a person's ability or motivation.**

If you rewrote sentence 5 beginning with

Height may be given so much consideration,

the next word would be

(1) nevertheless
(2) in fact
(3) because
(4) so that
(5) and

8. Sentence 8: **However though, these results have been interpreted as a possible source of prejudice and employment discrimination.**

Which of the following is the best way to write the underlined portion of this sentence? If you think the original is the best way, choose option (1).

(1) However though, these results
(2) However though these results,
(3) However, these results
(4) However; though these results
(5) However, these results,

9. Sentence 9: **Whatever the interpretation, height have been an important factor in employment decisions.**

What correction should be made to this sentence?

(1) change *Whatever* to *Whichever*
(2) remove the comma after *interpretation*
(3) insert a comma after *factor*
(4) change *have been* to *can be*
(5) no correction is necessary

10. Sentence 10: **U.S. News and World Report have said that height bias is ". . . a reality most must face at one time or another in their working lives."**

Which of the following is the best way to write the underlined portion of this sentence? If you think the original is the best way, choose option (1).

(1) *U.S. News and World Report* have said
(2) *U.S. News and World Report* has said,
(3) *U.S. News and World Report* have said,
(4) *U.S. News and World Report* has said
(5) *U.S. News and World Report*, has said,

Answers are on pages 254–255.

Chapter 4 Quiz

1. Described below are the tasks you complete when you use the 5-R method of editing. Write the name of each step after its description. Choose from these terms: *Reread, Reflect, Record, Read, Revise.*

   (1) Mark your answer. ____________
   (2) Choose an alternative. ____________
   (3) Determine meaning and organization. ____________
   (4) Check your choice. ____________
   (5) Locate the error. ____________

2. Next, list the steps in their correct order.

   (1) ____________
   (2) ____________
   (3) ____________
   (4) ____________
   (5) ____________

Directions: The following paragraph contains numbered sentences. These sentences may have errors in usage, sentence structure, and mechanics. Read the paragraph and answer the items that follow. For each item, choose the answer that would result in the most effective writing of the sentence.

Items 3 to 10 are based on the following paragraph.

(1) One of the fastest-growing industries in our nation is the fast-food business. (2) The results of a study conducted by the Newspaper Advertising Bureau showed that the average American over 12 years old eat in a fast-food restaurant at least 9 times a month. (3) Having studied buying trends, market researchers conclude that fast-food restaurants are profitable because it fill a need. (4) While people began to patronize fast-food restaurants for their novelty. (5) They now frequent them because these types of restaurants are convenient, inexpensive, and saving time. (6) McDonald's for example, attempts to serve a typical meal of a hamburger, french fries, and a shake in about 50 seconds. (7) Burger King can broil a hamburger in 80 seconds and can produce over 700 Whoppers in an hour! (8) The bureau of Labor Statistics reports that in 1981 we spent 32.4 percent of our total food expenditures for restaurant meals. (9) Translating this percentage into dollars, the total sales for just McDonald's, Burger King, and Wendy's reached $12 billion in 1984. (10) In 1966 McDonald's billboards told us, "2 billion sold." (11) In 1984 they boasted, "45 billion sold." (12) Marketing forecasts show that these increasing numbers of fast-food sales are likely to continue.

3. Sentence 2: **The results of a study conducted by the Newspaper Advertising Bureau showed that the average <u>American over 12 years old eat</u> in a fast-food restaurant at least 9 times a month.**

Which of the following is the best way to write the underlined portion of this sentence? If you think the original is the best way, choose option (1).

(1) American over 12 years old eat
(2) American, over 12 years old, eat
(3) American over 12 years old eats
(4) American over 12 years old, eats
(5) American, over 12 years old eats

4. Sentence 3: **Having studied buying trends, market researchers conclude that fast-food restaurants are profitable because it fill a need.**

What correction should be made to this sentence?

(1) remove the comma after *trends*
(2) change *conclude* to *will conclude*
(3) insert a comma after *conclude*
(4) change the spelling of *profitable* to *profitible*
(5) replace *it* with *they*

5. Sentence 4: **While people began to patronize fast-food restaurants for their novelty.**

What correction should be made to this sentence?

(1) remove *While*
(2) replace *While* with *After*
(3) change *began* to *begun*
(4) insert a comma after *began*
(5) no correction is necessary

6. Sentence 5: **They now frequent them because these types of restaurants are convenient, <u>inexpensive, and saving time.</u>**

Which of the following is the best way to write the underlined portion of this sentence? If you think the original is the best way, choose option (1).

(1) inexpensive, and saving time.
(2) inexpensive and saving time.
(3) inexpensive and time-saving.
(4) inexpensive, and time-saving.
(5) inexpensive, and save time.

7. Sentence 6: **McDonald's for example, attempts to serve a typical meal of a hamburger, french fries, and a shake in about 50 seconds.**

What correction should be made to this sentence?

(1) insert a comma after *McDonald's*
(2) remove the comma after *example*
(3) change the spelling of *attempts* to *attemps*
(4) change *attempts* to *attempt*
(5) insert a comma after *shake*

8. Sentence 7: **Burger King can broil a hamburger in 80 seconds and can produce over 700 Whoppers in an hour!**

Which of the following is the best way to write the underlined portion of this sentence? If you think the original is the best way, choose option (1).

(1) seconds and can produce
(2) seconds and produced
(3) seconds, and can produce
(4) seconds and can, produce
(5) seconds and, can produce

9. Sentence 8: **The bureau of Labor Statistics reports that in 1981 we spent over 32.4 percent of our total food expenditures for restaurant meals.**

What correction should be made to this sentence?

(1) change *bureau* to *Bureau*
(2) change *reports* to *report*
(3) insert a comma after *reports*
(4) change *spent* to *spend*
(5) no correction is necessary

10. Sentences 10 & 11: **In 1966 McDonald's billboards told us, "2 billion sold." In 1984 they boasted, "45 billion sold."**

The most effective combination of sentences 10 and 11 would include which of the following groups of words?

(1) because in 1984 they boasted
(2) while in 1984 they boasted
(3) so that in 1984 they boasted
(4) consequently in 1984 they boasted
(5) in fact boasting that

Directions: The following paragraph contains numbered sentences. These sentences may have errors in usage, sentence structure, and mechanics. Read the paragraph and answer the items that follow. For each item, choose the answer that would result in the most effective writing of the sentence.

Items 11 to 20 are based on the following paragraph.

(1) The Summer months are the months when most people take their vacations. (2) Regardless of where you travel, you should always carry a first-aid kit. (3) Some items should be standard. (4) Antibiotic cream, bandage strips, and gauze pads are some standard items. (5) If someone in your family are allergic to insect stings, a special medicine is needed. (6) This meducine is a type of adrenaline. (7) Hydrogen peroxide was a good item to keep in the kit. (8) They can be used to clean a wound when soap and water aren't available. (9) Also carry

a small bottle of calamine lotion this helps relieve the itching of mosquito bites and poison ivy. (10) Be sure you have cotton balls or cotton swabs, too. (11) A well-stocked first-aid kit can keep accident's from ruining your vacation.

11. Sentence 1: **The Summer months are the months when most people take their vacations.**

What correction should be made to this sentence?

(1) replace *The* with *A*
(2) change *Summer* to *summer*
(3) insert a comma after *are*
(4) change *take* to *took*
(5) insert a comma after *their*

12. Sentence 2: **Regardless of where you travel, you should always carry a first-aid kit.**

Which of the following is the best way to write the underlined portion of this sentence? If you think the original is the best way, choose option (1).

(1) travel, you should always
(2) travel you should, always
(3) travel you should always
(4) travel. You should always
(5) travel, you should always,

13. Sentences 3 & 4: **Some items should be standard. Antibiotic cream, bandage strips, and gauze pads are some standard items.**

If you rewrote sentences 3 and 4 beginning with

Some items should be standard,

the next word(s) would be

(1) unless
(2) for
(3) because of
(4) even though
(5) such as

14. Sentence 5: **If someone in your family are allergic to insect stings, a special medicine is needed.**

What correction should be made to this sentence?

(1) replace *someone* with *everyone*
(2) replace *you* with *my*
(3) change *are* to *is*
(4) change the spelling of *allergic* to *allergick*
(5) change the spelling of *medicine* to *meducine*

15. Sentence 6: **This meducine is a type of adrenaline.**

What correction should be made to this sentence?

(1) change the spelling of *meducine* to *medicine*
(2) insert a comma after *meducine*
(3) replace *a* with *the*
(4) insert a comma after *type*
(5) replace the period with a question mark

16. Sentence 7: **Hydrogen peroxide was a good item to keep in the kit.**

Which of the following is the best way to write the underlined portion of this sentence? If you think the original is the best way, choose option (1).

(1) Hydrogen peroxide was
(2) Hydrogen peroxide has
(3) Hydrogen peroxide had
(4) Hydrogen peroxide will be
(5) Hydrogen peroxide is

17. Sentence 8: **They can be used to clean a wound when soap and water aren't available.**

(1) change *They* to *It*
(2) change *used* to *using*
(3) insert a comma after *wound*
(4) insert a comma after *water*
(5) change the spelling of aren't to are'nt

18. Sentence 9: **Also carry a small bottle of calamine lotion this helps relieve the itching of mosquito bites and poison ivy.**

Which of the following is the best way to write the underlined portion of this sentence? If you think the original is the best way, choose option (1).

(1) lotion this helps relieve
(2) lotion. This helps relieve
(3) lotion, this helps relieve
(4) lotion. This helps. Relieve
(5) lotion, this helps, relieve

19. Sentence 10: **Be sure you have cotton balls or cotton swabs, too.**

What correction should be made to this sentence?

(1) insert a comma after *sure*
(2) change *have* to *had*
(3) insert a comma after *balls*
(4) replace *or* with *with*
(5) no correction is necessary

20. Sentence 11: **A well-stocked first-aid kit can keep accident's from ruining your vacation.**

What correction should be made to this sentence?

(1) insert a comma after *well-stocked*
(2) insert a comma after *kit*
(3) change *accident's* to *accidents*
(4) change *your* to *our*
(5) no correction is necessary

Answers are on page 255.

Unit I Test

Directions: The items in this test are based on paragraphs that contain numbered sentences. Some of the sentences may contain errors in usage, sentence structure, or mechanics. **A few sentences, however, may be correct as written.** Read each paragraph and answer the items based on it.

Items 1 to 8 are based on the following paragraph.

(1) Home computers and television has made a tremendous impact on our society. (2) While even though some would argue that electronic advances have aided the education of our youth, others point out that these machines represent the growing trend of passive activity. (3) A 1985 survey was conducted by the President's Council on Physical Fitness and Sports. (4) It showed the results of a lack of enough active participation in exercise. (5) A total of 18,857 boys and girls, ages 6 though 17, were studied. (6) Of these, 40 percent of the boys, and 70 percent of the girls could not do more than one pull-up. (7) In addition, About 50 percent of the girls and 30 percent of the boys, ages 6–12, couldn't run a mile in less than 10 minutes. (8) Medically, these results illustrate a problem because poor fitness in childhood increased the likelihood of heart attacks and other health-related problems in adulthood. (9) Accordingly, we need to educate children's bodies as well as his mind.

Directions: Answer the following multiple-choice questions. Choose the answer that best fits the meaning and tone of the paragraph.

1. Sentence 1: **Home computers and television has made a tremendous impact in our society.**

   What correction should be made to this sentence?

   (1) insert a comma after *computers*
   (2) insert a comma after *television*
   (3) change *has* to *have*
   (4) change the spelling of *tremendous* to *tremendus*
   (5) no correction is necessary

2. Sentence 2: **While even though some would argue that electronic advances have aided the education of our youth, others point out that these machines represent the growing trend of passive activity.**

Which of the following is the best way to write the underlined portion of this sentence? If you think the original is the best way, choose option (1).

(1) While even though some would argue
(2) While some would argue,
(3) While even though some would argue,
(4) While some would argue
(5) While, even some would argue,

3. Sentences 3 and 4: **A 1985 survey was conducted by the President's Council on Physical Fitness and Sports. It showed the results of a lack of enough active participation in exercise.**

The most effective combination of sentences 3 and 4 would include which of the following groups of words?

(1) , conducted by the President's Council on Physical Fitness and Sports, showed the results of a lack
(2) conducted by the President's Council on Physical Fitness and Sports, showed the results of a lack
(3) , conducted by the President's Council on Physical Fitness and Sports showed the results of a lack
(4) , survey conducted by the President's Council on Physical Fitness and Sports showed the results of a lack
(5) , survey conducted by the President's Council on Physical Fitness and Sports, showed the results of a lack

4. Sentence 5: **A total of 18,857 boys and girls, ages 6 though 17, were studied.**

What correction should be made to this sentence?

(1) insert a comma after 18,857
(2) insert a comma after *boys*
(3) remove the comma after *girls*
(4) change *ages* to *age*
(5) replace *though* with *through*

Directions: Answer the following completion questions. Write the answer that best fits the meaning and tone of the paragraph you have just read. If the sentence needs correcting, write out the entire sentence with its correction. If the sentence does not need correcting, write "no correction is necessary."

5. Sentence 6: **Of these, 40 percent of the boys, and 70 percent of the girls could not do more than one pull-up.**

The best correction for this sentence is: ____________

6. Sentence 7: **In addition, About 50 percent of the girls and 30 percent of the boys, ages 6–12, couldn't run a mile in less than 10 minutes.**

The best correction for this sentence is: ____________

7. Sentence 8: **Medically, these results illustrate a problem because poor fitness in childhood increased the likelihood of heart attacks and other health-related problems in adulthood.**

The best correction for this sentence is: ____________

8. Sentence 9: **Accordingly, we need to educate our children's bodies as well as his mind.**
The best correction for this sentence is: ____________

Items 9 to 17 are based on the following paragraph.

(1) Many people who make the mistake of accepting the first job that is offered to them. (2) They often became frustrated and unfulfilled. (3) They find out too late that the job neither meets their needs nor uses their full potential. (4) The book *Career Planning: Skills to Build Your Future* provide a new approach to the matter of knowing when a job is right for you. (5) This approach is called P.L.A.C.E. (6) You gather information about a particular job, and you should think about these ideas. (7) First, (P) position is important, know the job description and its duties. (8) Second, (L) location should be considered for both the geographical locale, and the physical working environment. (9) Third, (A) advancement opportunities and job security should be considered. (10) Fourth, (C) conditions of employment should be made clear. (11) These include salary, hours, and benefits. (12) Fifth, (E) entry skills must be known they include specific education and training requirements. (13) This data will help you evaluate whether or not a specific job meets you're expectations and goals.

Directions: Answer the following multiple-choice questions. The best answer must be consistent with the meaning and tone of the rest of the paragraph.

9. Sentence 1: **Many people who make the mistake of accepting the first job that is offered to them.**

What correction should be made to this sentence?

(1) insert a comma after *people*
(2) remove the word *who*
(3) change the spelling of *mistake* to *misteak*
(4) insert a comma after *job*
(5) change *them* to *themselves*

10. Sentence 2: **They <u>often became frustrated</u> and unfulfilled.**

Which of the following is the best way to write the underlined portion of this sentence? If you think the original is the best way, choose option (1).

(1) often became frustrated
(2) , often, became frustrated
(3) often, become frustrated
(4) often become frustrated
(5) often became frustrated,

11. Sentence 3: **They find out too late that the job neither meets their needs nor uses their full potential.**

What correction should be made to this sentence?

(1) insert a comma after *late*
(2) change *meets* to *will meet*
(3) change *needs* to *need*
(4) insert a comma after *needs*
(5) no correction is necessary

12. Sentence 4: **The book Career Planning: Skills to Build Your Future provide a new approach to the matter of knowing when a job is right for you.**

Which of the following is the best way to write the underlined portion of this sentence? If you think the original is the best way, choose option (1).

(1) provide a new approach
(2) , provides a new approach
(3) provides a new approach
(4) provides a new approach,
(5) , provides a new approach,

13. Sentence 6: **You gather information about a particular job, and you should think about these ideas.**

If you rewrote sentence 6 beginning with

As you gather information about a particular job,

the next word would be

(1) thinking
(2) and
(3) because
(4) you
(5) however

Directions: Answer the following completion questions. Write the answer that best fits the meaning and tone of the paragraph you have just read. If the sentence needs correcting, write out the entire sentence with its correction. If the sentence does not need correcting, write "no correction is necessary."

14. Sentence 7: **First, (P) position is important, know the job description and its duties.**

The best correction for this sentence is: ______________

15. Sentence 8: **Second, (L) location should be considered for both the geographical locale, and the physical working environment.**

The best correction for this sentence is: ______________

16. Sentence 12: **Fifth, (E) entry skills must be known they include specific education and training requirements.**

The best correction for this sentence is: ____________

17. Sentence 13: **This data will help you evaluate whether or not a specific job meets you're expectations and goals.**

The best correction for this sentence is: ____________

Items 18 to 25 are based on the following paragraph.

(1) Computer languages are as unique as computers themselves. (2) A computer must use a language to process data and instructions. (3) Each of the languages are unique in its purpose and has its own specialized function. (4) LOGO is used to teach programming to children. (5) It is a specialized language that uses both graphics and words. (6) On the other hand, PASCAL, named after the 17th-century Mathematician Blaise Pascal, is a high-level language used to teach the principles of computer programming. (7) Three widely used languages are actually "acronyms," which are words formed from the first letters of several words. (8) BASIC stands for Beginner's All-Purpose Symbolic Instruction Code. (9) Commonly used with smaller computers this versatile language is noted for being easy to learn and use. (10) COBOL or Common Business Oriented Language is used mainly for data processing and business applications. (11) FORTRAN is used for mathematical and scientific applications, an acronym for Formula Translator. (12) As different needs arise, different languages evolved. For this reason, new computer languages are continually being developed.

Directions: Answer the following multiple-choice questions. The best answer must be consistent with the meaning and tone of the rest of the paragraph.

18. Sentence 1: **Computer languages are as unique as computers themselves.**

What correction should be made to this sentence?

(1) change *are* to *is*
(2) remove the word *as* after *are*
(3) insert a comma after *unique*
(4) change *themselves* to *theirselves*
(5) no correction is necessary

19. Sentence 3: **Each of the languages are unique in its purpose and has its own specialized function.**

Which of the following is the best way to write the underlined portion of this sentence? If you think the original is the best way, choose option (1).

(1) are unique in its purpose
(2) is unique in its purpose
(3) are unique in it's purpose
(4) is unique in its purpose,
(5) are unique in its purpose,

20. Sentences 4 and 5: **LOGO is used to teach programming to children. It is a specialized language that uses both graphics and words.**

The most effective combination of sentences 4 and 5 would include which of the following groups of words?

(1) which use both graphics and words
(2) and use both graphics and words.
(3) with both graphics and words.
(4) that uses both graphics and words,
(5) in order to use graphics and words.

21. Sentence 6: **On the other hand, PASCAL, named after the 17th-century Mathematician Blaise Pascal, is a high-level language used to teach the principles of computer programming.**

What correction should be made to this sentence?

(1) remove the comma after *hand*
(2) insert a comma after *century*
(3) change *Mathematician* to *mathematician*
(4) insert a comma after *language*
(5) replace *principles* with *principals*

Directions: Answer the following completion questions. Write the answer that best fits the meaning and tone of the paragraph you have just read. If the sentence needs correcting, write out the entire sentence with its correcttiion. If the sentence does not need correcting, write "no correction is necessary."

22. Sentence 7: **Three widely used languages are actually "acronyms," which are words formed from the first few letters of several words.**

The best correction for this sentence is: ____________

23. Sentence 9: **Commonly used with smaller computers this versatile language is noted for being easy to learn and use.**

The best correction for this sentence is: ____________

24. Sentence 11: **FORTRAN is used for mathematical and scientific applications, an acronym for Formula Translators.**

The best correction for this sentence is: ____________

25. Sentence 12: **As different needs arise, different languages evolved.**

The best correction for this sentence is: ____________

Items 26 to 28 are based on the following paragraph.

(1) A word processor is a computer that is useful, easy to learn and easy to use. (2) Compared with writing in longhand, the word processor lets you enter text, edit, and print much more quickly. (3) A word processor allows a writer to perform the following procedures: delete, insert, retrieve, change type styles, and print format. (4) It also permits you to store pages of text like a file cabinet. (5) If you were to keep a daily journal, you could obtain a printed copy of all your entries, for a week, a month, or a whole year! (6) You can go back to material and make changes at a later date. (7) Imagine having to mail the same letter to twenty different people. (8) The printer will print each letter separately you only have to insert the name and address. (9) A few programs, especially educational software, has a built-in dictionary. (10) If you discover an error, the word processor allows you to go back through your writing and will correct the misspelled word each time it appears.

26. Sentence 7: **Imagine having to mail the same letter to twenty different people.**

What correction should be made to this sentence?

(1) change the spelling of *having* to *haveing*
(2) replace *mail* with *send*
(3) change the spelling of *different* to *diffrent*
(4) replace the period with a question mark
(5) no correction is necesssary

27. Sentence 8: **The printer will print each letter separately you only have to insert the name and address.**

Which of the following is the best way to write the underlined portion of this sentence? If you think the original is the best way to write the sentence, choose option (1).

(1) separately you
(2) seperately you
(3) separately. You
(4) one at a time, you
(5) and you the writer

28. Sentence 9: **A few programs, especially educational software, has a built-in dictionary.**

Which of the following is the best way to write the underlined portion of this sentence? If you think the original is the best way to write the sentence, choose option (1).

(1) software, has
(2) software, have
(3) software have
(4) software, is having
(5) software, had

Answers are on pages 255–256.

UNIT I TEST
Performance Analysis Chart

Directions: Circle the number of each item that you got correct on the Unit I Test. Count how many correct items there are in each row. Write the amount correct per row as the numerator in the fraction in the appropriate "Total Correct" box. (The denominators represent the total number of items in the row.) Write the grand total correct over the denominator, **28,** at the lower right corner of the chart. (For example, if you got 20 items correct, write *20* so that the fraction reads *20*/**28.**)

Item Type	*Usage (page 25)*	*Sentence Structure (page 55)*	*Mechanics (page 75)*	TOTAL CORRECT
Construction Shift (page 112)		13	3, 20	**/3**
Sentence Correction (page 111)	1, 18	9, 11	4, 21, 26	**/7**
Sentence Revision (page 112)	10, 12, 19, 28	2, 27		**/6**
Non-Multiple Choice	7, 8, 22, 25	14, 16, 24	5, 6, 15, 17, 23	**/12**
TOTAL CORRECT	**/10**	**/8**	**/10**	**/28**

The page numbers in parentheses indicate where in this book you can find the beginning of specific instruction about the areas of grammar and about the types of questions you encountered in the Unit I Test.

UNIT II

Writing Skills, Part II: Essay Writing

The purpose of this unit is to help you prepare for Part II of the Writing Skills Test. It is made up of chapters that are divided into lessons. It is important that you work through the unit in order.

The lessons in the first chapter offer several suggestions about ways you can help yourself become more comfortable with writing. The second chapter explains and demonstrates a process approach to essay writing. By doing all the activities in the lessons and using Chapter 3 as a review, you will get plenty of practice at developing compositions on topics like those assigned in GED testing centers.

For most of the activities in this unit, there are no entries in the book's Answers and Explanations section. However, there are discussions, examples, and guidelines provided within the activities to assist your evaluation of your writing.

As you work through this unit, it will probably help you to have the benefit of other people's reaction to your writing. A teacher or someone else may be able to help you judge your essays and other writing better than you could working alone.

As is stressed in this unit, the best way to develop skill at writing is to write. If you use the suggestions in this unit, you will develop your skills and write essays like the one you will be expected to write when you take the GED.

UNIT II PROGRESS CHART

Writing Skills, Part II: Essay Writing

Directions: Use the following chart to keep track of your work. When you complete a lesson and its activity, check the box to show you have completed that lesson.

Lesson	*Page*		
		CHAPTER 1: **Daily Writing**	
1	147	Introduction to Personal Writing	☐
2	148	Developing a Personal Writing Plan	☐
3	149	Keeping a Journal	☐
		CHAPTER 2: **The Writing Process**	
1	151	Introduction to Writing as a Process	☐
2	153	Understanding Essay Topics	☐
3	154	Generating Ideas	☐
4	157	Organizing Ideas	☐
5	159	Writing an Essay	☐
6	162	Revising an Essay	☐
7	167	Editing an Essay	☐
		CHAPTER 3: **Reviewing the Writing Process**	
1	171	Practice the Process	☐
2	175	The Writing Process: A Summary	☐

Chapter

1 Daily Writing

Objective

In this chapter you will be introduced to various techniques and processes for writing. The writing exercises you will work on are designed to help you

- Begin personal writing
- Establish a personal writing plan
- Keep a daily journal

Lesson 1 Introduction to Personal Writing

This chapter will show you how to become a more productive and effective writer. As you complete the activities in this chapter, you will find that writing becomes easier and more automatic.

Sometimes it can be difficult just to get started writing. A good way to break through this barrier is to practice a technique known as *fastwriting*. In fastwriting, you write as fast as possible and you do not worry about what you are writing or how correctly you are writing it. Your goal is simply to write. Fastwriting can be practiced every day, beginning with perhaps as little as five minutes and increasing the time every few days.

Lesson 1 Activity

For five minutes, use fastwriting to write about what you think the world would be like if there were no automobiles. If nothing comes to mind immediately, you may write about any other topic that occurs to you. The purpose of this activity is to practice the fastwriting method. Don't stop to correct your mistakes and don't pause to think of ways to make your writing better. Just write for five minutes. No one else will read what you have written.

Lesson 2 Developing a Personal Writing Plan

Fastwriting can be used to help you develop the habit of daily writing. As you become used to it, increase your writing time to ten minutes daily. You can write about anything at all, but remember that topics that are more personal will probably be more enjoyable for you to write about. These topics, therefore, will be easier to write about for longer periods of time. Should you have difficulty coming up with ideas, topics are suggested in this lesson.

Use a calendar to record your progress. Each day, record the number of words you have written and how long you spent writing. If you continue to write every day and record your progress, you will soon find that you are writing more each day.

Sunday	Monday	Tuesday	Wednesday	Thursday	Friday	Saturday
1	2	3	4	5	6	7
8	9	10	11	12	13	14

Lesson 2 Activity

Do at least ten minutes of fastwriting every day. Suggested topics follow. Either choose from among these or come up with your own ideas. Write about a different topic every day, but try to choose topics that interest you. You will find it easier to write about topics that are of personal interest.

Suggested Topics

1. Describe the things in the room where you are now sitting.
2. Write about one of your favorite movies.
3. Summarize a recent newspaper article you have read or a television program you have seen.
4. Write about what you intend to do when you have passed your GED exam.
5. Write about what kind of car you would buy if you could afford any car in the world. Explain why you would select that particular car.
6. Write about how our lives would be changed if gravity on earth were only one fourth what it is now.
7. Write about a pet that has meant a lot to you.

Lesson 3 Keeping a Journal

Many people find that keeping a daily record of their thoughts and feelings in a journal is a relaxing and interesting activity. It helps them clear their minds of things that may be bothering them, and sometimes it even helps them solve problems. Besides benefits such as these, journal writing is definitely a good way to improve your writing skills.

Try to make journal writing a daily habit. Set aside a time each day when you will have ten or fifteen minutes without interruptions. Remember that when you write in your journal, you are writing for no one else but yourself. You are writing a personal record of your thoughts, feelings, and experiences.

Read the following examples of journal entries.

EXAMPLE 1

". . . I'm especially looking forward to a summer vacation this year. It will be the first time where I might have enough money to go somewhere and do what I want to do. I still don't know where I'm going to go, but I know I will spend most of my time relaxing as much as I can. Of course, I'll still do some things other people might not consider relaxing that are relaxing to me. I plan to do some hiking and other outdoor things."

EXAMPLE 2

". . . I enjoyed the movie last night. I enjoy movies that are both funny and serious. I think most really good movies have funny scenes in them as well as sad scenes. I like to both laugh and cry when I go to the movies. But my favorite movies are the ones that make me laugh."

EXAMPLE 3

". . . I intend to let my brother know how much I appreciate his help over the years. When I was in school, he always gave me a little extra money to spend. He also used to take me to baseball games. Some of my friends' older brothers ignored them when they were little, but my brother never ignored me. I always felt important when he was around."

These examples are intended to show you that you can write about anything when you keep a journal. Remember that you do not have to worry about correctness, because you are keeping the journal for yourself only. Journal writing will help you write faster and more easily. As with any skill, writing practice will help you perform the activity better and with less effort.

Suggestions for Keeping a Journal

- Use a special notebook or blank bound book for your journal writing.
- Try to write in the same place and at the same time each day.
- Record the date of each journal entry.
- Write in your journal every day. Don't worry about grammar, spelling, or

punctuation. Write quickly without being concerned about whether your writing is perfect.

- Think of your journal writing as a time when you can enjoy thinking about yourself, other people, and the events in your life.

Lesson 3 Activity

Begin keeping a journal today. The first step is to find a comfortable place to write. Then choose a topic that interests you. The following suggestions may help you get started, but you should write about anything that is of personal interest to you.

For your first entries, try writing for at least ten minutes each time. As you become used to journal writing, increase the time, spending as much time as you need to get as many thoughts as possible on paper. Some topics that might be of interest to you are listed here.

- A law that you think isn't fair
- A conversation you had recently that bothered you
- An event that may have changed the course of your life
- The recent actions or behavior of someone in your family
- Something beautiful you have seen recently
- Your feelings about the place in which you are currently living
- A description of your dream house
- One thing in the world that you would most like to change, and why
- One thing about yourself that you would most like to change, and why

Chapter

2 The Writing Process

Objective

This chapter will take you through the development of a sample essay. Following the process will help you begin to develop your own writing skills and apply them to essay writing. In this chapter, you will also develop an essay using a five-step process to

- Generate ideas
- Organize ideas for essays
- Write essays
- Revise essays
- Edit essays

Lesson 1 Introduction to Writing as a Process

Writing can be viewed as a product or a process. Viewing it as a *product* causes the writer to focus on what the paper will look like when it is finished. This causes the writer to concentrate too heavily on correctness while writing. But viewing writing as a *process* helps the writer see the steps involved in writing. These steps are part of a simple process outlined in the following chart.

The Five Steps in the Writing Process

Step 1. Generate ideas

☐ Use brainstorming or clustering to generate ideas about your essay topic.

Step 2. Organize ideas

☐ Select the most appropriate ideas to support your point of view or opinion.

☐ Decide how to arrange your ideas for your audience (the reader).

☐ Decide which examples best support your point of view.

☐ Decide which examples to present first, second, and so on.

Step 3. Write essay

☐ Put your ideas in sentences and paragraphs following the organization you planned.

Step 4. Revise essay

☐ Make sure that your point of view or opinion is stated clearly and that your examples support your point of view.

☐ Add information needed for clarity.

☐ Remove information that is not needed.

Step 5. Edit essay

☐ Correct errors in usage, sentence structure, spelling, punctuation, and capitalization.

When you read through the chart, you may have noticed that you already use some or all of these steps when you write an essay. The activity that follows will help you determine exactly which steps you do and don't use. This will help you put the whole process together to write more effective essays.

Lesson 1 Activity

For this activity, use the essay you wrote for the Predictor Test (see pages 10–11). Answer the following questions to find out how many of the steps in the writing process you used to write the essay.

1. **Generating ideas.** Did you spend time thinking about ideas (brainstorming) to put in your essay? Did you write down these ideas?
2. **Organizing ideas.** If you did Step 1, did you take time to plan what to write first, second, third, and so on? Did you make notes about your plan?
3. **Writing.** If you did Step 1 and Step 2, did you follow your plan when you wrote your essay?
4. **Revising.** After you wrote your essay, did you read it to see how effectively you presented your ideas? Did you make any changes to increase the effectiveness of your essay?
5. **Editing.** Did you correct all the errors you could find in your essay—errors in usage, sentence structure, spelling, punctuation, and capitalization?

Discussion

Use your answers to the questions to help you write more effective essays. Every time you answered *yes* to one of the questions, you identified a step in the writing process that you are already using. Every time you answered *no*, you identified a step you should learn to use.

Lesson 2 Understanding Essay Topics

One of the skills involved in writing an effective essay is understanding the topic you are writing about. You will have forty-five minutes to write your 200-word GED essay. Some of that time should be spent making sure you understand the topic and its limits. This lesson will show you a method for reading topics carefully and developing a point of view about them.

When you are assigned a topic, take some time to think about it and make sure you understand it. The following chart suggests a process for understanding essay topics.

Steps for Understanding an Essay Topic

Step 1. Underline the important or key words in the topic.

Step 2. Make sure you understand all of the key points of the topic.

Step 3. Decide on your own point of view and state it in one sentence.

By practicing these three steps, you will learn to follow them automatically when reading essay topics. Read the following topic and follow the directions in the activity for this lesson.

TOPIC

In all of our lives there is a certain person who played a very important role in helping us understand something that will always be important to us. Describe a person in your life who played an important role in shaping your own view of the world and of the people around you. This person may be someone in your family who helped raise you or perhaps someone you came to know on your own. Explain the important role this person played in your life and how your life may have been changed by this person.

Lesson 2 Activity

1. In the topic, some of the key words are already underlined. Reread the topic and underline five additional key words or groups of words. Do not continue the lesson activity until you have underlined those five words or groups of words.

Discussion

Other words you might have underlined are: understand something, shaping, view of the world, raise, and know on your own. These words are important because your essay must be about someone who helped you **understand something** and was important in **shaping** your **view of the world.** This person may have **raised** you or may be someone you came to **know on your own.**

A good way to be sure that you have underlined all of the important concepts in the topic is to use the underlined words to form a question. Use as many of the underlined words as you can.

What person played an important role in helping you understand something and in shaping your view of the world?

As you continue with this chapter you will do all five steps in the writing process to write an essay on this topic.

2. Complete the following answer to the question about the topic.

"The person who played an important role in . . ." (Complete this sentence to indicate the person in your own life who played this important role.)

Discussion

The answer you completed acts as a focus for the topic. It will become the topic of the essay you will begin to plan in Lesson 3.

Lesson 3 Generating Ideas

In this lesson you will be introduced to the first part of the writing process that will help you write an essay for the GED Writing Skills Test. This is the planning stage of the process, in which you generate ideas about your topic.

Planning what you will write is perhaps the most important step in writing a good essay. Spend some time generating ideas *before* you begin to write. This will help you write a better organized and more effective essay. In this lesson you will learn two ways of generating ideas for your essay: brainstorming and clustering.

Brainstorming

Brainstorming is a way of gathering information for writing. When you brainstorm, you write all the words you can think of that relate to the topic you are going to write about. Even if a word or phrase doesn't seem to relate to the topic, you should write it down; you can always decide not to use it later if it does not work well in your essay. Spend anywhere from three to five minutes brainstorming to be sure you have covered all the thoughts you may have on the topic. The topic for this chapter will be used to illustrate how this strategy works.

TOPIC

In all of our lives there is a certain person who played a very important role in helping us understand something that will always be important to us. Describe a person in your life who played an important role in shaping your own view of the world and of the people around you. This person may be someone in your family who helped raise you or perhaps someone you came to know on your own. Explain the important role this person played in your life and how your life may have been changed by this person.

After thinking over the topic, one writer decided to write from this point of view.

The person who played an important role in shaping my life was Uncle Ned.

This writer then began to brainstorm and wrote down all the words that came to mind about the topic. Here are the results of his brainstorming.

uncle successful reads red convertible personality friends traveled girlfriends retired young had interesting jobs had freedom money teacher pet-store owner travel agent truck driver fine clothes knows a lot lecturer happy caring good to people paid attention to me

Clustering

Clustering is really another method of brainstorming and generating ideas. It helps you organize your ideas by focusing first on your point of view about the topic. When you cluster, you write your position or point of view in the center of a piece of paper and draw a circle around it. Next, you brainstorm supporting ideas and place those words on an extension off the circle.

Look at the cluster that follows. It uses the same topic and words as those in the brainstorming example.

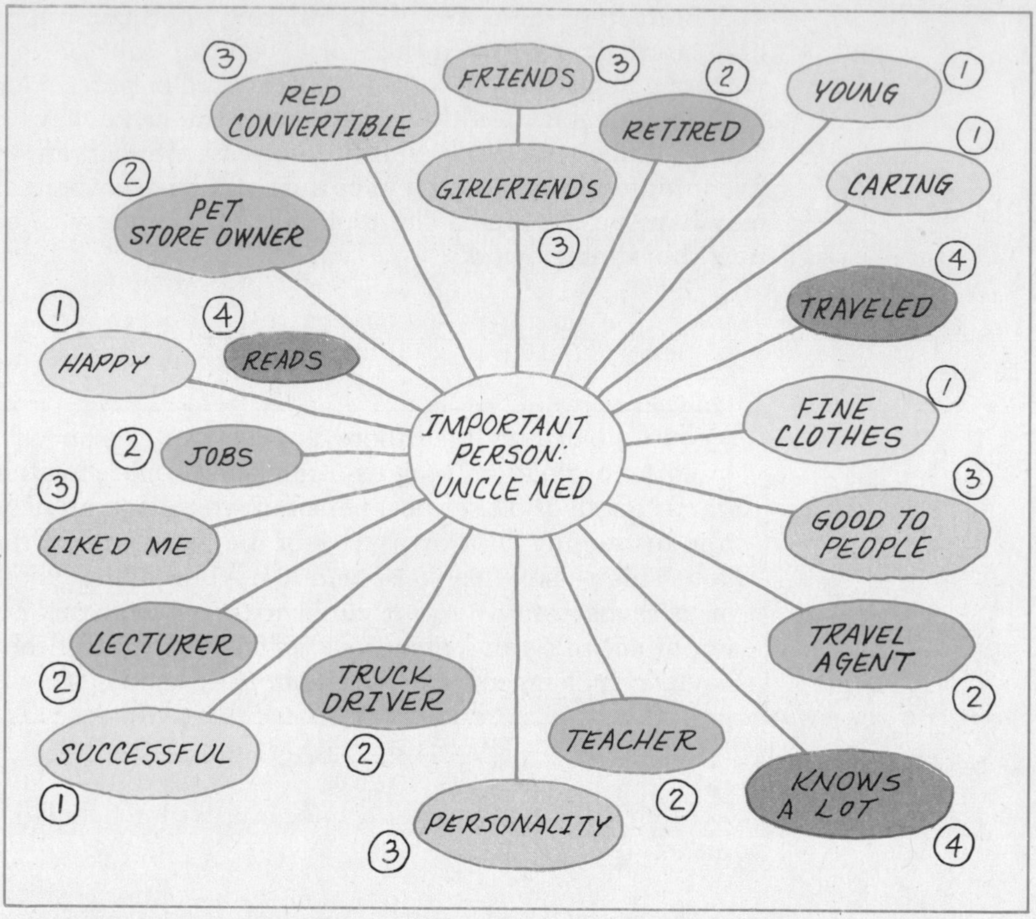

Clustering may help you organize your material better than brainstorming. It can be a great help when planning an essay.

Lesson 3 Activity

In this activity you will begin to plan the essay you are going to write on the "important person" topic. Read the topic again on page 155. Your essay will take this point of view.

The person who played an important role in shaping my life was ________________________.

1. Fill in the blank in the sentence and then brainstorm, keeping in mind the person you have chosen. Write at least ten words or phrases that come to mind about this person and the role he or she played in your life. (You may look at the example on page 155.)

2. Brainstorm again, keeping in mind the person *you* have chosen to write about. This time, however, cluster your ideas. Start by writing "Important Person" and that person's name in the middle of a piece of paper. Draw a circle around that phrase. Then write your ideas on extensions from the circle, grouping related ideas along the same extension. (You

may look at the cluster example just before the Lesson Activity.) Save this cluster to use as you work through the next lesson.

Lesson 4 Organizing Ideas

Brainstorming and clustering help you generate ideas and, to a certain extent, organize them. However, they do not help you decide how the essay will begin, how it will end, or exactly what information to include to get your point of view across. In this lesson, you will learn a strategy called mapping that you can use to organize your information and ideas.

Mapping

Mapping is a visual way of organizing information. It helps you to actually see the organization of your essay.

To make a map, take the words you have generated in your brainstorming and clustering activities and put them in categories. To categorize words, you find those words that relate to one another. For example, if you made a cluster, the first step in mapping would be to number or color-code the words in the cluster. All the ideas that go together would be given the same number or color, whichever works best for you. Depending on your topic and the number of ideas you wrote in your cluster, you may have two, three, four, or more different categories. The following example shows a cluster (the same one used in Lesson 3) that has both numbers and colors.

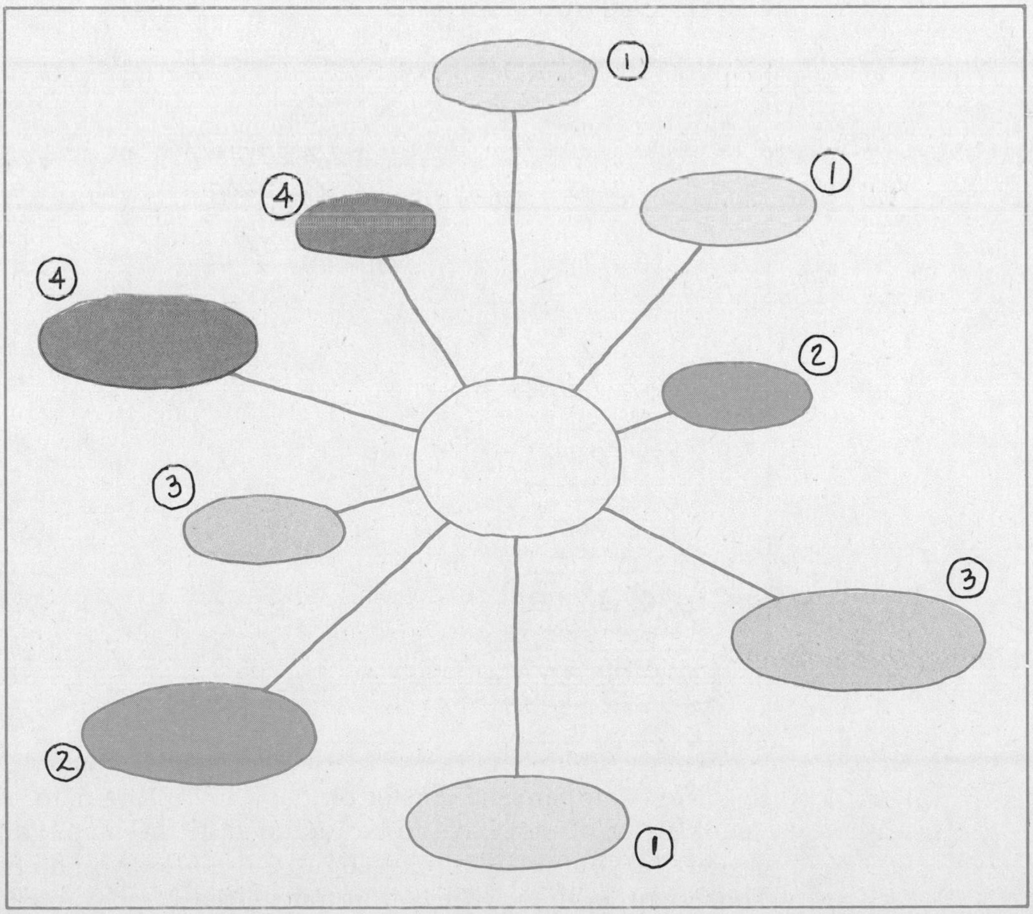

After you have numbered or color-coded the ideas in your cluster, the next step is to create a map.

Creating a Map

Step 1. Gather all the words from your brainstorming or clustering activities.

Step 2. Eliminate words that have similar meanings.

Step 3. Arrange words in categories. Give the categories titles. The titles will suggest your main ideas, and the words listed will be used as examples to support those ideas.

Step 4. Decide which paragraph should come first and label it. Because it is the introductory paragraph, remember to list the topics of the other paragraphs as they will be introduced by the first paragraph.

Step 5. Decide which paragraph should be second, third, fourth, and so on. Label each one.

A map based on the cluster on page 156 might look like the following.

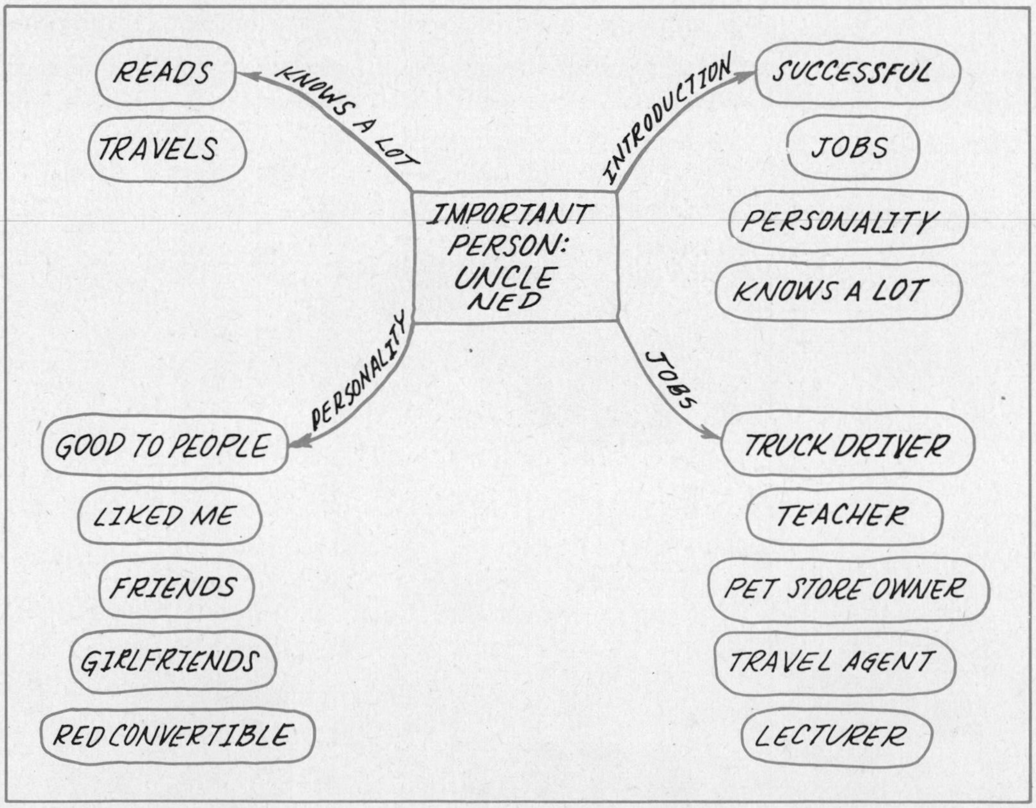

Now compare the cluster on page 157 to the map. All of the words in your cluster do not have to be included in the map. Part of the process of organizing your essay is to weed out those ideas you do not want to include. Those words, then, will not be transferred from your cluster to your map.

At the center of your map will be the point of view, in this case "Important Person: (Name)." The different categories extend from the center. Notice that the topics of the second, third, and fourth paragraphs—*jobs, personality*, and *knows a lot*—are listed as supporting ideas in the first paragraph.

Making a map for an essay may seem difficult at this stage. As you practice doing it, you will find that you can brainstorm and cluster ideas in your head; mapping will only take a few minutes.

Lesson 4 Activity

For this activity, use the cluster you made during the Lesson 3 Activity.

1. Number or color-code the ideas in your cluster. Find ideas that go together and give them the same number or color, whichever you prefer. How many different groups do you have?
2. Use your numbered or color-coded cluster to make a map. Keep your central point in mind—the important person who shaped your life. Use the map from this lesson as an example in creating your own map.

Discussion

Look at the map. Did you identify and label which paragraph comes first, second, and so on? Did you include all of the paragraph topics in the first paragraph's supporting ideas?

Lesson 5 Writing an Essay

Now that you have made a map for your essay, you are ready to begin writing. Following the plan you have made on your map, the opening of your essay should give the reader your point of view or key idea. The next paragraphs will give the reasons that explain or describe your point of view or key idea. To effectively explain your point of view, you should use specific examples that support what you are saying. The following chart outlines the steps involved in writing an essay.

Writing an Essay

Step 1. In the opening paragraph, immediately state your point of view about the topic. Then give your reasons for your point of view.

Step 2. In the second, third, and following paragraphs, develop supporting examples to explain each of the reasons for your point of view.

Step 3. In the final paragraph, restate and explain why you hold your point of view.

The essay that follows is based on the sample map in Lesson 4. To the left of the essay are comments that indicate how it follows the map. Following the essay is an explanation of how the essay was written according to the steps outlined in the chart on writing essays.

As you read this essay, you may notice some errors in usage, sentence structure, and mechanics. Remember that this is only a first draft and the writer is concentrating on getting the ideas on paper in an organized manner. In lessons 6 and 7, this essay will be revised and edited.

SAMPLE ESSAY

Central point of view is stated: "Uncle Ned was important person."

First reason for point of view: "jobs"

Second reason for point of view: "friends"

Third reason for point of view: "smart"

One of the people who was most important in shaping my life was my Uncle Ned. He was important because he was different from my immediate family. He had many different kinds of jobs and he have many different kinds of friends and he also was very smart. I always thought his life was much more interesting than the rest of my families. I wanted to be like him to have a lot of jobs and friends and be educated from my experiences and travels and other things.

Gives examples in support of first reason for point of view: "pet-store owner, travel agent, truck driver, teacher, lecturer"

My Uncle had more jobs than anyone I ever knew. My father used to say that he had so many jobs because he couldn't keep a job, but I think that he just got bored with things after a while. He owned a pet store until he sold the store and decided to travel. When he came back after a few years he became a travel agent. Then he he was a truck driver for a while. After that, he taught in a private school, and he lectured for a while for a book club in town.

Gives examples in support of second reason for point of view: "good to people, good to me, lots of friends, girlfriends, red convertible"

He was good to people and he was especially good to me. He had lots of friends and he had lots of girlfriends who used to come around the house. He had a red convertible in those days and I always wanted to have a red convertible too.

Gives examples in support of third reason for point of view: "traveled, read a lot"

Everyone thought that he was very smart. I guess he got smart from all of his travels all over the world and all over the United States too. And he read a lot of books and other kinds of things like magazines. Uncle Ned was always reading one book or another. He told me that every time he read a book he learned something he didn't know before. He once told me that because of all the characters he met in the novels he read that he never met a person in real life that he hadn't already met in a book he had read. He said that gave you an advantage when you met people.

Restates point of view and concludes

He had lots of jobs, lots of friends and was very smart. I always wanted to be like that too. I think each of the things he had meant something to me when I was small. All the jobs meant freedom and the friends meant never being lonely. Being smart meant always being able to take care of yourself. I guess that my uncle meant the good life to me. Though I am different from my uncle, I too have tried to keep my freedom, have lots of friends, and become educated in my own way. I never got a red convertible though; it's a green one.

Discussion

Refer to the chart on the steps in writing an essay and to the essay itself. Following the guidelines in the chart, the first paragraph begins by presenting the central point of view or key idea.

One of the people who was most important in shaping my life was my Uncle Ned.

The paragraph continues with the three main reasons why Uncle Ned was important in this person's life: (1) He had so many different jobs; (2) He had many friends; and (3) He was very intelligent.

The paragraphs that follow elaborate on the points made in the first paragraph by giving specific examples of each point. The second paragraph tells of the many jobs Uncle Ned has held and gives a little information about each. The third paragraph gives details about the components of Uncle Ned's personality. The fourth paragraph gives details about why Uncle Ned was so well educated. Finally, the essay concludes with a last paragraph that restates the key idea and briefly summarizes how Uncle Ned has affected the writer's life.

Lesson 5 Activity

Write an essay of approximately 200 words in length, using as your key idea a person who was important in shaping your life.

To develop your essay, follow the map you made in the Lesson 4 Activity. Also review the chart on Writing an Essay (page 159) before you begin. Do not worry about writing a perfect essay. For now, concentrate on getting your ideas on paper in an organized manner. Write your essay quickly. You will have a chance to change what you don't like about it later, when you revise it.

When you have finished writing this draft of your essay, keep it to make revisions when you do the Lesson 6 Activity.

Lesson 6 Revising an Essay

Now that you have a first draft of your essay, you will want to revise it. This is an important part of the writing process for *all* writers. Even the best writers write and revise many times before they are satisfied with their work. This lesson will give you guidelines for improving your essay. It will also show you some useful techniques for making your writing clearer.

As you revise an essay, bear in mind that the essay is written for others to read. It must be well organized and clear enough for your audience to be able to follow the points you are making. Unlike a conversation, in which the other person can interrupt and ask questions, your reader must get all of the information from what you have written.

Some suggestions for things to look for when revising an essay are given in the following chart.

Chart for Revising Essays

Key Ideas

- ☐ Did you state the central idea of your essay in one sentence?
- ☐ Is the central idea or point of view stated clearly enough that any reader would be able to restate it?

Content

- ☐ Did you use specific examples that support your point of view?
- ☐ Are your examples explained clearly enough that your reader can see how they support your point of view?
- ☐ Did you consider the opinions of a person who might not agree with your point of view? If so, did you answer that argument?

Organization

- ☐ Did you state your point of view right away?

- ☐ Did you present two or three important supporting ideas?
- ☐ Would your reader be able to restate what the important supporting ideas are?
- ☐ Did you use words that show how your supporting ideas relate to the central idea and to each other?

Summary or Conclusion

- ☐ Does your summary or conclusion restate your point of view and supporting ideas so that the reader is reminded of them?
- ☐ Does your summary or conclusion follow logically from what you said in your essay?

Demonstration

The essay on Uncle Ned will be used to demonstrate how to use the revising chart to improve an essay. For this demonstration, the essay from Lesson 5 is printed again, paragraph by paragraph, just as it was written. It is shown with handwritten changes made during revision. The *Discussion* about each paragraph refers to the revising chart to explain why the changes were made. The sentences from the original essay are numbered to make the discussion easier to follow.

Take the time to study this demonstration. You will soon be revising your own essay about the important person who shaped your life.

PARAGRAPH 1

(1) One of the people who was most important in shaping my life was my Uncle Ned. (2) He was important because he was different from my immediate family. (3) He had many different kinds of jobs and he have many different kinds of friends and he also was very smart. (4) I always thought his life was much more interesting than the rest of my families. (5) I wanted to be like him to have a lot of jobs and friends and be educated from my experiences and travels and other things.

PARAGRAPH 1 REVISED

(1) One of the people who was most important in ~~shaping~~ my life was my Uncle Ned. (2) He was important because he was different from my immediate family. (3) He had many different ~~kinds of~~ jobs ~~and he have~~ many different ~~kinds of~~ friends and he ~~also~~ was very smart. (4) I always thought his life was much more interesting than the rest of my families.

(5) I wanted to be like him. ^I wanted^ to have a lot of jobs and friends and be educated from my experiences and travels. ~~and other things.~~

Discussion

Looking back at the chart on revising essays (page 162), it suggests that the central idea should be stated immediately, in one sentence, and that it be stated clearly.

The first revision, Sentence 1, was made because the writer did not want to limit himself to ways his uncle *shaped* his life.

In Sentence 3, the words that have been crossed out do not add meaning to the sentence. In Sentence 5, the last words were deleted because they did not give the reader specific information.

With these changes, Paragraph 1 clearly and immediately presents the key idea and introduces the three supporting ideas that the next three paragraphs discuss.

PARAGRAPH 2

(1) My Uncle had more jobs than anyone I ever knew. (2) My father used to say that he had so many jobs because he couldn't keep a job, but I think that he just got bored with things after a while. (3) He owned a pet store until he sold the store and decided to travel. (4) When he came back after a few years he became a travel agent. (5) Then he he was a truck driver for a while. (6) After that, he taught in a private school, and he lectured for a while for a book club in town.

PARAGRAPH 2 REVISED

(1) My Uncle had more jobs than anyone I ever knew. ~~(2) My father used to say that he had so many jobs because he couldn't keep a job, but I think that he just got bored with things after a while.~~ (3) He owned a pet store until he sold the store and decided to travel. (4) When he came back after a few years he became a travel agent. (5) Then he was a truck driver for a while. (6) After that, he taught in a private school, and he lectured for a while for a book club in town. ^ All these different jobs made my uncle an interesting man to know.

Discussion

Sentence 2 has been deleted because it is not central to the key idea of the paragraph or the essay. The last sentence has been added to tell the reader more about why the writer thought his uncle and all his uncle's jobs were so interesting.

These changes make it clearer to the reader how the ideas in this paragraph relate to the key idea of the essay. They also show the logic of the writer's ideas, making it easier for the reader to understand the writer's point of view.

PARAGRAPH 3

(1) He was good to people and he was especially good to me. (2) He had lots of friends and he had lots of girlfriends who used to come around the house. (3) He had a red convertible in those days and I always wanted to have a red convertible too.

PARAGRAPH 3 REVISED

(1) He was good to ~~people and~~ he was especially good to me. ~~(2) He had lots of friends and he had lots of girlfriends who used to come around the~~

~~house.~~ (3) He had a red convertible in those days ~~and I always wanted to have a red convertible too.~~ It was just like him: not flashy, just nice looking and comfortable. He took me everywhere in it -- movies, bowling, even a horse race. I loved that convertible.

Discussion

Paragraph 3 explains a second reason the writer feels his uncle was important in his life. The changes in Sentence 1 link the two ideas together in a more logical way.

The writer decided to delete Sentence 2 because he wanted to concentrate on his relationship with his uncle, rather than talk about his uncle's friends.

The last part of Sentence 3 was deleted because it is not central to the key idea. As it stands, the paragraph is short and lacking in substance. The writer then added the last three sentences to show the reader why the red convertible was important and exactly what it had to do with Uncle Ned's personality, which is the key idea of this paragraph.

All the changes serve to make Uncle Ned's importance to the writer clearer to the reader.

PARAGRAPH 4

(1) Everyone thought that he was very smart. (2) I guess he got smart from all of his travels all over the world and all over the United States too. (3) And he read a lot of books and other kinds of things like magazines. (4) Uncle Ned was always reading one book or another. (5) He told me that every time he read a book he learned something he didn't know before. (6) He once told me that because of all the characters he met in the novels he read that he never met a person in real life that he hadn't already met in a book he had read. (7) He said that gave you an advantage when you met people.

PARAGRAPH 4 REVISED

(1) Everyone thought that he was well educated. ~~very smart~~. (2) I guess from ~~he got smart from all of~~ his travels all over the world and his reading, he became an educated man. ~~all over the United States too. (3) And he read a lot of books and other kinds of things like magazines.~~ (4) Uncle Ned was always reading ~~one book or another. (5) He told me that every time he read a book he learned something he didn't know before.~~ (6) He once told me ~~that because of all the characters he met in the novels he read~~ that he never met a person in real life that he hadn't already met in a book he had read. (7) He said that gave you an advantage when you met people.

Discussion

Paragraph 4 presents the third reason Uncle Ned was so important in the writer's life. In Sentence 1, the writer decided to change *very smart* to *well educated* because it is truer to the meaning he is trying to convey; people can be smart but not well educated. Uncle Ned was both.

The changes in Sentences 2 and 3 were done to clean up the writing. It is not necessary to say he traveled all over the world and then say he traveled all over the United States (all over the world includes the United States). The changes in Sentences 4 through 6 also eliminate repetition and unnecessary information. Cleaning up the writing in this paragraph serves to make the supporting ideas clearer to the reader.

PARAGRAPH 5

(1) He had lots of jobs, lots of friends and was very smart. (2) I always wanted to be like that too. (3) I think each of the things he had meant something to me when I was small. (4) All the jobs meant freedom and the friends meant never being lonely. (5) Being smart meant always being able to take care of yourself. (6) I guess that my uncle meant the good life to me. (7) Though I am different from my uncle, I too have tried to keep my freedom, have lots of friends, and become educated in my own way. (8) I never got a red convertible though; it's a green one.

PARAGRAPH 5 REVISED

(1) He had lots of jobs, lots of friends and was very smart. (2) I ~~always~~ wanted to be like that too. (3) I think each of these things ~~he had meant~~ symbolized something to me when I was small. (4) All the jobs meant freedom and the friends meant never being lonely. (5) Being smart meant always being able to take care of yourself. (6) ~~I guess that~~ My uncle meant the good life to me. (7) Though I am different from my uncle, I too have tried to keep my freedom, have lots of friends, and become educated in my own way. (8) I never got a red convertible though; it's a green one.

Discussion

The concluding paragraph sums up the ideas in the essay, reminding the reader of what the point of view was. It ties the whole essay together and leaves the reader with a sense of completion and understanding of what the writer has said.

The changes made in this last paragraph were made to clean up the writing. This corrected sentence gives the reader a good sense of why Uncle Ned was important to the writer and an understanding of what kind of person Uncle Ned was.

There are still some errors in grammar, sentence structure, and mechanics in the essay. These will be corrected in the next step in the writing process—editing.

Lesson 6 Activity

Now that you have seen how the revision step works, use the Chart for Revising Essays (page 162) to revise your own essay. Remember that your goal in revising is to make your ideas and point of view clear to your reader.

Ask yourself the questions on the chart and do what is necessary to improve your essay. When you believe you have made all the improvements you can, keep your revised version of the essay. You will be editing it in the Lesson 7 Activity.

Lesson 7 Editing an Essay

The last step in the writing process is to edit your essay. To edit, read over your essay, concentrating on errors in spelling, punctuation, and grammar. Use the editing skills you learned in Part I of the Writing Skills Test. At this point, you can make other changes if you wish, but try to concentrate on correctness. The effect you are trying to achieve is polishing—making the paper read smoothly and flawlessly, with no errors or awkward wording that will jar the reader's attention. A polished essay is an effective essay, and the more effective your essay, the higher your score will be on the GED Writing Skills Test.

There are several ways to approach editing, all of which should be used to make sure that you have caught all your errors. The first is to read your essay aloud, or in a whisper if there are others in the room. Sometimes it is easier to spot a mistake when you actually hear it. Perhaps you will naturally pause at a place in your essay where a comma should be inserted. Hearing the pause will alert you to insert the comma. Other errors, such as overlong sentences, can also be picked up this way. First try reading your essay at a normal reading speed. See which errors you find. Then try reading it slowly, word for word. You may find it easier to catch errors at this speed. Try both speeds and see which works better for you.

Another good editing strategy is the 5-R method you learned in Unit I of this book. This method gives you a systematic way of checking for errors in your writing. If you have forgotten the method, go back and review it before you begin editing your essay.

Spelling errors can be especially difficult to see. Sometimes words look right because you *expect* to see them a certain way. This becomes increasingly true when you have read the same thing many times. One way to avoid this trap is to read your essay backward, from the bottom of the page to the top. Doing this forces you to concentrate on each word. Reading backward can also help you spot words that you may have written twice in a row by mistake.

The editing chart that follows summarizes the strategies you can use.

Editing Chart

Step 1. Read your essay aloud or in a whisper.

Step 2. Read at the speed—normal or slow—that works best for you.

Step 3. Use the 5-R editing method.

Step 4. Read your essay backward while you concentrate on finding spelling errors.

Demonstration

The revised essay from Lesson 6 (pages 163–166) was edited using suggestions from the Editing Chart. Portions of the revised essay are shown below with editorial changes. Notice how these changes help polish the essay.

PARAGRAPH 1

He had many different jobs, many different friends, and ~~he was very smart.~~ was well educated. I always thought his life was much more interesting than the rest of my famil~~ies.~~ y's

PARAGRAPH 2

My ~~U~~ncle had more jobs than anyone I ever knew. . . . When he returned from his travels ~~came back after a few years~~ he became a travel agent.

PARAGRAPH 3

~~He~~ My uncle was good to everybody, but he was especially good to me.

PARAGRAPH 4

~~I guess from~~ Uncle Ned was educated through his ~~travels all over the~~ world travels and all his reading ~~he became an educated man.~~ He was always reading and once told me that he never met a person in real life that he hadn't ~~didn't~~ already met in ~~know from~~ a book he had read. He said that gave him ~~you~~ an advantage when he ~~you~~ met people.

PARAGRAPH 5

He had lots of jobs, lots of friends and was very intelligent ~~smart.~~ . . . I never got a red convertible though ~~; it's~~ mine is a green one.

In Paragraph 1, commas are needed between *jobs* and *many* and between *friends* and *and*. The writer changed *very smart* to *well-educated* to show that his uncle was a learned man, not just an intelligent man. Another mechanical error was fixed by changing the incorrectly used plural *families* to the correctly used possessive *family's*.

Paragraph 2 begins with an error in mechanics. The word *Uncle* should not be capitalized unless it is part of the person's name. A sentence was also changed to make it sound less awkward: *When he returned from his travels* sounds much better than *When he came back after a few years. . . .*

Paragraph 3 originally began with an indefinite pronoun, *he*. Who is *he*? Because the essay is about Uncle Ned, the reader assumes *he* is Uncle Ned, but it is better to use the specific noun here, *My uncle*.

In Paragraph 4, the first sentence is structurally poor and reads better changed to: *Uncle Ned was educated through his world travels and all his reading*. The last sentence in this paragraph has a pronoun shift. The two instances of the word *you* should be changed respectively to *him* and *he*.

In the concluding paragraph, the first sentence needs a comma between *friends* and *and*. The writer also decided to change *very smart* to *intelligent*, which is a higher-level word. In the last sentence, *it's* is changed to *mine* to correct an unclear pronoun reference.

After the editing and the last-minute revisions were completed, the essay was in its final form, as follows.

> One of the people who was most important in my life was my Uncle Ned. He was important because he was different from my immediate family. He had many different jobs, many different friends, and was well educated. I always thought his life was much more interesting than the rest of my family's. I wanted to be like him. I wanted to have a lot of jobs and friends and be educated from my experiences and travels.
>
> My uncle had more jobs than anyone I ever knew. He owned a pet store until he sold the store and decided to travel. When he returned from his travels, he became a travel agent. Then he was a truck driver for a while. After that, he taught in a private school, and he lectured for a while for a book club in town. All these different jobs made my uncle an interesting and fascinating person to know.
>
> My uncle was good to everybody, but he was especially good to me. He had a red convertible in those days. It was just like him: not flashy, just nice looking and comfortable. He took me everywhere in it—the movies, bowling, even a horse race. I loved that convertible.
>
> Uncle Ned was educated through his world travels and all his reading. He was always reading and once told me that he never met a person in real life that he hadn't already met in a book he had read. He said that gave him an advantage when he met people.
>
> He had lots of jobs, lots of friends, and was very intelligent. I wanted to be like that too. I think each of these things symbolized something to me when I was small. All the jobs meant freedom and the friends meant never being lonely. Being smart meant always being able to take care of yourself. My uncle meant the good life to me. Though I am different from my uncle today, I too have tried to keep my freedom, have lots of friends, and become educated in my own way. I never got a red convertible though: mine is a green one.

What you have just read is an effective essay. It is the result of the five-step writing process that includes clustering, mapping, writing, revising, and editing. However, saying that this essay is effective is not saying that it is perfect. There really is no such thing as a perfect essay. The essay makes its point, it is clear, and its supporting ideas are logical. There are still some mechanical and structural errors—awkward phrases, repetition of ideas, and the like.

The final, edited version of this essay is longer than 200 words. If it had been written for Part II of the GED Writing Skills Test, its score would not have been affected by its length. Since it is longer than 200 words, but not *that* much longer, it would be scored on a basis of its effectiveness. It is difficult to write an essay that is exactly 200 words long, or any particular length, for that matter. As you practice writing essays, you will become more able to judge the length of what you are writing and tailor it accordingly. Your main task, however, should be concentrating on writing effectively.

In the next chapter you will have an opportunity to practice writing essays. When you have completed this lesson's Activity, think about your completed essay. Is it better than others you have written? Are the ideas clearer? Do they flow in a more logical and organized manner?

Ideally, the answer to these questions will be *yes*. You will find that the more you write and use the techniques you have just learned, the more effective your writing will become, and the easier it will be for you to write well.

Lesson 7 Activity

Edit the essay that you revised in the Lesson 6 Activity. Follow the suggestions in the Editing Chart on page 167. When you have finished this Activity, you will have developed an essay that uses every step in the writing process. You should then go to Chapter 3 to practice what you have learned by writing other essays.

Chapter 3

Reviewing the Writing Process

Objective

In this chapter you will

- Review the steps in the writing process
- Practice the writing process by developing several essays on your own

Lesson 1 Practice the Process

If you find the process of writing to be difficult, it may seem hard to believe that, with practice, writing will become increasingly easy. You may even find at some point that you actually enjoy writing. In this lesson there are suggestions and tools that can help make writing a habit and help you prepare for the GED.

No one can *force* you to improve your writing. It is something you must want to do for yourself. One way to help yourself improve your writing is to continue writing in your journal every day. If you have stopped daily writing, start again.

Journal writing, however, is not enough for the GED. You need to practice writing essays, as that is the form of writing on which you will be judged. For the GED, you will be assigned a topic to write about. For this reason, it would be wise to practice writing on assigned topics. Furthermore, when you practice writing, use all five steps of the writing process. This will help you write an effective essay for the GED.

In Lesson 2 of this chapter, there is a summary of the activities you should do at each step in the writing process. This summary is provided as a reference for you to use as you develop more essays. For a detailed review of the writing process, you may find it helpful to refer to Chapter 2.

Lesson 1 ends with a list of topics for you to use when you practice writing essays. The following are some suggestions for using this topic list.

Ways to Use the Topic List

1. Read all the topics in the list. Choose the topics that interest you most and write about them first. Save the topics that interest you least to write about later when your skill and confidence have increased.
2. Keep the topics a secret from yourself. Write on Topic 1 first, Topic 2

next, and so on. Look at each topic only when you are ready to write an essay.

3. Have someone else assign topics from the list to you.

You might decide that you want to write on the same topic more than once, perhaps because you want to approach it from a different angle or just to see if you can improve on your first essay by starting again. Whatever your reasons, this would be a good way to measure your progress.

As you write essays and become more comfortable with the writing process, set time limits for your writing. Gradually, you should aim for completing essays in no more than 45 minutes—the time allotted for the GED essay.

The following is the list of assigned topics for this chapter.

TOPIC LIST

TOPIC 1

To help fight the war on pollution, recyling centers for glass, aluminum, and paper have sprung up in communities around the country. For such efforts to make a real difference, some people think that individuals should be fined if they don't use these centers. Others argue that such laws are hard to enforce, and that using recycling centers should be voluntary.

Give your own opinion as to whether or not using recycling centers should be voluntary or mandatory. Be specific. Use reasons and examples to support your view.

TOPIC 2

In modern history, people have sealed objects from their time and place into time capsules for future generations to discover. The objects may have been wooden shoes, a souvenir from the 1939 World's Fair, or a Beatle wig. Select a typical item from your generation and write an essay to explain why you would want to include it in a time capsule. Include reasons that support your explanation.

TOPIC 3

It is almost impossible to go through a day without coming into contact with computers. You must deal with them in offices, banks, city hall, and even in the checkout line at the supermarket. How do you feel about the way computers affect your life? In your explanation, give two or three main ideas and support each idea with two or three details.

TOPIC 4

Some people think that being the oldest child, a middle child, or the youngest child affects them for their entire life. Do you think this makes any difference? Write an essay to express your opinion. Be specific, and use examples and reasons to support your essay.

TOPIC 5

Some people in restaurants have been saved from choking to death because another diner knew just what to do. Some heart attack victims have had their lives saved because someone who was present knew what steps to take. Do you think that lifesaving techniques like these should be mandatory training? Explain your opinion and give reasons and examples for your explanation.

TOPIC 6

Many corporate leaders say that the secret of their company's success is teamwork. When employees work together as a team, they achieve success. Are you a member of a team? It may be at home, in the office, at school, or in some outside activity. In an essay, describe a team effort you are involved in. In your opinion, are the biggest strides forward made by group efforts or by individual efforts? Give supporting details for your opinion.

TOPIC 7

Recently, many school systems have been forced to cut back programs outside the regular course of study because of economics. Sports programs have been hardest hit. Do you agree with these cutbacks? Or should schools try to find other ways to save money. In an essay, give your own position on this issue and back it up with reasons and examples.

TOPIC 8

Some apartment complexes today advertise their apartments for adults only. Should landlords have the right to discriminate against families with small children? Do you agree or disagree with this practice? Explain your position and back it up with reasons and examples.

TOPIC 9

Some people think that fairy tales may be harmful to children because they are often violent. Others say that fairy tales help to develop a child's imagination.

Write an essay to present your own view about the harm or benefit fairy tales may bring to children. Support your opinion with specific examples and reasons.

TOPIC 10

More people are taking responsibility for their health today than ever before. Some stop smoking. Others change their eating habits. Why do you think more people today are meeting the challenge of changing bad health habits? Give your own opinion and support it with specific examples and reasons.

TOPIC 11

Many men today have to buy groceries and prepare meals—whether they are single or married. They have to take responsibility for general household chores in a way their fathers and grandfathers weren't required to. Do you think high school boys should be encouraged to enroll in a home economics class? Write an essay to express your opinion. Support your essay with reasons and examples.

TOPIC 12

Recently many cities have begun to crack down on parking ticket violators. Some drivers suddenly are forced to pay long-overdue fines of thousands of dollars. Is this fair?

State your view in an essay. Give specific details to support your position.

TOPIC 13

Many countries around the world use the metric system of weights and measures. There has been a debate in the country for some time about whether or not we should adopt this system. How well could Americans adapt if they were suddenly forced to measure in centimeters and meters instead of inches and feet? If this change were to happen, what benefits could you foresee? What problems? Use reasons and examples to support your opinion.

TOPIC 14

Americans have been encouraged to buy American-manufactured goods instead of products made in other countries. Do you agree or disagree with this? Be specific, and use examples to support your opinion.

TOPIC 15

Some people find that they have a much easier time overcoming difficulties in their lives if they have the support of a group. They may face problems such as drinking, smoking, or losing weight. Or they may even be the victim of a violent crime. Do you think these support groups are effective? Or do you think overcoming a particular problem is solely up to the individual? In an essay, give your opinion. Use reasons and examples to support your view.

Lesson 1 Activity

1. Keep your journal on a daily basis.
2. Whenever the opportunity arises, write something that you intend for other people to read (for example, notes, letters, or reports).
3. Set a schedule that will allow you to develop essays on all 15 topics listed in this lesson before you take the GED.
4. Decide how you will use the Topic List to assign yourself topics.

Before you develop any more essays, read Lesson 2 for a quick review of the writing process.

Lesson 2 The Writing Process: A Summary

Use this lesson as a guide when you develop the essays in this chapter. It summarizes all steps in the writing process that you learned in Chapter 2.

When you have become more adept at writing essays using the writing process, you will probably find that you need to refer to the guide less and less. At this point, you will know that you are well on the way to becoming an efficient and effective writer.

Before Beginning the Process

Before you can begin Step 1 in the writing process, you must be sure you understand the assigned topic. Your next task is to decide on the point of view you want to take in your essay. To understand the topic, read it a few times. Then follow the steps in the following chart.

Steps in Reading a Topic Carefully and Developing a Point of View

Step 1. Underline the important or key words in the topic.

Step 2. Make sure you have noticed and understood all the key ideas or concepts in the topic.

Step 3. Decide on your own point of view and state it in one sentence.

STEP 2 One way to do Step 2 is to write a question that uses most of the words you underlined in Step 1.

STEP 3 To do Step 3, write an answer to the question you formulated in Step 2. Your answer will state the point of view you will present in your essay.

You are now ready to begin the writing process.

The Five Steps in the Writing Process

Step 1: Generate Ideas

- Use brainstorming or clustering to generate ideas about your essay topic.

To brainstorm, write down all the words that come to mind as you think about your point of view on the topic.

Clustering is another form of brainstorming. To cluster, follow these steps: (1) Using a few words, write your point of view on the topic in the center of a piece of paper. Circle your point of view. (2) Write the words that come to mind on extensions from the point-of-view circle. Circle each of these words or phrases.

All clusters will have a different number of circles, but in general they will look like this.

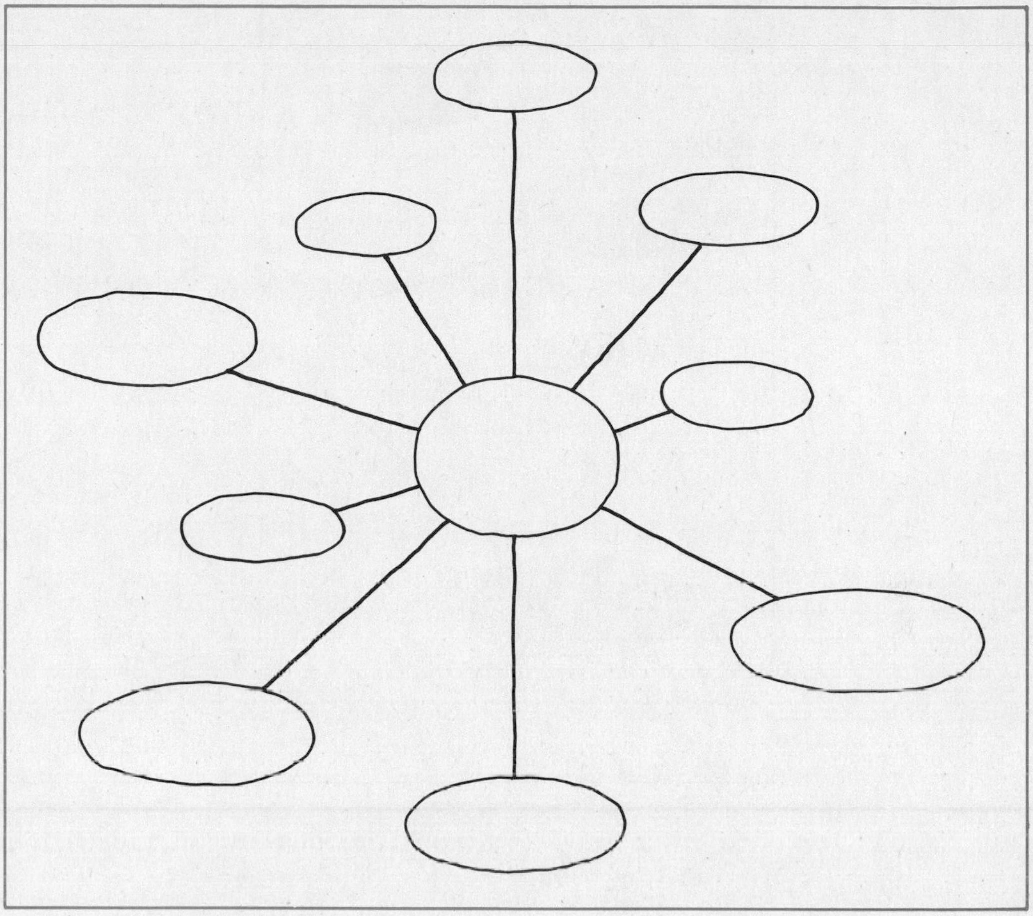

Step 2: Organize Your Ideas

- Select the most appropriate ideas to support your point of view or opinion.
- Decide how best to arrange your ideas for your audience.
- Decide which examples best support your point of view.
- Decide which examples to present first, second, and so on.

A good method of organizing ideas is mapping. Before you begin to map, number or color-code the ideas in your cluster. Use the same number or color for all ideas that are related. The following cluster is both numbered and color-coded.

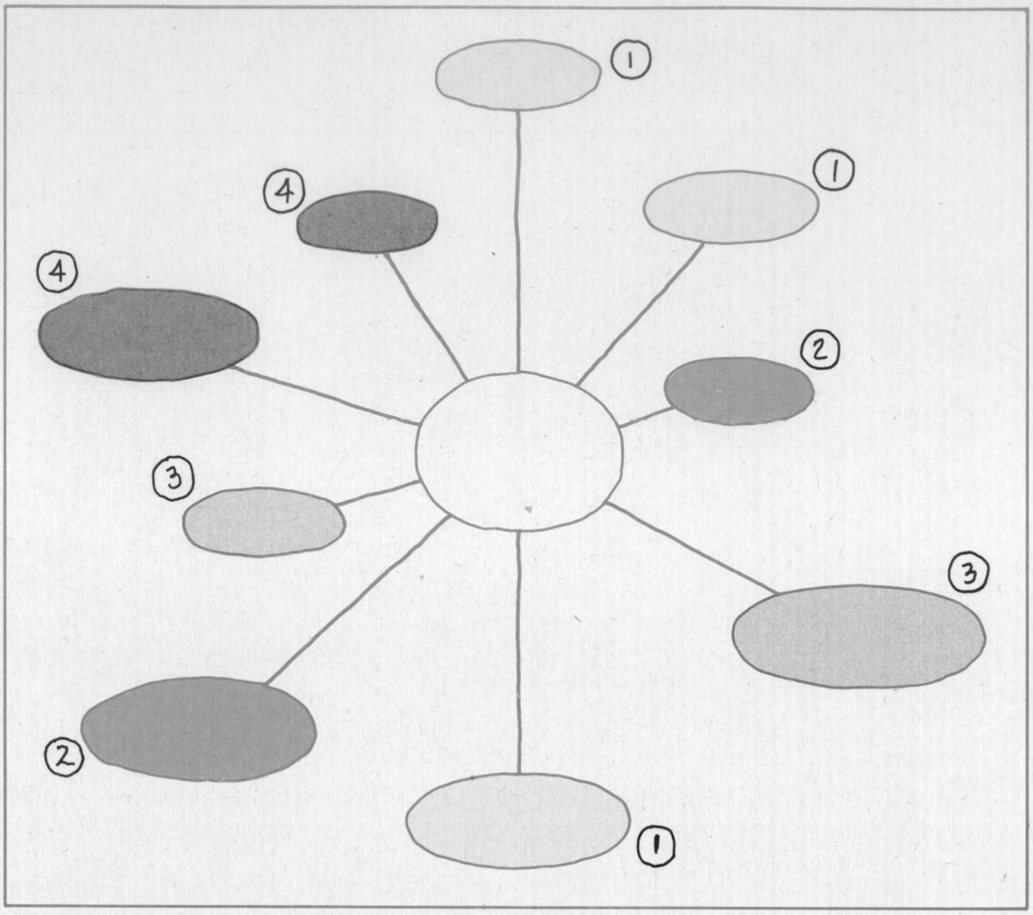

After you have grouped the ideas in your cluster, follow the steps below for creating a map.

Creating a Map

Step 1. Gather all the words from your brainstorming or clustering activities.

Step 2. Eliminate words that have similar meanings.

Step 3. Arrange words in categories and title the categories. The titles will suggest your main ideas, and the words listed will be used as examples to support those ideas.

Step 4. Decide which paragraph should come first and label it. Because it is the introductory paragraph, remember to list the topics of the other paragraphs as they will be introduced by the first paragraph.

Step 5. Decide which paragraph should be second, third, fourth, and so on. Label each one.

Following is the outline of a typical map.

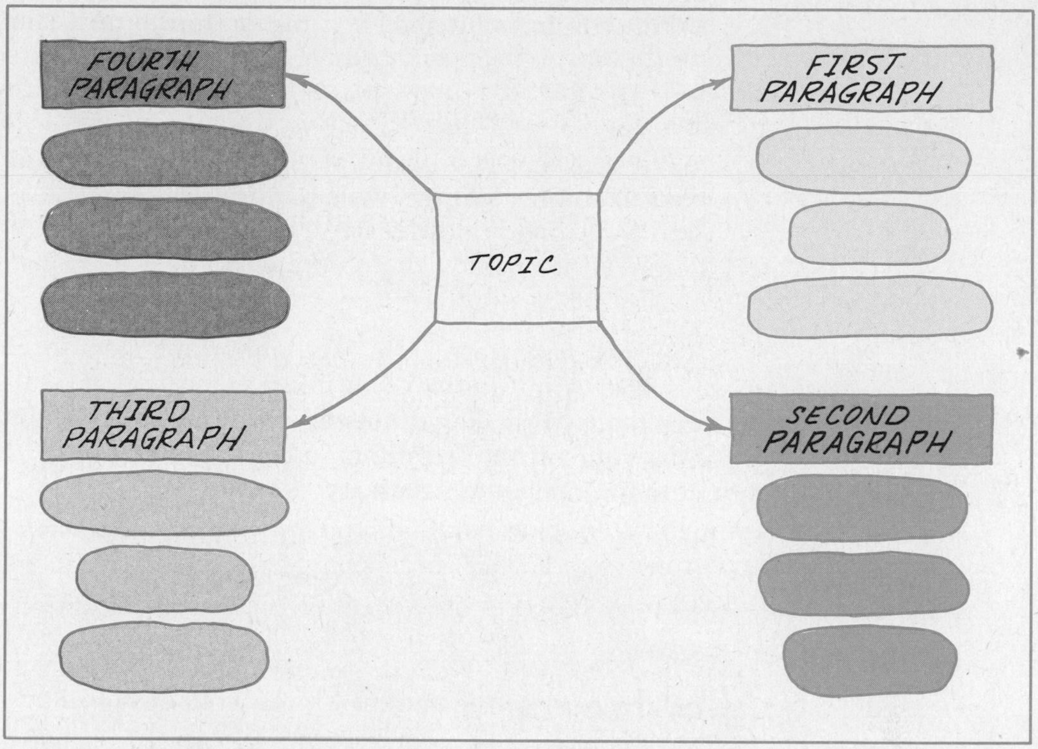

When you have finished mapping, go to the next step in the writing process.

Step 3: Write Your Essay

- Put your ideas in sentences and paragraphs, following the organization you planned.

Step 3 is the stage of the writing process in which you write the first draft of your essay. Since this is not the final version, at this point you should be concentrating on getting your ideas on paper in an organized fashion. Don't spend a lot of time changing what you have written. You'll have a chance to make all the changes you want in the next step.

When you write your essay, follow the instructions in this chart.

Writing Your Essay

Step 1. In the opening paragraph, state your central point of view about the topic immediately. Then give your reasons for your point of view.

Step 2. In the second, third, and following paragraphs, develop supporting examples to explain each of the reasons for your point of view.

Step 3. In the final paragraph, restate and explain why you hold your central point of view.

When you have finished writing, go to the next step.

Step 4: Revise Your Essay

- Make sure that your point of view or opinion is stated clearly and that your examples support your point of view.
- Add information needed for clarity.
- Remove information that is not needed.

The revision stage is a very important step in the writing process. Always keep your audience in mind when you revise an essay. Make any changes that will make your essay clearer and easier for someone to read.

Ask yourself the questions in the following chart. If you answer *no* to any of them, make the necessary changes.

Revising Your Essay

Key Ideas

- ☐ Did you state the central idea of your essay in one sentence?
- ☐ Is the central idea or point of view stated clearly enough that a reader would be able to restate it?

Content

- ☐ Did you use specific examples that support your point of view?
- ☐ Are your examples explained clearly enough that your reader can see how they support your point of view?
- ☐ Did you consider the opinions of a person who does not agree with your point of view? If so, did you answer that person's arguments?

Organization

- ☐ Did you state your point of view right away?
- ☐ Did you present two or three important supporting ideas?
- ☐ Would your reader be able to restate what the important supporting ideas are?
- ☐ Did you use words that show how your supporting ideas relate to the central idea and to each other?

Summary or Conclusion

- ☐ Does your summary or conclusion restate your point of view and supporting ideas so that the reader is reminded of them?
- ☐ Does your summary or conclusion follow logically from what you said in your essay?

After revising, your essay is almost in its final version. To polish it, do the next and last step in the writing process.

Step 5: Edit Your Essay

- Correct errors in usage, sentence structure, spelling, punctuation, and capitalization.

Your essay is almost completed now. However, when you revise your essay for organization, clarity, and effectiveness, you may overlook some mechanical errors. In this step, you will correct any errors you find.

Use the following suggestions to help you polish your essay.

Editing Your Essay

Step 1. Read your essay aloud or in a whisper.

Step 2. Read at the speed—normal or slow—that works best for you.

Step 3. Use the 5-R editing method.

Step 4. Read your essay backward while you concentrate on spelling.

When you have finished editing, your essay is in its final form.

Lesson 2 Activity

1. Continue making daily entries in your journal.
2. Without looking back at this lesson, write a brief summary of the major activities that belong in each of the five steps of the writing process. See how well you remembered by checking your summary against the summary in the lesson.
3. Before taking the Unit II Test, practice writing essays. Write an essay on all 15 of the topics provided in Lesson 1 of this chapter (pages 172–175). To develop each essay, follow the writing process summary in this lesson and refer to the sample of a developed essay in Chapter 2 (page 169).

Unit II Test

Directions: *This is a test to see how well you can write. In this test, you are asked to write an essay in which you present your opinions about an issue. In preparing your essay, you should take the following steps.*

Step 1. Read all of the information about the topic. Be sure that you understand the topic and that you write about only the assigned topic.

Step 2. Plan your essay before you write.

Step 3. Use scrap paper to make any notes.

Step 4. Write your essay on a separate sheet of paper.

Step 5. Read what you have written. Make sure that your writing is legible.

Step 6. Check your paragraphing, sentence structure, spelling, punctuation, capitalization, and usage; make any changes that will improve your essay.

TOPIC

The voting age has been lowered to eighteen. While efforts are made to recruit new voters, not everyone thinks that voting is worthwhile.

Write a composition of about 200 words in which you give your opinion on the importance of voting in national, state, or local elections. Give details to support your position.

When you take the GED test, you will have 45 minutes to write about the topic question you are assigned. Try to write the essay for this test within 45 minutes. Write legibly and use a ballpoint pen so that your writing will be easy to read. Any notes that you make on scrap paper will not be counted as part of your score.

After you complete this essay, you can judge its effectiveness by using the Essay Scoring Guide and Model Essays in the answer key to score your essay. They will be concerned with how clearly you make the main point of your essay, how thoroughly you support your ideas, and how clear and correct your writing is throughout the composition. You will receive no credit for writing about a question other than the one assigned.

Answers are on pages 257–259.

UNIT II TEST

Performance Analysis Record

Directions: After you have used the guidelines in the answer key to score your essay, make a record of your evaluation here.

Write your essay's score in the box at the right.

What were some of the strong points of your essay?

What were some of the weak points of your essay?

What improvements do you plan to make when you work on your next essay?

Practice

Introduction

When a person goes on a job interview, he or she often runs through practice interviews with a friend or family member. Pretending that it is an actual job interview, the interviewer asks questions that might be asked at a job interview, and the job seeker tries to answer in a way that would impress the interviewer. These mock interviews allow the job seeker to get useful interviewing practice, and helps him or her recognize strengths and weaknesses. If the practice interview does not go smoothly, the job seeker can practice some more to improve his or her interviewing skills. When the time for the real interview arrives, the job seeker will be as prepared as possible. The activities in this GED Practice section will serve you in the same way as the practice interview serves the job seeker. By completing the activities, you will get valuable practice at taking GED-type tests. When it comes time to take your test, you will be as prepared for the actual test as you can be.

This section is filled with GED-like test questions, or *items*. It provides valuable practice on the kinds of items found in the Writing Skills Test. There are two groups of items in this section, Practice Items and a Practice Test. Both groups contain 55 multiple-choice items, like those in Part I of the Writing Skills Test, and one essay topic just as in Part II of the test. Both groups of items are structured just like the GED.

By completing the Practice Items and the Practice Test, you will discover your strong points and weak points in writing skills. If you discover any weak points, you will be able to strengthen them. For the items in Part I of each section, the answer key provides correct answers to each practice question and explains why each answer is correct. There are model essays to help you evaluate the essay you write for Part II of the practices. The Performance Analysis Chart following each practice will direct you to parts of the book where you can review the skills that give you trouble.

You can use the Practice Items and the Practice Test in different ways. The introductions that precede the practices will provide you with choices for using them to best advantage. You may also wish to talk with your teacher to get suggestions about how best to make use of the Practice Items and Practice Test.

PRACTICE ITEMS

These Practice Items are similar to a real Writing Skills Test in many ways. The whole group of Practice Items is the same length as an actual GED test. The test items are as challenging as the real test items. Your results on the Practice Items will help you determine which skills you have mastered and which you should study further.

Using the Practice Items to Best Advantage

You can use the Practice Items in the following ways:

- After you finish Chapter 4 in Unit I, you can test your skill by completing Part I of the Practice Items. Or, you can save the Practice Items until you've completed Unit II.
- You may wish to do the Part I Practice Items one group at a time and then review the chapters for the areas in which you have difficulty. After your review, when you do another group of Part I items, your performance may improve.
- You can use the Practice Items as a practice test. To do this, complete the Practice Items in one sitting. Since the actual test allows you 120 minutes, you may want to time yourself. It is suggested that you begin with Part I of the Practice Items. If 75 minutes elapse and you have not yet finished Part I, you should proceed to Part II. If you finish Part II before 120 minutes have elapsed, you can go back to finish Part I. If 120 minutes elapse and you have not finished, note how far you have gotten and then continue. This way, you can find out whether you should work at the same or a different pace. You

also get a good reading on how well you will do if you work quickly enough to finish the GED.

Keep an accurate record of your performance. Write your answers to Part I neatly on a sheet of paper, or use an answer sheet provided by your teacher. Plan and write your essay on fresh sheets of paper.

Using the Answers and Explanations

The Answers and Explanations can be a very helpful study tool. Compare your answers for Part I to those beginning on page 260, and check each item you answered correctly. Whether you answer a multiple-choice item correctly or not, you should read through the solutions given. Doing this will reinforce your writing skills and develop your test-taking skills. For Part II, follow the directions that tell you how to score your essay. You might like to have a teacher or someone else score your essay as well.

How to Use Your Score

Regardless of how you use these Practice Items, you will gain valuable experience with GED-type items. After scoring your Part I work with the answer key, fill in the Performance Analysis Chart on page 204. The chart will help you determine which grammar and editing skills and item types you are strongest in, and direct you to parts of the book where you can review areas in which you need additional work. After you evaluate your Part II essay, you should record your evaluation on the Performance Analysis Chart. Refer back to the Unit II lessons that cover writing skills that you may have been weak in.

PRACTICE ITEMS
Part I

Directions: *The items in Part I of this test are based on paragraphs that contain numbered sentences. Some of the sentences may contain errors in sentence structure, usage, or mechanics.* **A few sentences, however, may be correct as written.** *Read each paragraph and then answer the items that follow it. For each item, choose the answer that would result in the most effective writing of the sentence or sentences. The best answer must be consistent with the meaning and tone of the rest of the paragraph.*

FOR EXAMPLE:

Sentence 1: **Although it may take only two hours to watch the average motion picture takes almost a year to make.**

What correction should be made to this sentence?

(1) replace it with they

(2) change take to have taken

(3) insert a comma after watch

(4) change almost to all most

(5) no change is necessary

The correct answer is **(3).** In this example, a comma is needed after the clause Although it may take only two hours to watch.

Items 1 to 9 are based on the following paragraph.

(1) Sports often have fascinating histories. (2) Volleyball, for example, was first developed for older men. (3) In 1895, William Morgan is a YMCA director in Holyoke, Massachusetts. (4) He seen that many games were too tiring for his classes of older males. (5) He set down the rules for the team sport we know as volleyball today. (6) Someone serves the ball by strikeing it over the net, and members of the other team try to hit the ball. (7) If they fail to get it back over the net, the serving team scoring a point. (8) During World Wars I and II, American military personnel introduced the game abroad, they introduced the game to foreign countries. (9) Men's volleyball was played in the Olympics during the 1960s it wasn't until over ten years later that women's volleyball became part of the Olympic Games. (10) The women's team from china won the gold medal in the exciting final match that year. (11) William Morgan would recognize the basic rules of Olympic volleyball but he might be surprised by how strenuous the games can be.

1. Sentence 1: **Sports often have fascinating histories.**

If you rewrote sentence 1 beginning with

The history of sports

the next word should be

(1) fascinating
(2) have
(3) has
(4) is
(5) are

2. Sentence 3: **In 1895, William Morgan is a YMCA director in Holyoke, Massachusetts.**

Which of the following is the best way to write the underlined portion of this sentence? If you think the original is the best way, choose option (1).

(1) Morgan is a YMCA director in
(2) Morgan been a YMCA director in
(3) Morgan was a YMCA director in
(4) Morgan is a YMCA director, in
(5) Morgan is a YMCA director; in

3. Sentence 4: **He seen that many games were too tiring for his classes of older males.**

What correction should be made to this sentence?

(1) change *seen* to *saw*
(2) change *were* to *was*
(3) change *too* with *to*
(4) insert a comma after *tiring*
(5) replace *males* with *male's*

4. Sentence 6: **Someone serves the ball by strikeing it over the net, and members of the other team try to hit the ball.**

What correction should be made to this sentence?

(1) change *serves* to *serve*
(2) change the spelling of *strikeing* to *striking*
(3) remove the comma after *net*
(4) change *team* to *Team*
(5) change *try* to *tries*

5. Sentence 7: **If they fail to get it back over the net, the serving team scoring a point.**

Which of the following is the best way to write the underlined portion of this sentence? If you think the original is the best way, choose option (1).

(1) net, the serving team scoring a point.
(2) net the serving team score a point.
(3) net, the serving team score a point.
(4) net, the serving team scores a point.
(5) net, the serving team scored a point.

6. Sentence 8: **During World Wars I and II, American military personnel introduced the game abroad, they introduced the game to foreign countries.**

What correction should be made to this sentence?

(1) change *American* to *american*
(2) change the spelling of *personnel* to *personal*
(3) remove the comma after *abroad*
(4) remove *the game abroad, they introduced*
(5) change *foreign* to *Foreign*

7. Sentence 9: **Men's volleyball was played in the Olympics during the 1960s it wasn't until over ten years later that women's volleyball became part of the Olympic Games.**

What correction should be made to this sentence?

(1) replace *Men's* with *Mens'*
(2) change *Olympics* to *olympics*
(3) insert a comma after *1960s*
(4) replace *1960s it* with *1960s. It*
(5) no correction is necessary

8. Sentence 10: **The women's team from china won the gold medal in the exciting final match that year.**

What correction should be made to this sentence?

(1) change *women's* to *womens'*
(2) change *china* to *China*
(3) replace *won* with *were the winners of*
(4) insert a comma after *medal*
(5) no correction is necessary

9. Sentence 11: **William Morgan would recognize the basic rules of Olympic volleyball but he might be surprised by how strenuous the games can be.**

Which of the following is the best way to write the underlined portion of this sentence? If you think the original is the best way, choose option (1).

(1) volleyball but he might be surprised
(2) volleyball but, he might be surprised
(3) volleyball. But he might be surprised
(4) volleyball, but he might be surprised
(5) volleyball; but he might be surprised

Items 10 to 19 are based on the following paragraph.

(1) Television plays a strong role in deciding who wins an election. (2) The fastest way for politicians to get most of the American population's attention was to go on television. (3) We see the faces of candidates frequently on TV as November of any election year approaches. (4) People running for office appear in the news, in campaign advertisements, and to debate. (5) Those men and women which do not come across well on television often do not get the votes they need. (6) Those who are attractive and have good stage presence tends to be the ones who win an election. (7) Unfortunately, the people who give the most positive impression on TV is not always the best candidates. (8) There were excellent leaders among past American presidents. (9) Some of them probably would have seemed awkward and plain on television. (10) On the other hand, people with good television personalities not necessarily making the best leaders. (11) Watching television, it is easy to forget that what politicians actually do is more important than how they look.

10. Sentence 1: **Television plays a strong role in deciding who wins an election.**

What correction should be made to this sentence?

(1) change *plays* to *playing*
(2) change the spelling of *role* to *roll*
(3) insert a comma after *role*
(4) replace *who* with *whom*
(5) no correction is necessary

11. Sentence 2: **The fastest way for politicians to get most of the American population's attention was to go on television.**

What correction should be made to this sentence?

(1) insert *most* after *The*
(2) change *American* to *american*
(3) change the spelling of *population's* to *populatian's*
(4) change *was* to *is*
(5) no correction is necessary

12. Sentence 3: **We see the faces of candidates frequently on TV as November of any election year approaches.**

If you rewrote sentence 3 beginning with

As November of any election year

the next word should be

(1) approaches,
(2) approaches;
(3) approaching,
(4) candidates,
(5) candidates;

13. Sentence 4: **People running for office appear in the news, in campaign advertisements, and to debate.**

What correction should be made to this sentence?

(1) change *appear* to *appears*
(2) change *news* to *News*
(3) change the spelling of *campaign* to *campain*
(4) remove the comma after *advertisements*
(5) replace *to debate* with *in debates*

14. Sentence 5: **Those men and women which do not come across well on television often do not get the votes they need.**

Which of the following is the best way to write the underlined portion of this sentence? If you think the original is the best way, choose option (1).

(1) Those men and women which do not
(2) Those men and women, which do not
(3) Those men and women who do not
(4) Those men and women who does not
(5) Those men, and women who do not

15. Sentence 6: **Those who are attractive and have good stage presence tends to be the ones who win an election.**

What correction should be made to this sentence?

(1) change *are* to *is*
(2) change the spelling of *presence* to *presents*
(3) insert a comma after *presence*
(4) change *tends* to *tend*
(5) replace *who* with *which*

16. Sentence 7: **Unfortunately, the people who give the most positive impression on TV is not always the best candidates.**

Which of the following is the best way to write the underlined portion of this sentence? If you think the original is the best way, choose option (1).

(1) on TV is not always the best candidates.
(2) on TV, is not always the best candidates.
(3) on TV is not the best candidates, always.
(4) on TV is not always the best canidates.
(5) on TV are not always the best candidates.

17. Sentences 8 & 9: **There were excellent leaders among past American presidents. Some of them probably would have seemed awkward and plain on television.**

The most effective combination of sentences 8 and 9 would include which of the following groups of words?

(1) There were some who were excellent
(2) American presidents in the past were
(3) In the past there were some who were
(4) who probably would have seemed awkward
(5) who probably would have seemed excellent

18. Sentence 10: **On the other hand, people with good television personalities not necessarily making the best leaders.**

What correction should be made to this sentence?

(1) insert *are* after *personalities*
(2) replace *not necessarily making* with *do not necessarily make*
(3) replace *necessarily making the* with *making the necessarily*
(4) change the spelling of *necessarily* to *necessaryly*
(5) insert *most* after *making the*

19. Sentence 11: **Watching television, it is easy to forget that what politicians actually do is more important than how they look.**

Which of the following is the best way to write the underlined portion of this sentence? If you think the original is the best way, choose option (1).

(1) Watching television, it is easy to
(2) Watching television, one easily
(3) Watching television, we may easily
(4) When you watch television, one may easily
(5) When one watches television, you may easily

Items 20 to 28 are based on the following paragraph.

(1) Scientists know that some illnesses are caused by tiny viruses. (2) Why would a doctor take a virus and injecting it into a patient? (3) Though when you may think the patient would then get the disease, the opposite is true. (4) In the early 1900s some doctors discovered something. (5) They found that patients given shots of cowpox virus were protected from smallpox. (6) Today we can often prevent patients from getting a disease by giving him a specific shot, called a vaccination. (7) Unfortunately, some vaccinations can have serious side effects. (8) There have been a few deaths associated with the whooping cough vaccine, for example. (9) Most doctors beleive that the dangers of this disease are worse than the risks posed by the vaccine. (10) The whooping cough vaccination, like many others, are only given with a parent's approval. (11) Many Doctors give parents literature about a particular vaccine before asking if it is all right to give it to the child. (12) Since more vaccines, are being developed each year, doctors will be asking parents this question more often.

20. Sentence 2: **Why would a doctor take a virus and injecting it into a patient?**

What correction should be made to this sentence?

(1) change *doctor* to *Doctor*
(2) change *take* to *took*
(3) insert a comma after *virus*
(4) replace *virus and* with *virus. An*
(5) replace *injecting* with *inject*

21. Sentence 3: **<u>Though when you may think the patient</u> would then get the disease, the opposite is true.**

Which of the following is the best way to write the underlined portion of this sentence? If you think the original is the best way, choose option (1).

(1) Though when you may think the patient
(2) Though you may think the patient
(3) Though when you may have thought the patient
(4) Though when you may think he
(5) Because you may think the patient

22. Sentences 4 & 5: **In the early 1900s some doctors discovered something. They found that patients given shots of cowpox virus were protected from smallpox.**

The most effective combination of sentences 4 and 5 would include which of the following groups of words?

(1) In the early 1900s they discovered
(2) They found in the early 1900s
(3) and they found that patients
(4) some doctors discovered that patients
(5) and they were protected in the early 1900s

23. Sentence 6: **Today we can often prevent patients from getting a disease <u>by giving him a specific shot, called</u> a vaccination.**

Which of the following is the best way to write the underlined portion of this sentence? If you think the original is the best way, choose option (1).

(1) by giving him a specific shot, called
(2) by given him a specific shot, called
(3) by giving him a spesific shot, called
(4) by giving them a specific shot, called
(5) by giving anyone a specific shot, called

24. Sentence 8: **There have been a few deaths associated with the whooping cough vaccine, for example.**

What correction should be made to this sentence?

(1) replace *There* with *Their*
(2) change *have* to *has*
(3) change the spelling of *associated* to *assosiated*
(4) remove the comma after *vaccine*
(5) no correction is necessary

25. Sentence 9: **Most doctors beleive that the dangers of this disease are worse than the risks posed by the vaccine.**

What correction should be made to this sentence?

(1) change the spelling of *beleive* to *believe*
(2) change *are* to *is*
(3) insert a comma after *disease*
(4) insert *more* after *are*
(5) replace *than* with *then*

26. Sentence 10: **The whooping cough vaccination, like many others, are only given with a parent's approval.**

Which of the following is the best way to write the underlined portion of this sentence? If you think the original is the best way, choose option (1).

(1) like many others, are only given
(2) like many other's, are only given
(3) like many others are only given
(4) like many others, is only given
(5) like many others is only given

27. Sentence 11: **Many Doctors give parents literature about a particular vaccine before asking if it is all right to give it to the child.**

What correction should be made to this sentence?

(1) change *Doctors* to *doctors*
(2) change *give* to *gave*
(3) change the spelling of *literature* to *litterature*
(4) insert a comma after *vaccine*
(5) change the spelling of *all right* to *alright*

28. Sentence 12: **Since more vaccines, are being developed each year, doctors will be asking parents this question more often.**

What correction should be made to this sentence?

(1) remove the comma after *vaccines*
(2) change the spelling of *developed* to *develloped*
(3) remove the comma after *year*
(4) change *will be* to *were*
(5) no correction is necessary

Items 29 to 37 are based on the following paragraph.

(1) Adults often ask how they can help a child in school. (2) One of the best ways to help a child in reading is by reading out loud togather. (3) Listening while you read offers the child several benefits he can look at words as you say them. (4) There have even been cases of children learning to read without any instruction because they listened as a brother sister, parent, or someone else read to them. (5) While reading, you may want to stop at times and talking with a child about letters, words, or the meaning of the story. (6) Many children refuse to read much on their own. (7) If you offer to take turns, the same children are often willing to read for quite a while. (8) The child enjoys spending time with you while you read; consequently, beginning to find reading a good experience. (9) Either your library or the bookstores nearby is sure to contain a book you and a child you know would both enjoy. (10) Somewhere on the bookshelves are the first half of a gift you might want to give a child. (11) When you sit down and read the book with him on his birthday, New Year's Day, or any other day, you are giving him the rest of the gift.

29. Sentence 2: **One of the best ways to help a child in reading is by reading out loud togather.**

What correction should be made to this sentence?

(1) change *reading* to *Reading*
(2) insert a comma after *in reading*
(3) change *is* to *are*
(4) replace *togather* with *to them*
(5) change the spelling of *togather* to *together*

30. Sentence 3: **Listening while you read offers the child several benefits he can look at words as you say them.**

Which of the following is the best way to write the underlined portion of this sentence? If you think the original is the best way, choose option (1).

(1) benefits he can look
(2) benefits, he can look
(3) benefits. He can look
(4) benefits they can look
(5) benefits; they can look

31. Sentence 4: **There have even been cases of children learning to read without any instruction because they listened as a brother sister, parent, or someone else read to them.**

What correction should be made to this sentence?

(1) change *have* to *has*
(2) replace *even been* with *been even*
(3) replace *they* with *he*
(4) insert a comma after *brother*
(5) change *read* to *reads*

32. Sentence 5: **While reading, you may want to stop at times and talking with a child about letters, words, or the meaning of the story.**

What correction should be made to this sentence?

(1) change the spelling of *While* to *Wile*
(2) replace *you may want* with *you wanted*
(3) change *talking* to *talk*
(4) remove the comma after *words*
(5) insert *discuss the* after *or*

33. Sentences 6 & 7: **Many children refuse to read much on their own. If you offer to take turns, the same children are often willing to read for quite a while.**

The most effective combination of sentences 6 and 7 would include which of the following groups of words?

(1) who refuse to read much
(2) which refuse to read much
(3) offer to take turns with him
(3) is often willing to read
(4) were often willing to read

34. Sentence 8: **The child enjoys spending time with you while you read; consequently, beginning to find reading a good experience.**

Which of the following is the best way to write the underlined portion of this sentence? If you think the original is the best way, choose option (1).

(1) you read; consequently, beginning to find
(2) one reads; consequently, beginning to find
(3) you read, consequently, beginning to find
(4) you read; consequently, he begins to find
(5) you read; consequently, he began to find

35. Sentence 9: **Either your library or the bookstores nearby is sure to contain a book you and a child you know would both enjoy.**

Which of the following is the best way to write the underlined portion of this sentence? If you think the original is the best way, choose option (1).

(1) library or the bookstores nearby is
(2) Library or the bookstores nearby is
(3) library, or the bookstores nearby is
(4) library or the bookstores nearby, is
(5) library or the bookstores nearby are

36. Sentence 10: **Somewhere on the bookshelves are the first half of a gift you might want to give a child.**

What correction should be made to this sentence?

(1) insert a comma after *bookshelves*
(2) change *are* to *is*
(3) change the spelling of *half* to *haft*
(4) replace *you* with *they*
(5) no correction is necessary

37. Sentence 11: **When you sit down and read the book with him on his birthday, New Year's Day, or any other day, you are giving him the rest of the gift.**

What correction should be made to this sentence?

(1) insert a comma after *down*
(2) change *New Year's Day* to *new year's day*
(3) remove the comma after *other day*
(4) change *are giving* to *gave*
(5) no correction is necessary

Items 38 to 47 are based on the following paragraph.

(1) As anyone who has growed up in a military family can tell you, military children face some special challenges. (2) For one thing, many military families make frequent moves. (3) Having to change schools especially in the middle of the year, can be difficult. (4) Take the case of a child who is learning to do long division. (5) Just as he is being taught this, his father is transferred from Germany to California. (6) The child's new class in San Diego may be in the middle of fractions, the child may get confused. (7) On the other hand, he will probably know more than his classmates about European geography and the german language. (8) Neither this child nor his parents enjoy leaving old friends, but they may learn to make friends faster than other people. (9) Another problem for some military children is the absence of a parent for long periads of time. (10) This separation is more common if the parent, usually the father, is in the Navy or Marine Corps, Army and Air Force personnel are sent away on duty less often. (11) Each branch of the military has set up family service centers. (12) It offers assistance with a variety of problems.

38. Sentence 1: **As anyone <u>who has growed up in a military family</u> can tell you, military children face some special challenges.**

Which of the following is the best way to write the underlined portion of this sentence? If you think the original is the best way, choose option (1).

(1) who has growed up in a military family
(2) which has growed up in a military family
(3) who have growed up in a military family
(4) who has grown up in a military family
(5) who has growed up, in a military family

39. Sentence 2: **For one thing, many military families make frequent moves.**

What correction should be made to this sentence?

(1) change *make* to *made*
(2) change the spelling of *frequent* to *freequint*
(3) change *families* to *family*
(4) change *make* to *makes*
(5) no correction is necessary

40. Sentence 3: **Having to change <u>schools especially in the middle</u> of the year, can be difficult.**

Which of the following is the best way to write the underlined portion of this sentence? If you think the original is the best way, choose option (1).

(1) schools especially in the middle
(2) schools; especially in the middle
(3) schools and especially in the middle
(4) schools but especially in the middle
(5) schools, especially in the middle

41. Sentences 4 & 5: **Take the case of a child who is learning to do long division. Just as he is being taught this, his father is transferred from Germany to California.**

The most effective combination of sentences 4 and 5 would include which of the following groups of words?

(1) For example, just as he is being taught
(2) Take the case of his being transferred just
(3) division and just as he is being taught
(4) division; and just as he is being taught
(5) when his father is transferred from Germany

42. Sentence 6: **The child's new class in San Diego may be in the middle of fractions, the child may get confused.**

What correction should be made to this sentence?

(1) replace *in San Diego* with *at San Diego*
(2) change *San Diego* to *san diego*
(3) remove the comma after *fractions*
(4) insert *and* after *fractions,*
(5) change *may get* to *may have gotten*

43. Sentence 7: **On the other hand, he will probably know more than his classmates about European geography and the german language.**

What correction should be made to this sentence?

(1) replace *know* with *no*
(2) replace *more than* with *more as*
(3) change *European* to *european*
(4) change *german* to *German*
(5) no correction is necessary

44. Sentence 8: **Neither this child nor his parents enjoy leaving old friends, but they may learn to make friends faster than other people.**

What correction should be made to this sentence?

(1) change *enjoy* to *enjoys*
(2) change the spelling of *friends* to *freinds*
(3) remove the comma after *friends*
(4) replace *they* with *families who move a lot*
(5) insert *more* after *friends*

45. Sentence 9: **Another problem for some military children is the absence of a parent for long periads of time.**

What correction should be made to this sentence?

(1) insert a comma after *children*
(2) change *is* to *are*
(3) change the spelling of *absence* to *absense*
(4) change the spelling of *periads* to *periods*
(5) no correction is necessary

46. Sentence 10: **This separation is more common if the parent, usually the father, is in the Navy or Marine Corps, Army and Air Force personnel are sent away on duty less often.**

Which of the following is the best way to write the underlined portion of this sentence? If you think the original is the best way, choose option (1).

(1) Navy or Marine Corps, Army and Air Force
(2) Navy, or Marine Corps, Army and Air Force
(3) Navy or Marine Corps; Army and Air Force
(4) Navy or Marine Corps, Army, and Air Force
(5) Navy or Marine Corps and Army and Air Force

47. Sentences 11 & 12: **Each branch of the military has set up family service centers. It offers assistance with a variety of problems.**

The most effective combination of sentences 11 and 12 would include which of the following groups of words?

(1) in order to serve the purpose of
(2) and it offers assistance with
(3) to offer its assistance with a
(4) to assist with a variety
(5) with a variety of different

Items 48 to 55 are based on the following paragraph.

(1) When computers were first invented, many people are really frightened of them. (2) One fear was that everyone's job would be took by computers. (3) In addition, the thought of working with more computers and fewer people, made many workers anxious. (4) The first worry turned out to be needless, in most cases; the use of computers has actually increased the total number of jobs. (5) There is some basis for the second concern. (6) Employees in the automobile industry in detroit, for example, often work with computers. (7) Robots who are controlled by computers now do many of the repetitive tasks in factories. (8) These tasks used to be done by employees working side by side in an assembly line. (9) One good side of this whole thing is that because of them the workplace is safer. (10) In an acsident that might have injured a worker in the past, there might only be damage to a robot today.

48. Sentence 1: **When computers were first invented, many people are really frightened of them.**

Which of the following is the best way to write the underlined portion of this sentence? If you think the original is the best way, choose option (1).

(1) invented, many people are really frightened
(2) invented many people are really frightened
(3) invented; many people are really frightened
(4) invented, many people were really frightened
(5) invented, many people are real frightened

49. Sentence 2: **One fear was that everyone's job would be took by computers.**

Which of the following is the best way to write the underlined portion of this sentence? If you think the original is the best way, choose option (1).

(1) job would be took by computers.
(2) job, would be took by computers.
(3) job were took by computers.
(4) job will be took by computers.
(5) job would be taken by computers.

50. Sentence 3: **In addition, the thought of working with more computers and fewer people, made many workers anxious.**

What correction should be made to this sentence?

(1) insert a comma after *thought*
(2) replace *fewer* with *less*
(3) remove the comma after *people*
(4) replace *made* with *making*
(5) change the spelling of *anxious* to *angshous*

51. Sentence 4: **The first worry turned out to be needless, in most cases; the use of computers has actually increased the total number of jobs.**

What correction should be made to this sentence?

(1) change the spelling of *first* to *furst*
(2) replace *cases; the* with *cases, unless the*
(3) insert a comma after *computers*
(4) change *has* to *have*
(5) no correction is necessary

52. Sentence 6: **Employees in the automobile industry in detroit, for example, often work with computers.**

What correction should be made to this sentence?

(1) change the spelling of *automobile* to *autamobile*
(2) change *detroit* to *Detroit*
(3) remove the comma after *example*
(4) insert *to* after *often*
(5) change *work* to *works*

53. Sentence 7: **Robots who are controlled by computers now do many of the repetitive tasks in factories.**

What correction should be made to this sentence?

(1) replace *who* with *that*
(2) change the spelling of *controlled* to *controled*
(3) replace *controlled by* with *under the control*
(4) insert a comma after *tasks*
(5) no correction is necessary

54. Sentence 9: **One good side of this whole thing is that because of them the workplace is safer.**

If you rewrote sentence 9 beginning with

Fortunately, the workplace has been made safer

the next word should be

(1) by
(2) from
(3) that
(4) however
(5) and

55. Sentence 10: **In an acsident that might have injured a worker in the past, there might only be damage to a robot today.**

Which of the following is the best way to write the underlined portion of this sentence? If you think the original is the best way, choose option (1).

(1) In an acsident that might have injured
(2) In a acsident that might have injured
(3) In an accident that might have injured
(4) In an acsident who might have injured
(5) In an acsident that might injuring

Answers are on pages 260–261.

Part II

Directions: *This is a test to see how well you can write. In this test, you are asked to write an essay in which you present your opinions about an issue. In preparing your essay, you should take the following steps.*

Step 1. Read all of the information about the topic. Be sure that you understand the topic and that you write about only the assigned topic.

Step 2. Plan your essay before you write.

Step 3. Use scrap paper to make any notes.

Step 4. Write your essay on a separate sheet of paper.

Step 5. Read what you have written. Make sure that your writing is legible.

Step 6. Check your paragraphing, sentence structure, spelling, punctuation, capitalization, and usage; make any changes that will improve your essay.

TOPIC

Hobbies may help develop an outside interest, or just allow enjoyable time away from normal routine. Many people feel that having a hobby enriches their lives.

Write an essay, approximately 200 words long, in which you give your opinion on the importance of a hobby. Be specific and use examples to support your opinion.

When you take the GED test, you will have 45 minutes to write about the topic question you are assigned. Try to write the essay for this test within 45 minutes. Write legibly and use a ballpoint pen so that your writing will be easy to read. Any notes that you make on scrap paper will not be counted as part of your score.

After you complete this essay, you can judge its effectiveness by using the Essay Scoring Guide and Model Essays in the answer key to score your essay. They will be concerned with how clearly you make the main point of your essay, how thoroughly you support your ideas, and how clear and correct your writing is throughout the composition. You will receive no credit for writing about a question other than the one assigned.

Answers are on pages 262–263.

PRACTICE ITEMS
Performance Analysis Chart

Part I

Directions: Circle the number of each item that you got correct on the Practice Items. Count how many items you got correct in each row; count how many items you got correct in each column. Write the amount correct per row and column as the numerator in the fraction in the appropriate "Total Correct" box. (The denominators represent the total number of items in the row or column.) Write the grand total correct over the denominator, **55,** at the lower right corner of the chart. (For example, if you got 48 items correct, write *48* so that the fraction reads *48*/**55.**)

Item Type	*Usage (page 25)*	*Sentence Structure (page 55)*	*Mechanics (page 75)*	TOTAL CORRECT
Construction Shift (page 112)	1, 38	12, 17, 22, 41, 47, 54		**/8**
Sentence Correction (page 111)	3, 11, 15, 24, 36, 39, 44, 53	6, 7, 13, 18, 20, 21, 32, 42, 51	4, 8, 10, 25, 27, 28, 29, 31, 37, 43, 45, 50, 52	**/30**
Sentence Revision (page 112)	2, 14, 16, 23, 26, 35, 38, 48, 49	5, 19, 30, 34, 46	9, 40, 55	**/17**
TOTAL CORRECT	**/19**	**/20**	**/16**	**/55**

The page numbers in parentheses indicate where in this book you can find the beginning of specific instruction about the areas of grammar and about the types of questions you encountered in the Practice Items.

Part II

Write your essay's score in the box at the right. [ ]

What were some of the strong points of your essay?

What were some of the weak points of your essay?

What improvements do you plan to make when you work on your next essay?

PRACTICE TEST

This Practice Test is like the actual test. There are 55 items in Part I and one essay topic in Part II. By taking the Practice Test, you can gain valuable test-taking experience and you will know what to expect when you sit down to take the actual Writing Skills Test.

Using the Practice Test to Best Advantage

You can use the Practice Test in the following ways:

- To get hands-on, test-taking experience, you may wish to take the Practice Test under conditions similar to those of the actual test. To do this, do the Practice Test in one sitting and try to complete it within the 120-minute time limit. Although you can complete the test in any order you choose, it is to your advantage to begin with Part I. If 75 minutes elapse and you have not yet finished Part I, you should proceed to Part II. If you finish Part II before 120 minutes have elapsed, you can go back to the items in Part I. If 120 minutes elapse and you have not finished, note how far you have gotten and continue. You will learn whether you need to change your pace to complete the test. You will also learn about how well you will do if you complete the Writing Skills Test.
- If you want, you can take the Practice Test in sections. One way to do this is to do Parts I and II at different times. You can also break Part I of the test into smaller sections. For example, you can complete one set of Part I items at a time. Then you can write your Part II essay in one sitting. While this does not simulate the actual testing situation, your results

still will give you a pretty good idea of how well you would do on the real test.

When you take the Practice Test, write your answers for Part I neatly on a sheet of paper, or use an answer sheet provided by your teacher. If you don't know how to answer a question, skip it and come back to it after you have answered the other questions. Plan and write your Part II essay on fresh sheets of paper. Express your thoughts as clearly as possible. Remember that this is not the actual test, just some helpful practice. If you relax, you may discover that you actually perform better!

Using the Answers and Explanations

Compare your answers for Part I to those in the Answers and Explanations on page 264, and check each item you answered correctly. Whether you answer a multiple-choice item correctly or not, you should read through the explanations. Doing this will reinforce your writing skills and develop your test-taking skills. For Part II, follow the directions that tell you how to score your essay. You might like to have a teacher or someone else score your essay as well.

How to Use Your Score

Regardless of how you use the items in the Practice Test, your final score will point out your strengths and weaknesses in writing and editing. After scoring your Part I work with the answer key, fill in the Performance Analysis Chart on page 221. This chart will help you determine which grammar and editing skills and item types you are strongest in, and direct you to parts of the book where you can review areas in which you need additional work. Record your evaluation of your essay on the Performance Analysis Chart. If you discover weaknesses while evaluating your Part II essay, you should refer back to the Unit II lessons that cover the composition skills you had difficulty with.

PRACTICE TEST
Part I

Directions: *The items in Part I of this test are based on paragraphs that contain numbered sentences. Some of the sentences may contain errors in sentence structure, usage, or mechanics.* **A few sentences, however, may be correct as written.** *Read each paragraph and then answer the items that follow it. For each item, choose the answer that would result in the most effective writing of the sentence or sentences. The best answer must be consistent with the meaning and tone of the rest of the paragraph.*

FOR EXAMPLE:

Sentence 1: **Although it may take only two hours to watch the average motion picture takes almost a year to make.**

What correction should be made to this sentence?

(1) replace it with they

(2) change take to have taken

(3) insert a comma after watch

(4) change almost to all most

(5) no change is necessary

The correct answer is **(3).** In this example, a comma is needed after the clause Although it may take only two hours to watch.

Items 1 to 9 are based on the following paragraph.

(1) At graduations, birthdays, and a wedding celebration, people often receive gifts of money. (2) Calculators can make good presence on such occasions; these devices help make decisions about spending easier. (3) Suppose the members of a family decides to go to a restaurant for Sunday dinner. (4) Using a calculator, the tip can easily be figured out. (5) Perhaps a husband and wife are going to buy living room furniture. (6) Before they decide whether to pay all at once, they used a calculator to find the total cost of paying in installments. (7) Maybe they are going to spend some money on painting their kitchen. (8) If they have a calculator, they will have no problem determining how much paint they need to buy. (9) Imagine that the couple plans to go to the grand canyon for a vacation. (10) A calculator will prove handy in figuring out the cost of driving staying in a motel, and taking a tour. (11) Of course, paper and pencil can be used to do all this math; but however, using a calculator is a lot more convenient.

1. Sentence 1: **At graduations, birthdays, and a wedding celebration, people often receive gifts of money.**

What correction should be made to this sentence?

(1) change *graduations* to *Graduations*
(2) change *birthdays* to *birthday*
(3) change *a wedding celebration* to *wedding celebrations*
(4) change *gifts* to *gift's*
(5) no correction is necessary

2. Sentence 2: **Calculators also make good presence on such occasions; these devices help make decisions about spending easier.**

What correction should be made to this sentence?

(1) change the spelling of *presence* to *presents*
(2) insert *because* after *occasions;*
(3) change the spelling of *devices* to *devises*
(4) change *help* to *helping*
(5) replace *easier* with *easily*

3. Sentence 3: **Suppose the members of a family decides to go to a restaurant for Sunday dinner.**

What correction should be made to this sentence?

(1) replace *Suppose* with *If*
(2) change *decides* to *decide*
(3) change the spelling of *restaurant* to *restaraunt*
(4) insert a comma after *restaurant*
(5) change *Sunday* to *sunday*

4. Sentence 4: **<u>Using a calculator</u>, the tip can easily be figured out.**

Which of the following is the best way to write the underlined portion of this sentence? If you think the original is the best way, choose option (1).

(1) Using a calculator,
(2) To use a calculator,
(3) Relying on the use of a calculator,
(4) With a calculator,
(5) By using a calculator.

5. Sentence 6: **Before they decide whether to pay all at once, they used a calculator to find the total cost of paying in installments.**

Which of the following is the best way to write the underlined portion of this sentence? If you think the original is the best way, choose option (1).

(1) once, they used
(2) once; they used
(3) once, they can use
(4) once they used
(5) once, one used

6. Sentence 8: **If they have a calculator, they will have no problem determining how much paint they need to buy.**

If you rewrote sentence 7 beginning with

Determining how much paint

the next word should be

(1) if
(2) you
(3) will
(4) to
(5) so

7. Sentence 9: **Imagine that the couple plans to go to the grand canyon for a vacation.**

What correction should be made to this sentence?

(1) change *plans* to *planned*
(2) change *plans* to *plan's*
(3) insert a comma after *plans*
(4) change *grand canyon* to *Grand Canyon*
(5) no correction is necessary

8. Sentence 10: **A calculator will prove handy in figuring out the cost of driving staying in a motel, and taking a tour.**

Which of the following is the best way to write the underlined portion of this sentence? If you think the original is the best way, choose option (1).

(1) driving staying in a motel
(2) to drive, staying in a motel
(3) driving or staying in a motel
(4) driving and staying in a motel
(5) driving, staying in a motel,

9. Sentence 11: **Of course, paper and pencil can be used to do all this math; but however, using a calculator is a lot more convenient.**

Which of the following is the best way to write the underlined portion of this sentence? If you think the original is the best way, choose option (1).

(1) this math; but however,
(2) this math; but although,
(3) this math. But however,
(4) this math; however,
(5) this math, however,

Items 10 to 19 are based on the following paragraph.

(1) Are you trying to learn about careers, your public library is a good place to start. (2) Try to find the *Occupational Outlook Handbook*, published by the U. S. Department of Labor. (3) They will give you helpful descriptions of many different jobs. (4) If in case you want more information about specific jobs, look in the card catalog. (5) Arranged in alphabetical order by subject is cards that tell you where to look for the books you want. (6) There may even be magazines or journels about the career in which you are interested. (7) Find out if the library had filmstrips, tapes, or computerized information about jobs. (8) Always ask yourself who wrote the information and why. (9) An example of the reason why is that employers sometimes pay writers to write pamphlets about a company. (10) The pamphlets may exaggerate job benefits. (11) They may fail to mention problems with the job. (12) It is better to find out the drawbacks of a job now than discovering them later.

10. Sentence 1: **Are you trying to learn about <u>careers, your public</u> library is a good place to start.**

Which of the following is the best way to write the underlined portion of this sentence? If you think the original is the best way, choose option (1).

(1) careers, Your public
(2) careers? Your public
(3) careers. Your public
(4) careers, then your public
(5) careers, and your public

11. Sentence 3: **<u>They will give you</u> helpful descriptions of many different jobs.**

Which of the following is the best way to write the underlined portion of this sentence? If you think the original is the best way, choose option (1).

(1) They will give you
(2) They gives you
(3) They gave you
(4) It will give you
(5) They will give people

12. Sentence 4: **If in case you want more information about specific jobs, look in the card catalog.**

What correction should be made to this sentence?

(1) remove *in case*
(2) change *want* to *wanted*
(3) insert a comma after *information*
(4) change *look* to *looking*
(5) replace *jobs, look* with *jobs; look*

13. Sentence 5: **Arranged in alphabetical order by subject is cards that tell you where to look for the books you want.**

What correction should be made to this sentence?

(1) Change the spelling of *Arranged* to *Aranged*
(2) change *is* to *are*
(3) insert a comma after *cards*
(4) replace *that* with *who*
(5) replace *you want* with *one wants*

14. Sentence 6: **There may even be magazines or journels about the career in which you are interested.**

What correction should be made to this sentence?

(1) insert a comma after *magazines*
(2) change the spelling of *journels* to *journals*
(3) replace *in which* with *that*
(4) change *you are* to *one is*
(5) no correction is necessary

15. Sentence 7: **Find out if the library had filmstrips, tapes, or computerized information about jobs.**

What correction should be made to this sentence?

(1) change *library* to *Library*
(2) change *had* to *has*
(3) remove the comma after *filmstrips*
(4) change *jobs* to *job's*
(5) no correction is necessary

16. Sentence 8: **Always ask yourself who wrote the information and why.**

Which of the following is the best way to write the underlined portion of this sentence? If you think the original is the best way, choose option (1).

(1) Always ask yourself who wrote
(2) Ask yourself who always wrote
(3) Always ask oneself who wrote
(4) Always ask yourself whom wrote
(5) Always ask yourself who had written

17. Sentence 9: **An example of the reason why is that employers sometimes pay writers to write pamphlets about a company.**

If you rewrote sentence 9 beginning with

Sometimes, for example,

the next word should be

(1) the
(2) that
(3) employers
(4) payment
(5) putting

18. Sentences 10 & 11: **The pamphlets may exaggerate job benefits. They may fail to mention problems with the job.**

The most effective combination of sentences 10 and 11 would include which of the following groups of words?

(1) There may be a benefits exaggeration
(2) An exaggeration and a failure
(3) and there also may be a failure
(4) as well as there being a failure
(5) may exaggerate and fail

19. Sentence 12: **It is better to find out the drawbacks of a job now than discovering them later.**

Which of the following is the best way to write the underlined portion of this sentence? If you think the original is the best way, choose option (1).

(1) than discovering them later.
(2) then discovering them later.
(3) if you discover them later
(4) than to discover them later.
(5) instead of discovering them later.

Items 20 to 28 are based on the following paragraph.

(1) To make sure that high school graduates have basic computer skills, computer literacy is a requirement in many schools. (2) Such skills as English and math have always been important; now knowlege of computers is needed for more and more jobs. (3) Even if computers are not needed for a particular job at present, in the future they probably are. (4) You can probably picture computers being used by people who work in such places as banks or business offices. (5) You might think that truckers, artists, and, musicians would not use computers, but many of them do. (6) Students learn about computers in special computer classes. (7) They also learn about computers in regular classes. (8) When schools order textbooks in the spring or summer they often buy accompanying computer programs. (9) Students taking french, for example, may learn some of the vocabulary and grammar from a computer. (10) There is computer programs, known as software, that deal with everything from applying for a bank loan to taking a driving test. (11) The workplace is only one of many areas computers have entered; their use in a variety of areas is becoming more widespread every day.

20. Sentence 1: **To make sure that high school graduates have basic computer skills, computer literacy is a requirement in many schools.**

Which of the following is the best way to write the underlined portion of this sentence? If you think the original is the best way, choose option (1).

(1) computer literacy is a requirement in many schools.
(2) computer literacy being a requirement in many schools.
(3) computer literacy is a requirement, in many schools.
(4) many school officials have made computer literacy a requirement.
(5) many are requiring computer literacy.

21. Sentence 2: **Such skills as English and math have always been important; now knowlege of computers is needed for more and more jobs.**

What correction should be made to this sentence?

(1) change *math* to *Math*
(2) change *have* to *has*
(3) replace *important; now* with *important, now*
(4) change the spelling of *knowlege* to *knowledge*
(5) change *is* to *being*

22. Sentence 3: **Even if computers are not needed for a particular job at present, in the future they probably are.**

Which of the following is the best way to write the underlined portion of this sentence? If you think the original is the best way, choose option (1).

(1) they probably are.
(2) computers probably are.
(3) they are probably.
(4) they probably will be.
(5) their need is probable.

23. Sentence 5: **You might think that truckers, artists, and, musicians would not use computers, but many of them do.**

What correction should be made to this sentence?

(1) insert a comma after *think*
(2) insert a comma after *that*
(3) remove the comma after *and*
(4) replace *but* with *however*
(5) replace *do* with *have*

24. Sentences 6 & 7: **Students learn about computers in special computer classes. They also learn about computers in regular classes.**

The most effective combination of sentences 6 and 7 would include which of the following groups of words?

(1) Students learn about them
(2) Learning about computers,
(3) in both special computer classes and
(4) in special computer classes both
(5) and they also learn about computers

25. Sentence 8: **When schools order textbooks in the spring or summer they often buy accompanying computer programs.**

What correction should be made to this sentence?

(1) change *spring or summer* to *Spring or Summer*
(2) insert a comma after *summer*
(3) replace *they often buy* with *one often buys*
(4) change the spelling of *accompanying* to *acompanying*
(5) no correction is necessary

26. Sentence 9: **Students taking french, for example, may learn some of the vocabulary and grammar from a computer.**

What correction should be made to this sentence?

(1) change *french* to *French*
(2) remove the comma after *example*
(3) change *learn* to *have learned*
(4) insert a comma after *vocabulary*
(5) change the spelling of *grammar* to *grammer*

27. Sentence 10: **There is computer programs, known as software, that deal with everything from applying for a bank loan to taking a driving test.**

Which of the following is the best way to write the underlined portion of this sentence? If you think the original is the best way, choose option (1).

(1) There is computer programs, known
(2) There are computer programs, known
(3) There are computer programs known
(4) Computer programs are known
(5) Computer programs is known

28. Sentence 11: **The workplace is only one of many areas computers have entered; their use in a variety of areas is becoming more widespread every day.**

What correction should be made to this sentence?

(1) replace *The* with *Because the*
(2) change *their use* to *they're use*
(3) change *is becoming* to *are becoming*
(4) insert a comma after *widespread*
(5) no correction is necessary

Items 29 to 37 are based on the following paragraph.

(1) Most of us have received at least one notice in the mail announcing that you've won a valuable prize. (2) The news usually comes in a letter, on a post card, or a computer form arrives. (3) When someone from a television audience wins a prize, they sometimes shrieks or faints. (4) Unlike the ecstatic winner on television, you may have your doubts about what you've won, you should. (5) The note of congratulations you've been sent, is most likely from someone who is trying to sell you something. (6) In bold letters at the top of the page often describing a vacation that can be yours. (7) You are offered the opportunity to travel to Florida, the Gulf of Mexico, Ulster County, or the Pocono Mountains, for example. (8) In fine print at the bottom or on the back is the catch. (9) First you have to listen to a sales pitch about buying land or vacation property may be for rent. (10) Absent altogether is any mention of the fact that you are responsible for air fare, meals, and other expenses. (11) Some unfortunate people have their time and money wasted on these scams; don't be one of them. (12) Before throwing away your notice, make a complaint to the Better Business Bureau.

29. Sentence 1: **<u>Most of us have received</u> at least one notice in the mail announcing that you've won a valuable prize.**

Which of the following is the best way to write the underlined portion of this sentence? If you think the original is the best way, choose option (1).

(1) Most of us have received
(2) Most of us has received
(3) Most all of us have received
(4) Most of you have received
(5) Probably having received

30. Sentence 2: **The news usually comes in a letter, on a post card, or a computer form arrives.**

What correction should be made to this sentence?

(1) change the spelling of *usually* to *usuelly*
(2) change *comes* to *come*
(3) remove *on*
(4) remove the comma after *card*
(5) replace *a computer form arrives* with *on a computer form*

31. Sentence 3: **When someone from a television audience wins a prize, they sometimes shrieks or faints.**

What correction should be made to this sentence?

(1) remove the comma after *prize*
(2) replace *they* with *the person*
(3) change the spelling of *shrieks* to *shreiks*
(4) replace *shrieks or faints* with *shriek or faint*
(5) no correction is necessary

32. Sentence 4: **Unlike the ecstatic winner on television, you may have your doubts about what you've won, you should.**

What correction should be made to this sentence?

(1) insert a comma after *winner*
(2) replace *you* with *one*
(3) change *your* to *you're*
(4) replace *won, you* with *won. You*
(5) insert *have one's doubts* after *should*

33. Sentence 5: **The note of congratulations you've been sent, is most likely from someone who is trying to sell you something.**

What correction should be made to this sentence?

(1) replace *been sent* with *sent*
(2) remove the comma after *sent*
(3) replace *is* with *are*
(4) insert a comma after *someone*
(5) replace *to sell* with *and sell*

34. Sentence 6: **In bold letters at the top of the page often describing a vacation that can be yours.**

Which of the following is the best way to write the underlined portion of this sentence? If you think the original is the best way, choose option (1).

(1) page often describing a vacation
(2) page, often describing a vacation
(3) page; often describing a vacation
(4) page are often a description of a vacation
(5) page is often a description of a vacation

35. Sentence 7: **You are offered the opportunity to travel to Florida, the Gulf of Mexico, Ulster County, or the Pocono Mountains, for example.**

What correction should be made to this sentence?

(1) change the spelling of *offered* to *oferred*
(2) insert a comma after *opportunity*
(3) change *County* to *county*
(4) change *Mountains* to *mountains*
(5) no correction is necessary

36. Sentence 9: **First you have to listen to a sales pitch about buying land or vacation property may be for rent.**

Which of the following is the best way to write the underlined portion of this sentence? If you think the original is the best way, choose option (1).

(1) buying land or vacation property may be for rent
(2) buying land; or vacation property may be for rent.
(3) buying land or renting vacation property.
(4) buying land or rented vacation property.
(5) buying land, or vacation property that is rented.

37. Sentence 11: **Some unfortunate people have their time and money wasted on these scams; don't be one of them.**

If you rewrote sentence 11 beginning with

Don't be one of those unfortunate people

the next word should be

(1) which
(2) who
(3) having
(4) these
(5) and

Items 38 to 47 are based on the following paragraph.

(1) An increasing number of employers are hiring temporary employees. (2) The jobs these workers are given anywhere from one day to several weeks. (3) Temporaries are hired to fill in for absint file clerks, typists, bookkeepers, and truck loaders, among other workers. (4) Agencies that handle temporary jobs are advertised in the telephone book. (5) They are also advertised in the classified section of your newspaper. (6) When you call the Agency, someone there will set up an appointment for you to come in and take a test. (7) An agency that handles clerical jobs, for example, probably tested your spelling, grammar, and typing speed. (8) Weigh the pros and cons before deciding whether or not one wants to work for a temporary agency (9) There is an advantage in that agencies usually pay you within a week or two of the week you work. (10) On the other hand, paychecks are fairly small, because as a result the agency takes a large percentage of your earnings. (11) You may become more versatile as you train for many different jobs but you may not enjoy making frequent job changes. (12) Having decided that the benefits of working for a temporary agency would outweigh the drawbacks, it might be worth a try.

38. Sentence 2: **The jobs these workers are given anywhere from one day to several weeks.**

Which of the following is the best way to write the underlined portion of this sentence?

(1) The jobs these workers gave anywhere
(2) The jobs who these workers are given anywhere
(3) The jobs, these workers are given, anywhere
(4) The jobs given these workers anywhere
(5) The jobs these workers are given last anywhere

39. Sentence 3: **Temporaries are hired to fill in for absint file clerks, typists, bookkeepers, and truck loaders, among other workers.**

What correction should be made to this sentence?

(1) replace *are hired to* with *which are hired*
(2) change the spelling of *absint* to *absent*
(3) insert *and* after *typists*
(4) remove the comma after *bookkeepers*
(5) no correction is necessary

40. Sentences 4 & 5: **Agencies that handle temporary jobs are advertised in the telephone book. They are also advertised in the classified section of your newspaper.**

The most effective combination of sentences 4 and 5 would include which of the following groups of words?

(1) They are advertised in the telephone book
(2) Agencies also advertise in the classified
(3) Temporary agencies who are advertised
(4) or they also are found
(5) and in the classified section

41. Sentence 6: **When you call the Agency, someone there will set up an appointment for you to come in and take a test.**

What correction should be made to this sentence?

(1) replace *you call* with *you called*
(2) change *Agency* to *agency*
(3) replace *there* with *their*
(4) insert a comma after *in*
(5) no correction is necessary

42. Sentence 7: **An agency that handles clerical jobs, for example, probably tested your spelling, grammar, and typing speed.**

What correction should be made to this sentence?

(1) replace *that* with *who*
(2) change *jobs* to *jobs'*
(3) remove the comma after *example*
(4) replace *probably tested* with *will probably test*
(5) remove the comma after *grammar*

43. Sentence 8: **Weigh the pros and cons before deciding whether or not one wants to work for a temporary agency.**

Which of the following is the best way to write the underlined portion of this sentence? If you think the original is the best way, choose option (1).

(1) one wants to work
(2) one will be wanting
(3) a person wants to work
(4) you want working
(5) you want to work

44. Sentence 9: **There is an advantage in that agencies usually pay you within a week or two of the week you work.**

If you rewrote sentence 9 beginning with

One of the advantages is that you

the next word should be

(1) are
(2) and
(3) or
(4) pay
(5) who

45. Sentence 10: **On the other hand, paychecks are fairly small, because as a result the agency takes a large percentage of your earnings.**

What correction should be made to this sentence?

(1) remove the comma after *small*
(2) remove *because*
(3) remove *as a result*
(4) replace *agency takes* with *agency's taking*
(5) replace *your* with *one's*

46. Sentence 11: **You may become more versatile as you train for many different jobs but you may not enjoy making frequent job changes.**

Which of the following is the best way to write the underlined portion of this sentence? If you think the original is the best way, choose option (1).

(1) jobs but you may not enjoy
(2) jobs; but you may not enjoy
(3) jobs, but you may not enjoy
(4) jobs but not enjoying
(5) jobs and you may not enjoy

47. Sentence 12: **Having decided that the benefits of working for a temporary agency would outweigh the drawbacks, it might be worth a try.**

Which of the following is the best way to write the underlined portion of this sentence? If you think the original is the best way, choose option (1).

(1) Having decided that the benefits of working
(2) Having decided that, the benefits of working
(3) Having decided that the benefits, of working
(4) If you decide that the benefits of working
(5) If one decides that the benefits of working

Items 48 to 55 are based on the following paragraph.

(1) Pets make popular Easter gifts, but you should think carefully before we give an animal as a present. (2) Your little niece might love getting a chick for Easter, but how would her mother feel about it? (3) Besides, after the chick grows to full size, it won't be happy staying in a small pen. (4) Your elderly aunt lives alone. (5) You might think that she needs a guard dog. (6) Before giving her a lively Great Dane for christmas, consider whether she will be able to handle such a large dog. (7) The turtle might seem like the perfect gift for your brother that crawled into your yard. (8) Did you realize that wild turtles often carry disease? (9) You may be certain that your sister would enjoy owning a Siamese kitten. (10) Have you think about whether she may be allergic to cat hairs or how the cat will get along with her pet mice? (11) Once the cat is hers, will your sister mind the expense of food vaccinations, and emergency trips to the veterinarian? (12) Before you decide to give an animal as a present your best bet is to check first with the potential owner.

48. Sentence 1: **Pets make popular Easter gifts, but you should think carefully before we give an animal as a present.**

What correction should be made to this sentence?

(1) change the spelling of *popular* to *populer*
(2) change *Easter* to *easter*
(3) remove the comma after *gifts*
(4) replace *we* with *you*
(5) no correction is necessary

49. Sentence 3: **Besides, after the chick grows to full size, it won't be happy staying in a small pen.**

Which of the following is the best way to write the underlined portion of this sentence? If you think the original is the best way, choose option (1).

(1) grows to full size, it won't be
(2) grow to full size, it won't be
(3) grows to full size it won't be
(4) grows to full size it wo'nt be
(5) grows to full size, it won't being

50. Sentences 4 & 5: **Your elderly aunt lives alone. You might think that she needs a guard dog.**

The most effective combination of sentences 4 and 5 would include which of the following groups of words?

(1) Your elderly aunt might think
(2) Your aunt is elderly and lives
(3) You might think that she
(4) which lives alone is in need
(5) who lives alone needs

51. Sentence 6: **Before giving her a lively Great Dane for christmas, consider whether she will be able to handle such a large dog.**

What correction should be made to this sentence?

(1) change *whether* to *weather*
(2) change *christmas* to *Christmas*
(3) insert a comma after *she*
(4) replace *consider* with *considering*
(5) change *will be* to *was*

52. Sentence 7: **The turtle might seem like the perfect gift for your brother that crawled into your yard.**

Which of the following is the best way to write the underlined portion of this sentence? If you think the original is the best way, choose option (1).

(1) might seem like the perfect gift for your brother that crawled into your yard.
(2) might seem like the perfect gift for your brother, that crawled into your yard.
(3) might seem like the perfect gift for your brother who crawled into your yard.
(4) that crawled into your yard might seem like the perfect gift for your brother.
(5) who crawled into your yard might seem like the perfect gift for your brother.

53. Sentence 10: **<u>Have you think about whether she</u> may be allergic to cat hairs or how the cat will get along with her pet mice?**

Which of the following is the best way to write the underlined portion of this sentence? If you think the original is the best way, choose option (1).

(1) Have you think about whether she
(2) Have we think about whether she
(3) Have you thinking about whether she
(4) Have you think about whether her
(5) Have you thought about whether she

54. Sentence 11: **Once the cat is hers, will your sister mind the expense of food vaccinations, and emergency trips to the veterinarian?**

What correction should be made to this sentence?

(1) replace *hers* with *her's*
(2) insert a comma after *food*
(3) insert a comma after *trips*
(4) change the spelling of *emergency* to *emergancy*
(5) change *veterinarian* to *Veterinarian*

55. Sentence 12: **Before you decide to give an animal as a present your best bet is to check first with the potential owner.**

What correction should be made to this sentence?

(1) replace *Before* with *To help*
(2) insert a comma after *present*
(3) replace *present your* with *present. Your*
(4) replace *your* with *you're*
(5) no correction is necessary

Answers are on pages 264–265.

Part II

Directions: *This is a test to see how well you can write. In this test, you are asked to write an essay in which you present your opinions about an issue. In preparing your essay, you should take the following steps.*

Step 1. Read all of the information about the topic. Be sure that you understand the topic and that you write about only the assigned topic.

Step 2. Plan your essay before you write.

Step 3. Use scrap paper to make any notes.

Step 4. Write your essay on a separate sheet of paper.

Step 5. Read what you have written. Make sure that your writing is legible.

Step 6. Check your paragraphing, sentence structure, spelling, punctuation, capitalization, and usage; make any changes that will improve your essay.

TOPIC

> Do you ever purchase one particular brand of an item over another because of the way it has been packaged?
>
> Write an essay approximately 200 words long, in which you give your opinion on the influence packaging has on consumer purchases. Be specific, and use examples to support your opinion.

When you take the GED test, you will have 45 minutes to write about the topic question you are assigned. Try to write the essay for this test within 45 minutes. Write legibly and use a ballpoint pen so that your writing will be easy to read. Any notes that you make on scrap paper will not be counted as part of your score.

After you complete this essay, you can judge its effectiveness by using the Essay Scoring Guide and Model Essays in the answer key to score your essay. They will be concerned with how clearly you make the main point of your essay, how thoroughly you support your ideas, and how clear and correct your writing is throughout the composition. You will receive no credit for writing about a question other than the one assigned.

Answers are on pages 266–267.

PRACTICE TEST

Performance Analysis Chart

Part I

Directions: Circle the number of each item that you got correct on the Practice Test. Count how many items you got correct in each row; count how many items you got correct in each column. Write the amount correct per row and column as the numerator in the fraction in the appropriate "Total Correct" box. (The denominators represent the total number of items in the row or column.) Write the grand total correct over the denominator, **55,** at the lower right corner of the chart. (For example, if you got 48 items correct, write 48 so that the fraction reads 48/**55.**)

Item Type	*Usage (page 25)*	*Sentence Structure (page 55)*	*Mechanics (page 75)*	TOTAL CORRECT
Construction Shift (page 112)	37, 44, 50	6, 17, 18, 24, 40		**/8**
Sentence Correction (page 111)	3, 13, 15, 28, 31, 42, 48	1, 12, 30, 32, 45, 55	2, 7, 14, 21, 23, 25, 26, 33, 35, 39, 41, 51, 54	**/26**
Sentence Revision (page 112)	5, 11, 16, 22, 27, 29, 43, 53	4, 9, 10, 19, 20, 34, 36, 38, 47, 49, 52	8, 46	**/21**
TOTAL CORRECT	**/18**	**/22**	**/15**	**/55**

The page numbers in parentheses indicate where in this book you can find the beginning of specific instruction about the areas of grammar and about the types of questions you encountered in the Practice Test.

Part II

Write your essay's score in the box at the right.

What were some of the strong points of your essay?

What were some of the weak points of your essay?

What improvements do you plan to make when you work on your next essay?

Simulation

Using the Simulated Test to Best Advantage

There is only one way you should take the Simulated Test. You should take the test under the same conditions as the real test.

- When you take the GED, you will have 120 minutes to complete both parts of the test.
- Do not talk to anyone or consult any books as you take the test. If you have a question on how to take the test, ask your instructor.
- If you have trouble answering a question, eliminate the choices that you know are wrong. Then mark the best remaining choice. On the real GED, you are not penalized more for wrong answers than for not answering. Guessing a correct answer will better your score.
- Although you can complete the test in any order you choose, it is to your advantage to begin with Part I. If 75 minutes elapse and you have not yet finished Part I, you should proceed to Part II. If you finish Part II before 120 minutes have elapsed, you can go back to the items in Part I. When time is up, if you have not finished, note how far you have gotten and then continue with the test.

As you take the Simulated Test, write your answers for Part I neatly on a sheet of paper, or use an answer sheet provided by your teacher. Write your Part II essay as neatly as you can on a fresh sheet of paper.

Using the Answers and Explanations

Use the Answers and Explanations (page 268) to check your answers. Mark each item in Part I that you answered correctly. Regardless of whether you correctly answer an item or not, you should look over each item explanation given. This will reinforce your testing skills and your understanding of the material. For Part II, follow the directions that tell you how to score your essay. You might like to have a teacher or someone else score your essay as well.

How to Use your Score

Your score on the Writing Skills Test will be made up of a combination of your scores on both parts of the test.

If you get 44 items or more in Part I correct, you will have done 80 percent or better. This shows that you are most likely working at a level that would allow you to do well in Part I of the actual Writing Skills Test. If you get a few less than 44 items correct, then you should spend time reviewing the lessons that will strengthen the areas in which you are weak. The Performance Analysis Chart at the end of the test will help you identify these areas.

If your essay merits a score of 4 or higher, you most likely will be able to write an essay on the actual test that will contribute to a passing score. If you essay earns a score of below 4, you should refer back to the Unit II lessons that cover the writing skills you had difficulty with and practice by writing essays about other appropriate topics.

SIMULATED TEST
Part I

TIME: *75 minutes*

Directions: *The items in Part I of this test are based on paragraphs that contain numbered sentences. Some of the sentences may contain errors in sentence structure, usage, or mechanics.* **A few sentences, however, may be correct as written.** *Read the paragraph and then answer the items that follow it. For each item, choose the answer that would result in the most effective writing of the sentence or sentences. The best answer must be consistent with the meaning and tone of the rest of the paragraph.*

FOR EXAMPLE:

Sentence 1: **Although it may take only two hours to watch the average motion picture takes almost a year to make.**

What correction should be made to this sentence?

(1) replace it with they

(2) change take to have taken

(3) insert a comma after watch

(4) change almost to all most

(5) no change is necessary

The correct answer is **(3).** In this example, a comma is needed after the clause Although it may take only two hours to watch.

Items 1 to 9 are based on the following paragraph.

(1) Millions of people are finding that it is often cheaper and more nutritious to pack a lunch than to buy them. (2) Packing a lunch used to mean putting a sandwich and a piece of fruit in a brown paper bag. (3) Lunch bags and lunch boxes now come in every shape, size, and color, you can imagine. (4) The range of possibilities for filling them is enormous, nevertheless, the rule of thumb for packing a healthful lunch hasn't changed. (5) Choose something from each food group. (6) There is protein contained in meat, fish, chicken, nuts, and beans. (7) In the grain group are such items as whole-wheat bread, crackers, and pita bread, a flat bread from the middle east. (8) It's a good idea to include one vegetable and one fruit, slices of carrot or green pepper are good sources of vitamin A. (9) An orange for dessert would meet your daily vitamin C requirement. (10) Either milk or a milk product such as cheese provide the calcium needed for strong bones. (11) Calcium, like all of the nutrients mentioned in the preceeding section, is needed by adults as well as children. (12) Whether you put the lunch in a plain paper bag or it was put in a lunch box, it's what's inside that counts.

1. Sentence 1: **Millions of people are finding that it is often cheaper and more nutritious to pack a lunch than to buy them.**

What correction should be made to this sentence?

(1) change the spelling of *Millions* to *Milions*
(2) change *are* to *is*
(3) insert *more* after *often*
(4) replace *to pack a lunch* with *packing a lunch*
(5) replace *them* with *one*

2. Sentence 3: **Lunch bags and lunch boxes now come in every <u>shape, size, and color, you</u> can imagine.**

Which of the following is the best way to write the underlined portion of this sentence? If you think the original is the best way, choose option (1).

(1) shape, size, and color, you
(2) shape, size, and color you
(3) shape, size and color, you
(4) shape, size, and color, that
(5) shape, size, and all the colors, you

3. Sentence 4: **The range of possibilities for filling them is enormous, nevertheless, the rule of thumb for packing a healthful lunch hasn't changed.**

What correction should be made to this sentence?

(1) change the spelling of *enormous* to *enoarmous*
(2) replace *enormous,* with *enormous;*
(3) remove the comma after *nevertheless*
(4) replace *healthful* with *healthy*
(5) no correction is necessary

4. Sentence 6: **There is protein contained in meat, fish, chicken, nuts, and beans.**

If you rewrote sentence 6 beginning with

Meat, fish, chicken, nuts, and beans

the next word should be

(1) contain
(2) contained
(3) contains
(4) are
(5) is

5. Sentence 7: **In the grain group are such items as whole-wheat bread, crackers, and pita bread, a flat bread from the middle east.**

What correction should be made to this sentence?

(1) change *are* to *is*
(2) replace *as* with *like*
(3) remove the comma after *pita bread*
(4) change *middle east* to *Middle East*
(5) no correction is necessary

6. Sentence 8: **It's a good idea to include one vegetable and one fruit, slices of carrot or green pepper are good sources of vitamin A.**

Which of the following is the best way to write the underlined portion of this sentence? If you think the original is the best way, choose option (1).

(1) fruit, slices
(2) fruit. Slices
(3) fruit slices
(4) fruit and slices
(5) fruit because slices

7. Sentence 10: **Either milk or a milk product such as cheese provide the calcium needed for strong bones.**

Which of the following is the best way to write the underlined portion of this sentence? If you think the original is the best way, choose option (1).

(1) product such as cheese provide
(2) product, such as cheese provide
(3) product such as cheese provides
(4) product such as cheese provided
(5) product such as cheese providing

8. Sentence 11: **Calcium, like all of the nutrients mentioned in the preceeding section, is needed by adults as well as children.**

What correction should be made to this sentence?

(1) replace *mentioned* with *mentioning*
(2) change the spelling of *preceeding* to *preceding*
(3) remove the comma after *section*
(4) change *is* to *was*
(5) replace *children* with *a child*

9. Sentence 12: **Whether you put the lunch in a plain paper bag or it was put in a lunch box, it's what's inside that counts.**

What correction should be made to this sentence?

(1) replace *you put* with *one puts*
(2) replace *plain* with *plane*
(3) remove *it was put*
(4) change *lunch box* to *lunch boxes*
(5) replace *it's* with *its*

Items 10 to 19 are based on the following paragraph.

(1) The presidency is an office that has changed substantially over the years. (2) Today's American president has not only more responsibilities than President George Washington ever had and more complex problems to handle. (3) Studies of recent Democratic and Republican presidents show that they have spent most of their time on foreign affairs. (4) Those financial matters concerning goods and services are called economic issues, and these issues have gotten less attention. (5) Domestic issues, questions concerning the quality of life in this country, the least presidential attention (6) Of course, many issues belong to two or three areas. (7) This country's drug problem, for example, was not only a domestic problem but also a foreign policy issue. (8) By working with Mexico and other countries, drugs are kept from being exported here. (9) Some critics say that presidents should divide their time more equally. (10) Other people feel there is some areas that will always deserve more of the president's attention than others. (11) In their judgment, for example, keeping peace in the Middle East should come first; whether or not to raise our minimum wage a few cents should come second. (12) Many people believe that presidents are expected to do too much, but they disagree about how to change the situation.

10. Sentence 2: **Today's American president has not only more responsibilities than President George Washington ever had and more complex problems to handle.**

What correction should be made to this sentence?

(1) change *American president* to *American President*
(2) change *has* to *have*
(3) replace *and* with *but also*
(4) replace *President George* with *president George*
(5) change the spelling of *responsibilities* to *responsability*

11. Sentence 3: **Studies of recent Democratic and Republican presidents show that they have spent most of their time on foreign affairs.**

What correction should be made to this sentence?

(1) change *Democratic and Republican* to *democratic and republican*
(2) change *presidents* to *Presidents*
(3) change *show* to *shows*
(4) replace *they* with *both*
(5) change the spelling of *foreign* to *forrin*

12. Sentence 4: **Those financial matters concerning goods and services are called economic issues, and these issues have gotten less attention.**

If you rewrote sentence 4 beginning with

Economic

the next word should be

(1) issues,
(2) issues;
(3) attention,
(4) attention;
(5) goods,

13. Sentence 5: **Domestic issues, questions concerning the quality of life in this country, the least presidential attention.**

What correction should be made to this sentence?

(1) remove the comma after *issues*
(2) insert *are* after *issues,*
(3) insert *and* after *country,*
(4) insert *receive* after *country,*
(5) replace *least* with *most least*

14. Sentence 7: **This country's drug <u>problem, for example, was not only</u> a domestic problem but also a foreign policy issue.**

Which of the following is the best way to write the underlined portion of this sentence? If you think the original is the best way, choose option (1).

(1) problem, for example, was not only
(2) problem for example, was not only
(3) problem, for example was not only
(4) problem, for example, is not only
(5) problem for example is not only

15. Sentence 8: **<u>By working with Mexico and other countries, drugs are kept</u> from being exported here.**

Which of the following is the best way to write the underlined portion of this sentence? If you think the original is the best way, choose option (1).

(1) By working with Mexico and other countries, drugs are kept
(2) By working with Mexico and other countries drugs are kept
(3) Having worked with Mexico and other countries, drugs are kept
(4) By working with Mexico and other countries, to keep drugs
(5) The U.S. has worked with Mexico and other countries to keep drugs

16. Sentence 9: **Some critics say that presidents should divide their time more equally.**

What correction should be made to this sentence?

(1) change *say* to *says*
(2) insert a comma after *that*
(3) replace *their* with *there*
(4) replace *equally* with *equal*
(5) no correction is necessary

17. Sentence 10: **Other people feel there is some areas that will always deserve more of the president's attention than others.**

What correction should be made to this sentence?

(1) change *feel* to *felt*
(2) replace *there* with *they're*
(3) change *is* to *are*
(4) change *president's* to *President's*
(5) no correction is necessary

18. Sentence 11: **In their judgment, for example, keeping peace in the Middle East should come first; whether or not to raise our minimum wage a few cents should come second.**

If you rewrote sentence 11 beginning with

For example, they feel that keeping peace in the Middle East should

the next words should be

(1) take priority
(2) be one
(3) raise our
(4) not be considered
(5) earn more

19. Sentence 12: **Many people believe that presidents are expected to do too much, but they disagree about how to change the situation.**

What correction should be made to this sentence?

(1) change *believe* to *believed*
(2) change *presidents* to *Presidents*
(3) remove the comma after *much*
(4) replace *they* with *everyone*
(5) replace *they disagree* with *there is disagreement*

Items 20 to 28 are based on the following paragraph.

(1) Experts in child psychology feel that many children watch too much television there is a lot of upsetting violence on television. (2) After watching actors yell and fight children may act this way. (3) Advertisements appear throughout most television programs. (4) If you discuss with children the reason behind advertising, they wo'nt be as likely to be swayed by ads. (5) Studies show that many children watch a lot of television and do poorly on reading tests. (6) Other children watch less television and do better on reading tests. (7) Television, rather than reading and homework, is occupying the time of frequent watchers. (8) Too many hours spent in front of saturday morning cartoons or weeknight movies can cause physical problems. (9) Children who sit or lay on the floor looking up at the television can develop neck and back problems. (10) Eyestrain and fatigue can result from watching television, especially in a darkened room. (11) If you have a child in the family, one should ask him to sit in a chair so that his eyes are level with the set. (12) Parents controlling their children's television viewing—what they watch, how much, and under what conditions.

20. Sentence 1: **Experts in child psychology feel that many children watch too much television there is a lot of upsetting violence on television.**

What correction should be made to this sentence?

(1) change the spelling of *psychology* to *phsycology*
(2) change *feel* to *feels*
(3) insert a comma after *that*
(4) replace *too* with *to*
(5) replace *television there* with *television. There*

21. Sentence 2: **After watching actors yell and fight children may act this way.**

What correction should be made to this sentence?

(1) insert a comma after *yell*
(2) replace *fight* with *fighting*
(3) insert a comma after *fight*
(4) replace *children may* with *you may see children*
(5) no correction is necessary

22. Sentence 4: **If you discuss with children the reason behind advertising, they wo'nt be as likely to be swayed by ads.**

What correction should be made to this sentence?

(1) change *discuss* to *discussed*
(2) remove the comma after *advertising*
(3) replace *they* with *he*
(4) replace *wo'nt* with *won't*
(5) replace *ads* with *them*

23. Sentences 5 & 6: **Studies show that many children watch a lot of television and do poorly on reading tests. Other children watch less television and do better on reading tests.**

The most effective combination of sentences 5 and 6 would include which of the following groups of words?

(1) that the more television children watch,
(2) that the more television they watch,
(3) a lot of television, and others watch less
(4) the less they watch, the worse
(5) some do poorly, and others do better

24. Sentence 7: **Television, rather than reading and homework, is occupying the time of frequent watchers.**

What correction should be made to this sentence?

(1) remove the comma after *Television*
(2) insert a comma after *reading*
(3) change *is* to *are*
(4) change the spelling of *frequent* to *frequant*
(5) no correction is necessary

25. Sentence 8: **Too many hours spent in front of saturday morning cartoons or weeknight movies can cause physical problems.**

What correction should be made to this sentence?

(1) replace *Too* with *Two*
(2) change *saturday* to *Saturday*
(3) insert a comma after *cartoons*
(4) insert a comma after *movies*
(5) replace *can cause* with *causing*

26. Sentence 9: **Children who sit or lay on the floor looking up at the television can develop neck and back problems.**

Which of the following is the best way to write the underlined portion of this sentence?

(1) replace *who* with *which*
(2) replace *lay* with *lie*
(3) replace *looking* with *having looked*
(4) insert a comma after *television*
(5) change the speling of *develop* to *devellop*

27. Sentence 11: **If you have a child in the family, <u>one should ask him to sit</u> in a chair so that his eyes are level with the set.**

Which of the following is the best way to write the underlined portion of this sentence? If you think the original is the best way, choose option (1).

(1) one should ask him to sit
(2) you should ask him to sit
(3) one should ask him, to sit
(4) one should ask them to sit
(5) you should ask them to sit

28. Sentence 12: **Parents <u>controlling their children's</u> television viewing—what they watch, how much, and under what conditions.**

Which of the following is the best way to write the underlined portion of this sentence? If you think the original is the best way, choose option (1).

(1) controlling their children's
(2) controlled their children's
(3) should control their children's
(4) controlling their childrens'
(5) controlling there children's

Items 29 to 37 are based on the following paragraph.

(1) Chances are that you will never have to help someone who's choking; yet you should know what to do, just in case. (2) Suppose someone is choking on something. (3) Before doing anything for the person, wait a moment to see if he coughs it up himself. (4) Show a small child how to raise both arms straight over his head. (5) If the person can't breath, however, you should try the Heimlich maneuver. (6) There are several ways to do this procedure, developed by Dr. Henry J. Heimlich. (7) One of the most common ways to start are by standing behind the person. (8) Wrap both your arms around him that your hands meet right below his ribs. (9) Clench one hand against his stomach so that beneath his bottom ribs are the thumb of your fist. (10) Cup your other hand over the fist, give a hard upward pull. (11) If the object does not come out of the person's throat, repeat the maneuver. (12) Fortunately, the Heimlich maneuver is extremely effective brain damage begins about four minutes after breathing stops.

29. Sentence 1: **Chances are that you will never have to help someone who's choking; yet you should know what to do, just in case.**

What correction should be made to this sentence?

(1) change *are* to *is*
(2) replace *who's* with *whose*
(3) replace *choking;* with *choking,*
(4) insert a comma after *yet*
(5) replace *you should* with *one should*

30. Sentences 2 & 3: **Suppose someone is choking on something. Before doing anything for the person, wait a moment to see if he coughs it up himself.**

The most effective combination of sentences 2 and 3 would include which of the following groups of words?

(1) Suppose someone who is choking
(2) Before one does anything for
(3) anything for someone who is
(4) which is choking on something
(5) for the person and wait a moment

31. Sentence 5: **If the person can't breath, however, you should try the Heimlich maneuver.**

What correction should be made to this sentence?

(1) change *can't* to *ca'nt*
(2) change the spelling of *breath* to *breathe*
(3) remove the comma after *however*
(4) change *Heimlich* to *heimlich*
(5) change the spelling of *maneuver* to *manuver*

32. Sentence 6: **There are several ways to do this procedure, developed by Dr. Henry J. Heimlich.**

What correction should be made to this sentence?

(1) change *are* to *is*
(2) replace *to* with *that one can*
(3) change the spelling of *procedure* to *proceedure*
(4) change *Dr.* to *dr.*
(5) no correction is necessary

33. Sentence 7: **One of the most common <u>ways to start are by standing</u> behind the person.**

Which of the following is the best way to write the underlined portion of this sentence? If you think the original is the best way, choose option (1).

(1) ways to start are by standing
(2) ways to start, are by standing
(3) ways to start are to stand
(4) ways to start is by standing
(5) ways to start is having stood

34. Sentence 8: **Wrap both your arms around <u>him that your hands meet</u> right below his ribs.**

Which of the following is the best way to write the underlined portion of this sentence? If you think the original is the best way, choose option (1).

(1) him that your hands meet
(2) him, that your hands meet
(3) him that one's hands meet
(4) him so that your hands meet
(5) him so that your hands met

35. Sentence 9: **Clench one hand against his stomach so that beneath his bottom ribs are the thumb of your fist.**

What correction should be made to this sentence?

(1) replace *one hand* with *one's hand*
(2) insert a comma after *that*
(3) change the spelling of *stomach* to *stomack*
(4) change *are* to *is*
(5) no correction is necessary

36. Sentence 10: **<u>Cup your other hand over the fist, give</u> a hard upward pull.**

Which of the following is the best way to write the underlined portion of this sentence? If you think the original is the best way, choose option (1).

(1) Cup your other hand over the fist, give
(2) Cup your other hand over the fist give
(3) With your other hand cupped over the fist, give
(4) With your other hand cupped over the fist give
(5) With your other hand cupped over the fist, giving

37. Sentence 12: **Fortunately, the Heimlich maneuver is extremely effective brain damage begins about four minutes after breathing stops.**

What correction should be made to this sentence?

(1) change the spelling of *extremely* to *extreemly*
(2) replace *is* with *being*
(3) insert a comma after *effective*
(4) replace *effective brain* with *effective; brain*
(5) change *begins* to *began*

Items 38 to 47 are based on the following paragraph.

(1) Holidays such as Thanksgiving, Christmas, and Hanukkah are traditionally times for families to gather. (2) When television families have these reunions, everyone usually has a wonderful time. (3) In real life, however, many people felt wretched after spending holidays with relatives. (4) Any arguing done by TV relatives usually taking the form of lighthearted kidding. (5) At real family gatherings, disagreements are not always in such an affectionate vein. (6) Anger may be suppressed for months or even years, and then it erupts when family members see each other again. (7) Fatigue and irritability goes hand in hand; thus, all the tiring traveling, cooking, and shopping that accompany holidays might make you irritable (8) If you're a parent who's just flown from the West Coast to Newark, you probably are exhausted and need a brake from your children. (9) Even if you've only driven from one part of Long island to another, the traffic has probably gotten you pretty tense. (10) Standing in line waiting to buy six pumpkin pies doesn't lead to feeling very relaxed, and baking six of them doesn't, either. (11) After spending more than you can afford on a Father's Day present your not sure your father will like, you may feel somewhat anxious. (12) The way TV families act on holidays is not wholly unrealistic, however keeping a sense of humor when tensions arise often does help.

38. Sentence 2: **When television families have these reunions, everyone usually has a wonderful time.**

Which of the following is the best way to write the underlined portion of this sentence? If you think the original is the best way, choose option (1).

(1) reunions, everyone usually has a
(2) reunions everyone usually has a
(3) reunions, everyone usually had a
(4) reunions, everyone usually have a
(5) reunions, everyone has a usually

39. Sentence 3: **In real life, however, many people felt wretched after spending holidays with relatives.**

What correction should be made to this sentence?

(1) remove the comma after *however*
(2) change *felt* to *feel*
(3) change the spelling of *wretched* to *retched*
(4) replace *spending holidays* with *holidays spended*
(5) change *holidays* to *Holidays*

40. Sentence 4: **Any arguing done by TV relatives usually taking the form of lighthearted kidding.**

Which of the following is the best way to write the underlined portion of this sentence? If you think the original is the best way, choose option (1).

(1) relatives usually taking
(2) relatives usually takes
(3) relatives usually take
(4) relatives usualy taking
(5) relatives, usually taking

41. Sentence 6: **Anger may be suppressed for months or even years, and then it erupts when family members see each other again.**

If you rewrote sentence 6 beginning with

Anger that has been suppressed for months or even years may

the next word should be

(1) be
(2) again
(3) erupt
(4) when
(5) erupted

42. Sentence 7: **Fatigue and irritability goes hand in hand; thus, all the tiring traveling, cooking, and shopping that accompany holidays might make you irritable.**

What correction should be made to this sentence?

(1) change the spelling of *Fatigue* to *Fatige*
(2) change *goes* to *go*
(3) replace *hand; thus,* with *hand, thus,*
(4) remove the comma after *cooking*
(5) change *accompany* to *accompanies*

43. Sentence 8: **If you're a parent who's just flown from the West Coast to Newark, you probably are exhausted and need a brake from your children.**

What correction should be made to this sentence?

(1) replace *who's* with *whose*
(2) change *flown* to *flew*
(3) change the spelling of *exhausted* to *exausted*
(4) change the spelling of *brake* to *break*
(5) no correction is necessary

44. Sentence 9: **Even if you've only driven from one part of Long island to another, the traffic has probably gotten you pretty tense.**

What correction should be made to this sentence?

(1) replace *if* with *whenever*
(2) replace *driven* with *drove*
(3) change *island* to *Island*
(4) change *gotten you* to *gotten one*
(5) no correction is necessary

45. Sentence 10: **Standing in line waiting to buy six pumpkin pies doesn't lead to feeling very relaxed, and baking six of them doesn't, either.**

If you rewrote sentence 10 beginning with

Neither waiting in line to buy six pumpkin pies nor baking six of them

the next word should be

(1) lead
(2) leads
(3) feel
(4) feels
(5) relax

46. Sentence 11: **After spending more than you can afford on a <u>Father's Day present your not sure</u> your father will like you may feel somewhat anxious.**

Which of the following is the best way to write the underlined portion of this sentence? If you think the original is the best way, choose option (1)

(1) Father's Day present your not sure
(2) Father's day present your not sure
(3) Father's Day present you're not sure
(4) Father's Day Present your not sure
(5) Father's Day present your aren't sure

47. Sentence 12: **The way TV families act on holidays is not wholly unrealistic, however keeping a sense of humor when tensions arise often does help.**

What correction should be made to this sentence?

(1) change *is* to *were*
(2) replace *wholly* with *holy*
(3) change the spelling of *families* to *familys*
(4) replace *however keeping* with *however; keeping*
(5) replace *sense* with *cents*

Items 48 to 55 are based on the following paragraph.

(1) Dentists' offices have changed in appearance over the years, but the dentist's role is basically unchanged. (2) There are many new pieces of equipment as well as new procedures, thanks to modern technology. (3) Some dentists ask their patients to sit in a chair that goes around in circles while X-rays of the jaw were taken. (4) Many dentists now have a device that used very high-pitched sound to clean your teeth. (5) Dentists who work with children often paint their teeth with a substance called fluoride, which helps prevent cavities. (6) One new and controversial proceedure involves attaching a computer chip to a child's tooth so that he could be identified if kidnapped or lost. (7) Still, the dentist's main goal is to help keep your teeth healthy, and the advice dentists give is pretty much what it has always been. (8) At least once a day, brush your teeth thoroughly and dental floss should be used. (9) If when you have a choice between fruit and a sticky dessert, you are better off taking the fruit. (10) Avoid cigarettes and brush once a week with baking soda to keep your teeth white. (11) Finally, the American Dental association recommends that you make an appointment to see your dentist every six months.

48. Sentence 1: **Dentists' offices have changed in appearance over the years, but the dentist's role is basically unchanged.**

If you rewrote sentence 1 beginning with

Although dentists' offices have changed in appearance over the years,

the next word should be

(1) but
(2) still
(3) the
(4) his
(5) roles

49. Sentence 3: **Some dentists ask their patients to sit in a chair that goes around in circles while X-rays of the jaw were taken.**

What correction should be made to this sentence?

(1) change *ask* to *asking*
(2) change the spelling of *patients* to *patience*
(3) change *were* to *are*
(4) change *taken* to *took*
(5) no correction is necessary

50. Sentence 4: **Many dentists now have a device <u>that used very high-pitched sound</u> to clean your teeth.**

Which of the following is the best way to write the underlined portion of this sentence? If you think the original is the best way, choose option (1).

(1) that used very high-pitched
(2) who used very high-pitched
(3) that use very high-pitched
(4) that has used very high-pitched
(5) that uses very high-pitched

51. Sentence 5: **Dentists <u>who work with children often paint their</u> teeth with a substance called fluoride, which helps prevent cavities.**

Which of the following is the best way to write the underlined portion of this sentence? If you think the original is the best way, choose option (1).

(1) who work with children often paint their
(2) which work with children often paint their
(3) who work with children, often paint their
(4) often paint children's
(5) often paints children's

52. Sentence 6: **One new and controversial proceedure involves attaching a computer chip to a child's tooth so that he could be identified if kidnapped or lost.**

What correction should be made to this sentence?

(1) change the spelling of *new* to *knew*
(2) change *child's* to *childs*
(3) change the spelling of *proceedure* to *procedure*
(4) replace *tooth so that he* with *tooth, he*
(5) no correction is necessary

53. Sentence 8: **At least once a day, brush your teeth thoroughly and dental floss should be used.**

Which of the following is the best way to write the underlined portion of this sentence? if you think the original is the best way, choose option (1).

(1) thoroughly and dental floss should be used.
(2) thoroghly and dental floss should be used.
(3) thoroughly and use dental floss.
(4) thoroughly and using dental floss.
(5) thoroughly, use dental floss.

54. Sentence 9: **If when you have a choice between fruit and a sticky dessert, you are better off taking the fruit.**

What correction should be made to this sentence?

(1) change the spelling of *dessert* to *desert*
(2) remove the comma after *dessert*
(3) remove the word *when*
(4) insert *more* after *are*
(5) change *taking* to *taken*

55. Sentence 11: **Finally, the American Dental association recommends that you make an appointment to see your dentist every six months.**

What correction should be made to this sentence?

(1) change *association* to *Association*
(2) change the spelling of *recommends* to *reccomends*
(3) replace *you* with *we*
(4) change *make* to *made*
(5) insert a comma after *appointment*

Answers are on pages 268–269.

Part II

TIME: *45 minutes*

Directions: *This is a test to see how well you can write. In this test, you are asked to write an essay in which you present your opinions about an issue. In preparing your essay, you should take the following steps.*

Step 1. Read all of the information about the topic. Be sure that you understand the topic and that you write about only the assigned topic.

Step 2. Plan your essay before you write.

Step 3. Use scrap paper to make any notes.

Step 4. Write your essay on a separate sheet of paper.

Step 5. Read what you have written. Make sure that your writing is legible.

Step 6. Check your paragraphing, sentence structure, spelling, punctuation, capitalization, and usage; make any changes that will improve your essay.

TOPIC

Traditionally, pioneers, war heroes, politicians, and movie stars have been models for young people to look up to because they have successfully achieved their goals. How important are role models to our culture today?

Write an essay, approximately 200 words long, in which you give your opinion on the importance of role models today. Be specific, and use examples to support your opinion.

When you take the GED test, you will have 45 minutes to write about the topic question you are assigned. Try to write the essay for this test within 45 minutes. Write legibly and use a ballpoint pen so that your writing will be easy to read. Any notes that you make on scrap paper will not be counted as part of your score.

After you complete this essay, you can judge its effectiveness by using the Essay Scoring Guide and Model Essays in the answer key to score your essay.

Answers are on pages 270–271.

SIMULATED TEST

Performance Analysis Chart

Part I

Directions: Circle the number of each item that you got correct on the Simulated Test. Count how many items you got correct in each row; count how many items you got correct in each column. Write the amount correct per row and column as the numerator in the fraction in the appropriate "Total Correct" box. (The denominators represent the total number of items in the row or column.) Write the grand total correct over the denominator, **55,** at the lower right corner of the chart. (For example, if you got 48 items correct, write *48* so that the fraction reads *48*/**55.**)

Item Type	*Usage (page 25)*	*Sentence Structure (page 55)*	*Mechanics (page 75)*	TOTAL CORRECT
Construction Shift (page 112)	4, 30, 45	18, 23, 41, 48	12	**/8**
Sentence Correction (page 111)	1, 11, 17, 19, 24, 35, 39, 42, 49	3, 9, 10, 13, 20, 37, 47, 54	5, 8, 16, 21, 22, 25, 29, 31, 32, 43, 44, 52, 55	**/30**
Sentence Revision (page 112)	7, 14, 26, 27, 33, 38, 40, 50, 51	6, 15, 28, 34, 36, 53	2, 46	**/17**
TOTAL CORRECT	**/21**	**/18**	**/16**	**/55**

The page numbers in parentheses indicate where in this book you can find the beginning of specific instruction about the areas of grammar and about the types of questions you encountered in the Simulated Test.

Part II

Write your essay's score in the box at the right.

What were some of the strong points of your essay?

What were some of the weak points of your essay?

What improvements do you plan to make when you work on your next essay?

Answers and Explanations

Introduction

In the Answers and Explanations section, you will find answers to all the questions in these sections of the book:

- Previews
- Lesson Exercises
- Skill Reviews
- Chapter Quizzes
- Unit Tests
- The Practice Items
- The Practice Test
- The Simulated Test

You will discover that the Answers and Explanations section is a valuable study tool. For grammar items, it not only gives you the correct answer, but explains why each answer is correct. It also points out the grammar topic each question tests. Even if you get a question right, it will help to review the explanation. The explanation will reinforce your understanding of the question and the skill it tests. Because you might have guessed a correct answer or answered correctly for the wrong reason, it can't hurt to review explanations. It might help a lot.

The answer section provides valuable tools to help you evaluate your essays. It will be advantageous for you to read everything the answer section has to offer on evaluating and scoring essays.

INSTRUCTION
UNIT I Grammar

Chapter 1 Usage

Skill 1 Preview

1. *Neither Denmark nor Norway* ***has*** *a shoreline on the Mediterranean Sea.* Because both parts of the compound subject are singular, the verb must be singular.
2. *There* ***are*** *two national anthems played at every All-Star baseball game.* The subject of this sentence is *anthems;* a plural verb, therefore, is required.
3. *Into the nearby tunnel* ***rushes*** *the frightened prairie dog.* This sentence is an example of inverted structure. The subject, *prairie dog,* requires a singular verb.
4. *An American man* ***spends*** *about four hours a year tying his necktie.* The singular subject, *man,* requires a singular verb.
5. *The most popular street name in the United States* ***is*** *Park Street.* The subject and verb have been separated by an interrupting phrase. The singular subject, *name,* requires a singular verb.

Lesson 1 Exercise

1. *The team* ***has*** *lost four games. Team* is considered one unit and takes a singular verb.
2. Correct. *Measles* is a singular noun.
3. *The pair of jeans* ***was*** *in the dryer.* Use a singular verb with the word *pair.*
4. Correct. *No one* is a singular indefinite pronoun.
5. *Tea leaves* ***need*** *to be stored in a tight container. Leaves* is plural and takes a plural verb.
6. *A correctly written résumé* ***lists*** *your most recent job first. Résumé* is singular and takes a singular verb.
7. *Many experts in the field* ***disagree*** *with that answer.* The subject *experts* is plural and takes a plural verb.
8. *Both* ***show*** *the same talent in music. Both* is a plural noun.
9. *Some of the senators* ***were*** *touring the flood-damaged area. Some* refers to more than one person and therefore takes a plural verb.
10. *They* ***realize*** *the importance of a healthy diet. They* is a plural pronoun.

Lesson 2 Exercise

1. Correct. The subject of the sentence, *broiling,* is singular, agreeing with the singular verb, *is.*
2. *Requirements for a driver's license* ***vary*** *from state to state. Requirements* is plural and takes a plural verb.
3. *Successful dieting, according to nutritionists,* ***demands*** *patience and determination. Dieting* is singular and takes a singular verb.
4. *One of the best salt substitutes* ***is*** *lemon juice. One* is singular and takes a singular verb.
5. *Foods with a high moisture content, such as lettuce,* ***do*** *not freeze well. Foods* is plural and takes a plural verb.

Lesson 3 Exercise

1. *At the bottom of the contract* ***was*** *the space for their signatures.* Cross out the interrupting phrase and invert the sentence to read, *The space for their signatures was at the bottom of the contract.* Change *were* to *was* to agree with *space.*
2. Correct. The subject of the sentence, *bills,* is plural.
3. ***Do*** *eggs boiled with vinegar resist cracking?* Cross out the interrupting phrase and invert the sentence to read, *Eggs boiled with vinegar do resist cracking.* Change *does* to *do* to agree with the plural *eggs.*
4. *In the shuttle* ***sit*** *the astronauts.* Invert the sentence to read, *The astronauts sit in the shuttle.* Change *sits* to *sit* to agree with the plural *astronauts.*
5. ***Are*** *the sun's rays as hot in the afternoon as in the morning?* Invert the sentence to read, *The sun's rays are as hot in the afternoon as in the morning.* Change *is* to *are* to agree with the plural *rays.*

Lesson 4 Exercise

1. Correct. The subject is *people* and the verb is *are.*
2. *Here* ***is*** *the map of the Hawaiian islands.* The subject is *map* and the verb is *is.*
3. *There* ***are*** *many ancient myths that explain forces in nature.* The subject is *myths* and the verb is *are.*
4. *Here* ***comes*** *the winner of the Boston Marathon.* The subject is *winner* and the verb is *comes.*
5. *There* ***are*** *players on each team in field hockey.* The subject is *players* and the verb is *are.*

Lesson 5 Exercise

1. Correct. The plural subject *diamonds* is closer to the verb; therefore, the verb must be plural.
2. *Either gravel or crushed rock* ***combines*** *with cement to form concrete.* The singular subject *crushed rock* is closer to the verb; therefore, the verb must be singular.
3. *The Rocky Mountains and the Andes* ***are*** *part of the same mountain chain.* Plural subjects joined by *and* take a plural verb.
4. *Both a blanket and warm clothing* ***are*** *recommended when traveling in the winter. Blanket* and *clothing* form a plural subject, requiring a plural verb.
5. *Neither creams nor lotions* ***are*** *effective in the prevention of wrinkles.* Because both subjects are plural, a plural verb is required.

Skill 1 Review

1. *Everyone* ***needs*** *a passport to travel in a foreign country. Everyone* is singular and takes a singular verb.

2. *Neither an ostrich nor a penguin* ***is*** *able to fly.* Singular subjects joined by *neither . . . nor* take a singular verb.
3. *There* ***are*** *more than 800,000 kinds of insects.* Kinds is plural and takes a plural verb.
4. *One of the most common diseases in the world* ***is*** *malaria.* One is singular and takes a singular verb.
5. *Both Robert De Niro and Dustin Hoffman* ***have*** *won Academy Awards.* Subjects joined by *both . . . and* take a plural verb.
6. ***Is*** *a group of lions called a herd or a pride?* The subject, group, refers to one unit; therefore, it takes a singular verb.
7. *On the Bonneville Salt Flats in Utah* ***is*** *an automobile racecourse. Racecourse* is singular and takes a singular verb.
8. *The whale shark, the largest fish in the world,* ***weighs*** *twice as much as an elephant. Shark* is singular and takes a singular verb.
9. Correct. The pronoun *you* always takes a plural verb.
10. *In cold climates, a caterpillar* ***takes*** *two or three years to reach the butterfly stage. Caterpillar* is singular and takes a singular verb.

Skill 2 Preview

1. *The Julian calendar* ***was developed*** *in 46* B.C. *by Julius Caesar.* The sentence refers to a historical event; the verb, therefore, must be in the past tense.
2. *The diameter of the moon is about 2,160 miles, and its surface area* ***is*** *14,650,000 square miles.* Because the sentence describes a current state, both verbs should be in the present tense.
3. Correct. The past tense verb *spent* is correct because the sentence concerns a historical event.
4. *Beethoven* ***had written*** *nine symphonies before his death in 1827.* The past participle of *write* is *written.*
5. *Tomorrow we* ***will learn*** *about Sir John A. Macdonald, the first Prime Minister of Canada.* The word *Tomorrow* provides a clue that the action should be expressed in the future tense.

Lesson 1 Exercise

The correct form of the verb is boldfaced in each of sentences 1 through 5.

1. *The Supreme Court* ***begins*** *each term on the first Monday in October.*
2. *Chester Gould* ***drew*** *the popular cartoon "Dick Tracy" for many years.*
3. *The Nile catfish* ***swims*** *upside down.*
4. *Most tornadoes* ***occurred*** *in the central section of the country.*
5. *Germany* ***broke*** *its treaty with the Soviet Union in 1941.*

The correct past participle is boldfaced in each of sentences 6 through 10.

6. *Birds* ***have built*** *their nests with many different materials.*
7. *Scientists* ***have done*** *experiments to determine the mineral composition of the moon.*
8. *The president of the company* ***had said*** *that the hiring freeze was temporary.*
9. *Native Americans* ***had taught*** *the colonists how to raise corn.*
10. *Many people* ***have written*** *to their representatives about the proposed law.*

Lesson 2 Exercise

1. *The first depression in the United States* ***happened*** *at the end of the Revolutionary War. The Revolutionary War* is a clue that the action has already taken place.
2. *Right now, we* ***import*** *more goods than we* ***export.*** The words *Right now* are a clue to use the present tense.
3. *During the next decade, new kinds of heart surgery* ***will be developed.*** The phrase *During the next decade* is a clue to use the future tense.
4. Correct. Both verbs are correctly written in the past tense.
5. *The last survivor of the* Mayflower ***was*** *John Alden.* Use the past tense; the sentence refers to a historical event.

Lesson 3 Exercise

Joseph Priestley, an eighteenth-century chemist, made several discoveries through his mistakes. For example, he ***invented*** *seltzer quite by accident. While performing an experiment, he added gas to water. Priestley was amazed at the new taste that* ***resulted*** *from the combination. As he was studying a certain type of tree sap, some of the substance dropped onto a piece of paper. He* ***noticed*** *the sap* ***made*** *pencil marks disappear from the paper. This* ***led*** *to the development of what we now call the* ***eraser.***

Lesson 4 Exercise

1. *The light from a laser is very powerful and* ***travels*** *in one direction.* The second verb in the sentence, *travels,* must be in the present tense to be consistent with the present tense form of *to be* in the first part of the sentence.
2. *The deepest lake in the world is Lake Baikal in Siberia, as it* ***measures*** *almost a mile deep in some places.* The present tense form of *measure* is consistent with the present tense form of *to be* in the first part of the sentence.
3. *A gorilla sleeps about 14 hours a day, whereas, an elephant* ***sleeps*** *about 2 hours.* The present tense form of *sleep* should be used in both parts of the sentence.
4. *Earth is closer to the sun in December than it* ***is*** *in July.* The present tense form of *to be* should be used in both parts of the sentence.
5. *The person who said, "If you can't stand the heat, get out of the kitchen"* ***was*** *Harry Truman.* Because the sentence is about an event in the past, both of the verbs used, *said* and *was,* are past tense forms.

Skill 2 Review

1. *The Puritans* ***thought*** *soap and water were bad for one's health.* The verb *think* should be changed to the past tense because the sentence is about a historical belief.
2. *The first American to fly in space was Alan Shepard, and he* ***flew*** *for a total of 15 minutes.* Both verbs in the sentence should be in the past tense.
3. *In 1804, Lewis and Clark* ***began*** *their expedition to the Northwest.* The date provides a clue that the past tense should be used.
4. *Yesterday the President* ***discussed*** *the new tax bill with several of his advisors.* The word *Yesterday* provides a clue that the past tense should be used.

5. Correct. The sentence is correct because both verbs, *invented* and *had*, are in the past tense.
6. *So far, how many people* ***have*** *successfully* ***swum*** *across the English Channel?* The correct past participle of the verb *swim* is *swum*.
7. *The words "Mankind must put an end to war or war will put an end to mankind"* ***were spoken*** *by John Kennedy.* The correct past participle of the verb *speak* is *spoken*.
8. Lochner v. New York *was a supreme court case that* ***gave*** *employees and employers the right to decide hours and wages without government interference.* Because the sentence is about a historical occurrence, the verb *give* should be changed to the past tense, *gave*.
9. *In 1930, Sinclair Lewis became the first American author who* ***won*** *the Nobel prize for literature.* Both verbs should be in the past tense because the sentence is about a historical event.
10. *Many people* ***believe*** *food production will be unable to keep up with population growth.* This sentence could also be rewritten this way: *Many people believed food production would be unable to keep up with population growth.* The verb tenses should be consistent within the sentence.

Skill 3 Preview

1. *The cornea is the only part of the human body* ***that*** *has no blood supply.* Change *who* to *that*. *Who* is used to refer only to people or animals, whereas *that* or *which* are used for people, animals, or things.
2. Correct. The pronoun *it* is correct because a singular pronoun is used to refer to two or more singular antecedents that are joined by *or*.
3. *We benefit from studying history because it helps* ***us*** *learn from past mistakes.* Change *you* to *us* to eliminate pronoun shift.
4. *An angler fish can swallow food twice* ***its*** *own size.* Change *their* to *its* to eliminate pronoun shift.
5. *After a new traffic light was installed at the intersection,* ***the intersection*** *was safer.* Replace *it* with a noun to eliminate the ambiguous pronoun reference.

Lesson 1 Exercise

1. Correct. The pronoun *their* agrees with its plural antecedent, *individuals*.
2. *A new cosmetic or a drug must be tested before* ***it*** *can be sold to the public.* Change *they* to *it* to agree with singular antecedents joined by *or*.
3. *People with a good sense of humor should be able to laugh at* ***themselves.*** Change *himself* to *themselves* to agree with the plural antecedent, *people*.
4. Correct. The pronoun, *he*, agrees with the closer antecedent, *manager*.
5. *The kangaroo and the opossum carry* ***their*** *young in a pouch.* Change *its* to *their* to agree with two antecedents joined by *and*.

Lesson 2 Exercise

The rule that governs all of these sentences is that pronoun shifts in person should be avoided.

1. *I exercise daily because physical exercise helps* ***me*** *maintain good health.*
2. Correct.
3. *When we are nervous,* ***our*** *pulse may quicken.*

OR

When ***you*** *are nervous, your pulse may quicken.*
4. *It is important for us to understand the new tax law before filing* ***our*** *tax returns.*

OR

It is important for ***you*** *to understand the new tax law before filing your tax returns.*
5. *People are more likely to be injured at home than if* ***they are*** *riding in a car.*

Lesson 3 Exercise

1. *Only people* ***who*** (or ***that***) *are registered blood donors may duel in Uruguay.* Use *who* or *that* to refer to people.
2. Correct. The relative pronoun *that* is correct when referring to animals.
3. *Ants and humans are the only two animal species* ***that*** *wage war on their own kind.* The use of *what* as a relative pronoun is incorrect. Because *species* is the antecedent, the pronoun *that* or *which* may be used.
4. *The state* ***that*** *uses the phrase "Land of Lincoln" on its license plates is Illinois.* *That* or *which* may be used to refer to things.
5. *The first American astronaut* ***who*** (or ***that***) *orbited Earth was John Glenn.* *Who* is correct, because it may be replaced by *he*.

Lesson 4 Exercise

The rewording of these sentences may vary.

1. *The machinist violated the company's policy by not wearing safety goggles.* Reword the sentence to eliminate *which*, which has no clear antecedent.
2. *On last night's weather forecast,* ***the weather forecaster*** *said there was an 80 percent chance of rain.* Substitute a noun for the pronoun *they*.
3. *Helium causes the pitch of the voice to rise by contracting the vocal cords.* Reword the sentence to eliminate *which*, which has no clear antecedent.
4. *My science textbook says that ten inches of snow equals one inch of rain.* Substitute a noun for the pronoun *it*.
5. ***Real estate developers*** *predict that during the next decade the price of housing will triple.* Substitute a noun for the pronoun *They*.

Lesson 5 Exercise

1. *Because the discussion leader and the secretary were responsible for the minutes of the meeting,* ***the discussion leader*** (or ***the secretary***) *was told to take accurate notes.* In the original sentence, it is not clear whether *he* refers to the discussion leader or the secretary.
2. *When* ***the supervisor*** *returned from vacation, she gave the employee additional responsibilities.*

OR

When the ***employee*** *returned from vacation, the supervisor gave her additional responsibilities.* In the original sentence, it is not clear whether *she* refers to the supervisor or the employee.
3. *The student asked the teacher if she,* ***the student,*** *could change the assignment.*

OR

The student asked the teacher if she, ***the teacher***, *could* change the assignment. In the original sentence, it is not clear whether *she* refers to the student or the teacher.

4. *If a child has an allergic reaction to a certain food, throw **the food** away.* It should be replaced with a noun to avoid an ambiguous pronoun reference.
5. *Mike told Randy that he, **Mike,** was the starting pitcher for tomorrow's game.*

   OR

   *Mike told Randy that he, **Randy,** was the starting pitcher for tomorrow's game.* In the original sentence, it is not clear whether *he* refers to Mike or Randy.

Skill 3 Review

The rewording of some sentences may vary.

1. *The purple color of amethysts may be caused by impurities such as iron or manganese.* Reword the sentence to eliminate *which.*
2. *A mosquito cannot beat **its** wings in temperatures below 60 degrees.* The singular subject *mosquito* uses a singular pronoun.
3. *A human being **who** [*or ***that***] is at rest breathes about 16 times per minute.* Do not use *which* as a relative pronoun when referring to people.
4. *The advisor was told by the president to cancel tomorrow's press conference.*

   OR

   The president was told by the advisor to cancel tomorrow's press conference. Eliminate the ambiguous pronoun, *she,* by rewording the sentence.
5. Correct. *Who* may be substituted for *that.*
6. *Frank Lloyd Wright was an architect **who** designed houses with low, horizontal shapes.* Who is correct as a relative pronoun, because it may be replaced by *he.*
7. *Animals that live in cold climates have smaller ears than **their** cousins in warmer climates.* *Animals,* the subject of the sentence, takes a plural pronoun.
8. *The legends **that** are told about King Arthur may be based on historical fact.* *What* is not a relative pronoun; *that* or *which* may be used.
9. *Neither potato chips nor candy bars give us the nutrition **we** need to stay healthy.*

   OR

   *Neither potato chips nor candy bars give **you** the nutrition you need to stay healthy.* Eliminate the pronoun shift.
10. *After World War II, the housing supply could not keep up with the demand because **the demand** grew so rapidly.* Eliminate the ambiguous use of the pronoun *it.*

Chapter 1 Quiz

The rewording of some sentences may vary.

1. ***This book says** that at one time ketchup was sold as a medicine in the United States.* Replace the vague pronoun *they* with a noun.
2. *Dinosaurs **lived** on Earth for 100 million years.* Change the verb to the past tense to be consistent with the logical meaning of the sentence.
3. *The people **who** live in Hawaii tend to live about four years longer than Americans who live in other states.* Do not use the relative pronoun *which* when referring to people.
4. Correct. The singular subject *reason* is in agreement with the singular verb *is.*
5. *The candidate **who** [*or ***that***] was elected won by a large majority.* *Who* is correct, because it may be replaced by *he* or *she.*
6. ***Does** everyone understand the directions?* The pronoun *everyone* is singular and uses a singular verb.
7. *In ancient Greece a woman counted her age from the date on which **she was** married.* Eliminate the pronoun shift.
8. *Mark Spitz **had broken** many Olympic swimming records.* Use the correct past participle form of the irregular verb *broke.*
9. *In 1864, Travelers Insurance Company **issued** the first insurance policy for two cents.* The words *in 1864* are a clue that the action should be expressed in the past tense.
10. *Ann and Linda told the staff that **the staff** would no longer need to work on Saturdays.*

    OR

    *Ann and Linda told the staff that **neither Ann nor Linda** would need to work on Saturdays.* Eliminate the ambiguous pronoun reference by rewording the sentence.
11. *The band rehearses three times a week before **its** performance.* In this sentence, *band* is considered a unit which requires a singular pronoun.
12. *The Liberty Bell is made of bronze and **weighs** over a ton.* Use verb tenses consistently within a sentence.
13. *The storm **has shaken** the leaves from the tree.* *Shaken* is the past participle of the irregular verb *to shake.*
14. ***Was** the tour of the art museums interesting?* Use the singular verb *was* to agree with the singular subject, *tour.*
15. *Many elephants are killed because **their** tusks are considered valuable.* The plural pronoun, *their,* agrees with its antecedent, *elephants.*
16. *Spiders **have been** found on the top of Mt. Everest.* The plural subject, *spiders,* takes the plural form of the verb *have.*
17. *Neither the book nor the movie **was** successful.* Singular subjects joined by *neither . . . nor* require a singular verb.
18. *As early as 700 A.D., fingerprints **were** taken for identification purposes.* The phrase *As early as 700 A.D.* is a clue that the past tense is required.
19. *Both civics and economics **are** listed as required courses in many schools.* The compound subject joined by *both . . . and* uses a plural verb.
20. *Injections for measles **are** being offered free at the clinic.* The plural subject, *injections,* requires a plural verb.

Chapter 2 Sentence Structure

Skill 1 Preview

There may be more than one correct way to edit some sentences.

1. *There are 206 bones in the human body; the thigh bone is the longest.* This is a run-on sentence. Add a semicolon or a period after *body.*
2. *The total shown on the receipt is incorrect.* This is a sen-

tence fragment. Add a verb and any other words needed to complete the meaning.

3. Correct. This compound sentence is correctly written. A comma and the connecting word *and* follow the first complete idea.
4. *Alfred sat in front of the television for five hours.* This is a sentence fragment. Add a subject.
5. *This dish can be heated in a microwave oven; it will not crack.* This is a comma splice. Add a semicolon or a period after *oven*.

Lesson 1 Exercise

There may be more than one correct way to edit some sentences.

1. Correct. This sentence has a subject, *cash registers*, and a verb, *are*, and expresses a complete thought.
2. *Even though I missed my usual train, I got to work on time.* Add words to complete the meaning.
3. *We stood and cheered the home team's victory.* Add a subject.
4. *The treasurer of the Hikers' Club resigned.* Add a verb.
5. *Tomatoes that are grown in hothouses have very little flavor.* Add a verb and words to complete the meaning.

Lesson 2 Exercise

Each run-on sentence or comma splice can be corrected by writing each complete thought as a separate sentence.

1. *Woodrow Wilson was our 28th president. He was the only president who had a Ph.D. degree.*
2. *The Nineteenth Amendment to the Constitution gave women the right to vote. It was adopted in 1920.*
3. *Congress established the first U.S. mint. It was located in Philadelphia.*
4. Correct. This sentence includes a compound verb but expresses only one complete thought.
5. *Pizza was first made by Roman soldiers. They used olive oil, cheese, and crackers.*

Lesson 3 Exercise

There may be more than one correct way to edit some sentences. If a semicolon is used after the first complete thought, a connecting word may also be used. If a comma is used after the first complete thought, a connecting word must be used.

1. *Egyptians made candy over 4,000 years ago; they used dates and honey.*
2. *England and France fought the longest war, for it lasted from 1337 to 1453 and was called the Hundred Years' War.*
3. *The first black American to become a Supreme Court justice was Thurgood Marshall, and he was appointed in 1967 by President Lyndon Johnson.*
4. Correct. This is not a compound sentence.
5. *This apartment needs some repairs; however, the rent is reasonable.* With *however* a semicolon must be used.
6. *The United States is the world's largest producer of cheese; France is second.*
7. Correct. The connecting word *nor* can be used with a comma.
8. *The first government employee strike was the Boston police strike; in fact, it happened in 1919.*
9. *Pluto takes 248 years to complete one orbit around the sun. Many comets orbit beyond Pluto.* Use separate sentences because the ideas are not closely related.
10. *Pretzels were invented by French monks, and they shaped the dough to represent arms folded in prayer.*

Skill 1 Review

There may be more than one correct way to edit some sentences.

1. *The world's oldest computer is located in Great Britain; it was built in 1949.* Or use a period, a semicolon and a connecting word, or a comma and a connecting word.
2. *The salt-water crocodile weighs approximately 1,100 pounds and grows to more than 12 feet long.* Do not use a comma between compound verbs.
3. *Shelley stayed indoors until the downpour stopped.* Add words to the sentence fragment to make the idea complete.
4. *Wilt Chamberlain holds the record for scoring the most points in a basketball game; he scored 100 points in a game against the New York Knicks.* Or use a period, a semicolon and a connecting word, or a comma and a connecting word.
5. *Ted added thinner to the can of paint.* Add a subject to the sentence fragment.
6. *William Taft was the 27th president of the United States; furthermore, he served as chief justice of the Supreme Court.* Use a comma after a connecting word that is used with a semicolon.
7. *That was the wildest ball game I have ever seen.* Add words to the sentence fragment to complete the thought.
8. Correct. This compound sentence is correctly written.
9. *The Grand Coulee Dam is the largest concrete dam in the United States, and it is located on the Columbia River.* With *and*, use a comma, not a semicolon.
10. *The first woman to be a member of a president's cabinet was Frances Perkins; Roosevelt appointed her secretary of labor in 1933.* Or use a period, a semicolon and a connecting word, or a comma and a connecting word.

Skill 2 Preview

1. *When the Depression occurred in 1931, Nevada legalized gambling.* Add a comma after *1931*.
2. *James Ritty invented the cash register because he wanted to keep a record of the sales in his restaurant.* Use only one connecting word. Either *because* or *when* is correct.
3. *The first electronic computer was developed in 1945. I am taking a programming course this fall.* Use separate sentences because the ideas are not closely related.
4. *William Henry Harrison was president of the United States for only 31 days, for he died of pneumonia in 1841.* Substitute *for* for *as a result* to show the correct relationship between ideas, and use a comma instead of a semicolon.
5. Correct. The first idea in this sentence is a subordinate, or incomplete, idea and is correctly followed by a comma.

Lesson 1 Exercise

1. *Irving Berlin wrote "White Christmas," the most popular song ever recorded; in fact, over 100 million copies have been sold.* Use a coordinator that gives a reason or an example.
2. *The Great Wall of China is 1,684 miles long; thus it is the longest wall in the world.* Use a coordinator that shows a result or a reason.

3. *O'Hare Airport in Chicago is the busiest in the world, and delays in landing there are common.* Change the second idea to one that is related to the first.
4. Correct. The coordinator *in fact,* which shows a reason, may be used with a semicolon.
5. *John Fitch designed the first steamboat; it looked like a canoe but had steam-driven paddles. He also built a boat that had paddle wheels on the side. However, he had difficulty finding people to back him financially, so his designs failed to be successful.* The original sentence has too many ideas. Divide the sentence into smaller units of information. This is one of several correct ways of doing so.

Lesson 2 Exercise

1. Correct. The subordinate idea is correctly followed by a comma.
2. *Even though some mushrooms are poisonous, others can be eaten safely.* Do not use a coordinator [but] along with a subordinator [even though].
3. *After the stock market crashed in 1929, many people refused to put their money in banks.* Use only one subordinator.
4. *When Shakespeare wrote his historical plays, he sometimes altered the truth to fit his story lines.* Use a comma after a subordinate idea that comes first in the sentence.
5. *Pollution will continue to be a major problem in many of our cities unless people show more concern for their environment.* Do not combine unrelated ideas.

Lesson 3 Exercise

1. *Seneca Lake and Cayuga Lake are in western New York State.* Use the plural verb *are* when compound subjects are joined by *and.*
2. *Mr. Wittenberg and Mr. Bush did not enjoy the concert.*

   OR

   Neither Mr. Wittenberg nor Mr. Bush enjoyed the concert. When using the paired coordinators *neither . . . nor,* do not also use *not.*
3. *You can buy that book in a hardcover edition or in paperback.* Or is a reasonable coordinator to use because a person would probably buy a book in only one form, hardcover or paperback.
4. *Roberta is making a skirt and a blazer.* Roberta is making one thing *and* another thing.
5. *Eliot fixed the faucet with a wrench and a screwdriver.* Eliot used one tool *and* another tool.

Skill 2 Review

1. *Before its building was completed, the United Nations met at Lake Success in New York.* Use a comma after a subordinate idea that begins the sentence.
2. *Ursa Major is one name of that constellation; in addition, it is also called the Big Dipper.* Use a coordinator that adds one idea to another or a coordinator, such as *however,* that shows contrast.
3. *As soon as you are well, you can leave the hospital.* Use only one subordinator. *When* could also be used.
4. *Whenever a new contract is being negotiated, tension among employees increases.* When using a subordinator [whenever], do not also use a coordinator [and].
5. *The highest golf course in the world is in Peru, and the lowest course in in Death Valley, California.* Use a coordinator that adds one idea to another.
6. *It is possible to solve the Rubik's Cube puzzle; in fact, the record for mastering the solution is 22.95 seconds.* Use a coordinator that gives an example or shows a reason.
7. *Jeanette Rankin was the first woman to be elected to Congress. I voted for Reagan in the last election.*

   OR

   Jeanette Rankin was the first woman to be elected to Congress, and she represented the state of Montana. Either use separate sentences for unrelated ideas, or change the second idea to one that relates to the first.
8. *Aristotle believed the heart was the body's center of intelligence; however, we now know the brain is.* Use correct punctuation in a compound sentence.
9. Correct. A comma correctly follows the subordinate idea that begins the sentence.
10. *Microwave ovens are very popular; in fact, estimates show that by 1990 three-quarters of American households will own one of these ovens. Accordingly, food manufacturers are developing new lines of frozen microwave products for people who want quick, easy meals. For example, single-serving pizzas are a new item.* The original sentence has too many ideas. Divide it into shorter sentences. This is one of several correct ways of doing so.

Skill 3 Preview

1. *Because he is so loyal, Al remains [or still is] my best friend.* Avoid wordiness: *continue* and *remain* have the same meaning.
2. Correct. The related ideas *to enjoy* and *to learn* are written in parallel form.
3. *Ms. Fischer gladly accepted the promotion.* Avoid wordiness. Choose only one of the ideas expressed by *joyful, happiness,* and *gladly* to describe Ms. Fischer's reaction.
4. *Flown from sunrise to sunset, the U.S. flag is displayed at the White House every day.* Move the words being modified closer to the modifier.
5. *Huffing and puffing, the wolf blew down the house.* Add a word that can be modified logically by *Huffing and puffing.*

Lesson 1 Exercise

1. *At last we had all the boxes packed and sealed.* Avoid wordiness.
2. *The supervisor told the employee that she, the supervisor, was being promoted.*

   OR

   The supervisor said to the employee, "You are being promoted." Avoid unclear pronoun reference.
3. Correct. The pronoun *they* refers to both the singer and the drummer.
4. *I have begun to write my autobiography.* Avoid wordiness: an autobiography is always about the writer.
5. *Last year we spent a very nice week in Florida.* Avoid unclear pronoun reference.

Lesson 2 Exercise

There may be more than one correct way to edit some sentences.

1. *Running into the end zone, the linebacker scored the winning touchdown.* Introduce a word that can be modified by *Running.*
2. Correct. *Wishing* modifies *Ernest.*

3. *A rainbow can be seen from an airplane as a complete circle.* Move *from an airplane* to a position where it clearly modifies *can be seen.*
4. *While lying on his back, Michelangelo painted the ceiling of the Sistine Chapel.* Introduce words to make the meaning of *on his back* clearer, and move the modifier closer to the word it modifies, *Michelangelo.*
5. *Wearing a disguise, the detective watched the suspect's house.* Move *wearing* closer to the word it modifies, *detective.*

Lesson 3 Exercise

1. *A U.S. senator must be at least 30 years old, be a U.S. citizen for a minimum of 9 years, and live in the state in which he or she seeks election.* Drop the word *to* to obtain parallel structure.
2. *Activities that strengthen the heart muscle include swimming, jogging, and riding a bike.* Change *to ride* to *riding* for parallel structure.
3. *I enjoy sports activities that are challenging, fast-paced, and inexpensive.* Change *don't need expensive equipment* to *inexpensive* for parallel structure.
4. *Is the birthstone of those born in July a ruby, a sapphire, or a diamond?* Change *the* to *a* for parallel structure.
5. Correct. The related ideas *to be treated* and *to be given* are written in parallel form.

Skill 3 Review

1. *It is a good idea to plan for the future.* Avoid wordiness: *ahead* is unnecessary with *for the future.*
2. *In case of a flood, leave your home at once.* Change or remove words that make the meaning unclear.
3. *So that I would learn to play the piano well, my teacher told me to practice often.*

   OR

   So that I would learn to play the piano well, my teacher often told me to practice. Move the modifier closer to the word being modified.
4. *While we were working with the computer, the telephone rang.* Add words to make the dangling modifier a subordinate idea.
5. *She enjoyed singing and dancing more than acting.* Change *to act* to *acting* for parallel structure.
6. *The human body has over 600 muscles; they account for 40 percent of the body's weight.* Use a pronoun, *they,* that clearly refers to the antecedent *muscles.*
7. Correct. The sentence expresses an idea clearly, without unnecessary words.
8. *The doctor explained the patient's symptoms, diagnosis, and treatment.* Change *what treatment would be used* to *treatment,* for parallel structure.
9. *The German scientist Martin Klaproth developed several uses for uranium, which was discovered in 1789.* Move the modifier closer to the word being modified.
10. *Excited and anxious, the child unwrapped the birthday gifts.* Introduce a word that can be modified by *Excited and anxious.*

Chapter 2 Quiz

There may be more than one correct way to edit some sentences.

1. *I visited the World's Fair taking place in New Orleans.* Move the modifier closer to the words it modifies, *World's Fair.*
2. *Davy Crockett was an early American folk hero; he eventually became a U.S. congressman.* Eliminate the run-on sentence.
3. *In the International Morse Code, the S.O.S. signal consists of three dots, three dashes, and three more dots.* Eliminate the words *then you use* for parallel structure.
4. *The volleyball and the basketball were invented in Massachusetts in the 1800s. Volleyball is a popular team sport.* Use separate sentences for ideas that are not closely related.
5. *My father is a loyal football fan, but he thinks the players are paid too much.* Eliminate the unclear pronoun reference by replacing the pronoun *they* with a noun.
6. *The house next door to ours has just been sold.* Eliminate the sentence fragment by adding words to complete the thought.
7. *My family and I visited the Basketball Hall of Fame, built in Springfield, Massachusetts.* Move the modifier closer to the words being modified.
8. *The monetary unit of China is the yuan; the monetary unit of Japan is the yen.* Eliminate the comma splice.
9. *The driver shouted furiously.* Avoid wordiness.
10. *Disney World is the largest amusement park in the world; it is located in Orlando, Florida.* Eliminate the run-on sentence.
11. *Riding in the car, I noticed that the fan belt broke.* Correct the dangling modifier by adding a word that can be modified logically by *riding.*
12. *The dentist who crowned Sam's tooth did a good job.* Add a verb and other words needed to complete the meaning of the sentence fragment.
13. Correct. A comma correctly follows the subordinate idea that begins the sentence.
14. *The stories of Edgar Allan Poe are unusual, exciting, and suspenseful.* Change *they have suspense* to *suspenseful* for parallel structure.
15. *An astronaut is an American space traveler; a cosmonaut is a Russian space traveler.* Eliminate the run-on sentence.
16. *Stephen Crane wrote* The Red Badge of Courage; *later, he died of tuberculosis at age 28.* Use a coordinator that expresses the relationship between ideas.
17. *Having studied for many hours, David found the test easy.* To eliminate the dangling modifier, introduce a word that can be modified logically by *Having studied.*
18. *While Lincoln was president, the first paper money was issued in the United States.* Use only one subordinator.
19. *Although Mrs. Rossi does not usually go to the movies, she occasionally enjoys one.* Add words to the sentence fragment to complete the meaning.
20. *The human body contains several chemical elements; these include carbon, hydrogen, nitrogen, and oxygen.* Eliminate the run-on sentence.

Chapter 3 Mechanics

Skill 1 Preview

1. *There are 26 letters in the* ***English*** alphabet. Capitalize a nationality.
2. *Dorothy's aunt in* The Wizard of Oz *was named* ***Aunt*** *Em.* Capitalize a title when it is part of a person's name.

3. Correct. Proper nouns that name clubs and organizations are capitalized.
4. *During the* ***American Revolution****, the Battle of Bunker Hill really was fought on Breed's Hill.* Capitalize proper nouns.
5. *Fred and Wilma Flintstone live at 39* ***Stone Canyon Way****.* Capitalize street addresses.

Lesson 1 Exercise

1. *The Mediterranean Sea is part of the* ***Atlantic Ocean.*** Capitalize the names of bodies of water.
2. Correct. Names of people, proper adjectives, and titles of books are capitalized.
3. *The* ***Presidential Medal of Freedom*** *was established in 1963.* Capitalize awards that are proper nouns.
4. *In 1865 a* ***steamboat*** *explosion on the Mississippi River killed 1,653 people.* Do not capitalize common nouns.
5. *Using his research ship* ***Calypso,*** *Jacques Cousteau explored the oceans.* Capitalize proper names of boats and ships.

Lesson 2 Exercise

1. *The first woman to be appointed to the Supreme Court was* ***Justice*** *Sandra Day O'Connor.* Capitalize titles when used as part of a person's name.
2. *Carnegie Hall is located at* ***Seventh Avenue and Fifty-Seventh Street*** *in New York City.* Capitalize the words in a street name.
3. Correct. A title that is not used as part of a person's name is not capitalized.
4. *While he was* ***president,*** *Herbert Hoover gave all of his paychecks to charity.* Do not capitalize the title president when it is not used as part of a person's name.
5. *Our new offices are located at 5310* ***South*** *27 Street.* Capitalize the words in an address.

Lesson 3 Exercise

1. *The word* ***"Monday,"*** *referring to the second day of the week, was taken from an Old English word that meant "moon's day."* Capitalize the days of the week.
2. *The first day of* ***winter*** *is usually on December 21.* Do not capitalize the seasons of the year.
3. *Socrates, the famous Greek philosopher, died in 399 B.C., but his ideas had a major influence on the philosophers of the* ***Christian Era.*** Capitalize the names of historical periods.
4. *Babe Ruth Day was held on* ***April*** *27, 1947, at Yankee Stadium.* Capitalize the months of the year.
5. Correct. A numerical designation of a century is not capitalized.

Skill 1 Review

1. *Cary Grant never won an* ***Academy Award.*** Capitalize the names of prizes and awards.
2. *Cleopatra, an* ***Egyptian*** *queen born in 69 B.C., married her brother.* Capitalize adjectives made from proper nouns.
3. *Peter O'Toole starred in the 1962 movie* Lawrence ***of*** Arabia. Do not capitalize the word *of* in a title, unless it is the first word.
4. *Old Kent Road and Park Lane are two of the squares in the* ***British*** *version of Monopoly.* Capitalize proper adjectives.
5. Correct. The names of holidays and titles used as part of a person's name are capitalized.

6. *Where are you going for your vacation this* ***summer?*** Do not capitalize the seasons of the year.
7. *The Tokyo World Lanes Bowling Center in* ***Japan*** *has 252 lanes.* Capitalize the names of countries.
8. *Sherlock Holmes' landlady was* ***Mrs.*** *Hudson.* Capitalize a title when it is part of a person's name.
9. *The* Apollo 11 *landed on the moon at 4:17* **P.M.** *on July 20, 1969.* Capitalize this indication of a specific time.
10. *Lucas Santomee was the first known* ***black*** *doctor in the United States.* Do not capitalize color distinction of a race of people.

Skill 2 Preview

1. *The first passengers to ride in a hot-air balloon* ***were a*** *duck, a sheep, and a rooster.* Do not use a comma before the first item in a series.
2. *The Statue of Liberty has special meaning to the United States,* ***for*** *it was a gift from France.* Use a comma before a coordinator in a compound sentence.
3. ***Because it didn't fade,*** *purple was the ancient color of royalty.* Use a comma after a subordinate idea at the beginning of a sentence.
4. Correct. Sentence interrupters are set off by commas.
5. *Laser beams are the* ***brightest artificial*** *light sources.* Do not use a comma after an adjective that modifies another adjective.

Lesson 1 Exercise

1. Sputnik 5, *a Russian satellite, orbited the earth with* ***two dogs and six mice*** *aboard.* Do not use a comma between only two items in a series.
2. *The tired, weary, and* ***hungry travelers*** *could not find a motel room.* Do not use a comma between the last adjective in a series and the noun that follows it.
3. *The background color of a flag is called the* ***"field" or "ground."*** Do not use a comma between only two items in a series.
4. Correct. Use commas to separate three or more items in a series.
5. *The five basic swimming strokes* ***are the*** *crawl, the backstroke, the breaststroke, the butterfly, and the sidestroke.* Do not use a comma before the first item in a series.

Lesson 2 Exercise

1. *Charles Dodgson wrote* Alice's Adventures in Wonderland, ***but he used the pen name*** *"Lewis Carroll."* Use a comma before the coordinator in a compound sentence.
2. *Scientists count the number of times fish cough, for it helps scientists determine the amount of water pollution.* Do not use a comma after a coordinator in a compound sentence.
3. *June is known as the month of romance and marriage, yet it also has one of the highest crime rates.* Do not use a comma after a coordinator in a compound sentence.
4. *I worked and he played.* If the two ideas expressed in a compound sentence are very short, the comma usually is omitted.
5. Correct. A comma is correctly used before the coordinator.

Lesson 3 Exercise

1. ***When it started in 1860,*** *the Pony Express mail service took ten days to deliver a letter from Missouri to California.* When a subordinate idea begins a sentence, it is followed by a comma.
2. ***Consequently,*** *a leap year has 366 days.* Follow an introductory element with a comma.
3. ***Gentlemen,*** *our program is ready to begin.* Follow a term of direct address with a comma.
4. ***No,*** *I did not know that there is a town in Arizona called Bumble Bee.* Follow an introductory element with a comma.
5. Correct. An introductory phrase of two words does not have to be set off by a comma.

Lesson 4 Exercise

1. *Baseball was introduced to Japan by Horace Wilson,* ***an American teacher.*** Set off a sentence interrupter that ends a sentence.
2. *A flashlight fish,* ***of course,*** *has lights beneath each eye that blink on and off.* Use a pair of commas to set off a sentence interrupter that is not essential to the main idea of the sentence.
3. ***I believe*** *that the Otis Elevator Company is the world's largest manufacturer of elevators.* Do not use a comma to set off words that are essential to the main idea of the sentence.
4. Correct. When a sentence interrupter is essential to the meaning of the sentence, it is not set off by commas.
5. *The Greater Antilles,* ***a group of islands in the West Indies,*** includes the islands of Cuba, Jamaica, and Puerto Rico. Use a pair of commas to set off an interrupter that falls in the middle of a sentence.

Lesson 5 Exercise

1. *In 1920 Elmer Smith of the Cleveland* ***Indians hit*** *the first grand-slam home run in a World Series game.* Do not use a comma to separate the subject and verb of a sentence.
2. *Dave DeBusschere played basketball for the New York Knicks* ***and*** *pitched for the Chicago White Sox.* Do not use a comma between two compound verbs joined by a coordinator.
3. *While playing water polo, one team wears white caps,* ***and*** *the opposing team wears blue caps.* Do not use a comma between two complete ideas without using a coordinator.
4. Correct. A comma correctly follows the introductory phrase.
5. *Bruce Jenner, Bill Toomey,* ***and Rafer Johnson*** *were all Olympic decathlon winners.* Do not use a comma after the last item in a series.

Skill 2 Review

1. *Both the Bering* ***Sea and*** *the Coral Sea are in the Pacific Ocean.* Do not use a comma between only two items in a series.
2. *An owl can turn its head 270 degrees,* ***but*** *it cannot move its eyes.* Use a comma before the coordinator in a compound sentence.
3. Correct. An introductory phrase of two words does not have to be set off by commas.
4. *The* ***first automobile*** *license plates were required by the state of New York.* Do not use a comma to separate an adjective that modifies another adjective.
5. *More dinosaur bones have been found in Canada,* ***for example,*** *than in any other place in the world.* A sentence interrupter is set off by commas from the rest of the sentence.
6. *The music for the song* ***"On Wisconsin"*** *was originally written for the University of Minnesota.* Words that are essential to the meaning of the sentence are not set off by commas.
7. ***Nevertheless,*** *a lizard that loses its tail can grow a new one.* Use a comma after an introductory element.
8. ***John,*** *is it true that over 60,000 bees can live in a single hive?* Use a comma after a word of direct address.
9. *The first space shuttle flight took place in 1981,* ***and*** *John Young was the commander.* Use a comma before a coordinator in a compound sentence.
10. *One hot dog* ***or*** *one ounce of cheese* ***or*** *one chicken drumstick provides seven grams of protein.* Do not use commas when the items in a series are joined by coordinating words such as *or*.

Skill 3 Preview

1. *Most of* ***Earth's*** *physical changes are so gradual that we do not notice them.* Add apostrophe to show possession.
2. *Only two city council members thought it was* ***all right*** *to raise parking fees. All right* is two words.
3. ***Besides*** *teaching, Larry enjoys coaching basketball.* Add an *s* to *beside,* to give the meaning "in addition to."
4. *There were several* ***misspelled*** *words in the letter. Misspelled* has two *s*'s.
5. Correct. The contraction *you'd* means "you would."

Lesson 1 Exercise

1. *Recent* ***discoveries*** *in medicine have changed the way people live.* The noun *discovery* ends in *y* preceded by a consonant. The plural is formed by replacing *y* with *i* and adding *es*.
2. *In many* ***cities,*** *trolleys once ran along main streets.* The noun *city* ends in *y* preceded by a consonant. Its plural is formed by replacing *y* with *i* and adding *es*. The noun *trolley* ends in *y* preceded by a vowel. Its plural is formed by adding *s*.
3. Correct. To form the *-ing* form of *arrive,* drop the final *e* before adding *-ing*.
4. *The candidates* ***running*** *for office appeared to have similar views.* To form the *-ing* form of *run,* double the final *n* before adding *-ing*
5. *Many families are* ***preparing*** *their children for school by helping them learn to read.* To form the *-ing* form of *prepare,* drop the final *e* before adding *-ing*.

Lesson 2 Exercise

1. *The only flag on the moon is* ***ours.*** Do not use an apostrophe with a possessive pronoun.
2. ***Americans*** *spend over $1 billion on gum each year.* An apostrophe is not needed, because the noun does not show possession.
3. Correct. The word *girls'* is the possessive of the plural noun *girls*.
4. *The anaconda, the world's largest snake, squeezes* ***its*** *prey to death and swallows it whole.* Do not use an

apostrophe with a possessive pronoun. The word "it's" is a contraction.

5. ***Beethoven's*** *music teacher criticized him for not having musical talent.* The possessive form of a singular noun is formed by adding an apostrophe and the letter *s* to the noun.

Lesson 3 Exercise

1. *A person* ***can't*** *jump higher than a horse.* Position the apostrophe to show exactly where letters have been omitted in the contraction of *cannot.*
2. ***There are*** *more telephones in the Pentagon than there are employees.* Do not confuse the possessive pronoun *their* with another similar word.
3. *Although it drinks huge amounts of water, a camel* ***doesn't*** *sweat.* Position the apostrophe to show exactly where letters have been omitted in the contraction of *does not.*
4. ***It's*** *a fact that light travels about 186,000 miles per second.* Use the apostrophe to form the contraction of *it is.*
5. Correct. *Isn't* is the contraction for *Is not.*

Lesson 4 Exercise

1. *It is* ***all right*** *to smile when you receive a* ***compliment.*** Change *alright* to *all right* and *complement* to *compliment.*
2. *In the* ***past,*** *I have always eaten dessert because I enjoy sweets a lot.* Change *passed* to *past.*
3. Correct. *Whose* is a pronoun that shows ownership.
4. *Next* ***week*** *the* ***council*** *will decide what* ***course*** *of action to take.* Change *weak* to *week, counsel* to *council,* and *course* to *course.*
5. *Don't* ***waste*** *stationery because it is* ***too*** *expensive.* Change *waist* to *waste* and *to* to *too.*

Lesson 5 Exercise

1.	change *abundence*	to *abundance*
	change *adress*	to *address*
	change *alright*	to *all right*
2.	change *auxilary*	to *auxiliary*
	change *benefitted*	to *benefited*
3.	change *calender*	to *calendar*
	change *cheif*	to *chief*
	change *committment*	to *commitment*
4.	change *coroborate*	to *corroborate*
	change *critisism*	to *criticism*
	change *dependant*	to *dependent*
5.	change *dissappoint*	to *disappoint*
	change *entrence*	to *entrance*
	change *exersice*	to *exercise*
	change *exhileration*	to *exhilaration*
6.	change *Febuary*	to *February*
	change *freind*	to *friend*
7.	change *grammer*	to *grammar*
	change *hankerchief*	to *handkerchief*
	change *manuever*	to *maneuver*
8.	change *newstand*	to *newsstand*
	change *occassion*	to *occasion*
	change *ommission*	to *omission*
9.	change *perserverance*	to *perseverance*
	change *shephard*	to *shepherd*
10.	change *unecessary*	to *unnecessary*
	change *vacuumm*	to *vacuum*
	change *wierd*	to *weird*

Skill 3 Review

1. *The flea can jump a distance that is 130 times the height of* ***its*** *body.* The possessive pronoun *its* is spelled without an apostrophe.
2. *Many lives were lost in the war for* ***independence*** *from England.* This is a frequently misspelled word.
3. *The Caterpillar Club is an organization* ***whose*** *members have used parachutes to save their lives.* The possessive pronoun *whose* is spelled without an apostrophe.
4. Correct. The frequently misspelled word *accommodate* and the word *principal,* meaning the head of a school, are spelled correctly as written.
5. *Orbiting* ***weather*** *satellites take pictures of cloud formations that surround the earth.* *Whether* and *weather* are homonyms; *weather* refers to climate.
6. *Solar energy is an* ***efficient*** *way to use the sun's energy.* This is a frequently misspelled word.
7. Correct. The frequently misspelled word *convenience* is correct as written.
8. *Honey* ***bees'*** *wings beat over 250 times a second.* The possessive of the plural noun *bees* is *bees'*
9. *The* ***development*** *of the popsicle is credited to an eleven-year-old boy.* This is a frequently misspelled word.
10. ***Didn't*** *you know that silver is made from the mineral "cinnabar"?* Position the apostrophe to show where the letter has been dropped to form the contraction for *Did not.*

Chapter 3 Quiz

1. *If you put a pat of butter on top of cooking liquid,* ***it'll*** *keep the liquid from boiling over.* Use the apostrophe to form the contraction of *it will.*
2. *The Lincoln Memorial is patterned after an ancient* ***Greek*** *temple.* Capitalize proper adjectives.
3. *When the North Pole tips toward the sun,* *summer occurs in the Northern Hemisphere.* Use a comma after a subordinate idea at the beginning of a sentence.
4. *A hurricane, a typhoon, and a cyclone* ***refer*** *to the same kind of storm.* Do not use a comma after the last item in a series.
5. *Pike's Peak, a famous tourist attraction in* ***Colorado,*** *stands 14,110 feet high.* Capitalize the name of a state.
6. *At the age of 26,* ***General*** *George Custer fought in the Civil War.* Capitalize a title that is used as part of a person's name.
7. *President* ***Kennedy's*** *two pet cats were named Kitten and Tom.* The possessive form of the singular noun *Kennedy* is formed by adding an apostrophe and the letter *s.*
8. Correct. *Their* is a possessive pronoun.
9. *During the* ***Middle Ages,*** *Europeans thought garlic would frighten away vampires.* Capitalize historical periods.
10. *Pong,* ***the first coin-operated video game,*** *was introduced in 1972.* Use a pair of commas to set off a sentence interrupter in the middle of a sentence.
11. *Birds that live in high places are* ***condors,*** *eagles, and hawks.* Do not use a comma before the first item in a series.
12. *The Lombardi Trophy is the prize given to the winning* ***team*** *of the Super Bowl.* Do not capitalize common nouns.
13. *The U.S.* ***battleship*** *Oregon was built very close to the*

dimensions of Noah's Ark. Do not capitalize common nouns.

14. *The Atacama Desert,* ***by the way,*** *is located in South America.* Use a pair of commas to set off a sentence interrupter in the middle of a sentence.
15. *In a* ***library's*** *Dewey Decimal Classification System, rare books can be found under the number 090.* The possessive form of the singular noun *library* is formed by adding an apostrophe and the letter *s*.
16. *Our universe contains billions of galaxies,* ***and*** *the nearest to our own is two billion light-years away.* Use a comma before the coordinator in a compound sentence.
17. *Neither Bolivia nor Paraguay borders on either the* ***Atlantic or Pacific oceans.*** Do not use a comma between only two items in a series. Also, do not use a comma when the word *or* connects items in a series.
18. *Ye****s,*** *the Hawaiian Islands are actually the tops of an underwater mountain range.* Use a comma after an introductory element at the beginning of a sentence.
19. ***Beginning*** *in 1943, income tax was withheld from workers' paychecks.* Change *begining* to *beginning*.
20. ***There*** *are over 20,000 kinds of fish, but we eat very few of them.* Do not confuse the possessive pronoun *their* with the expletive *there*.

Chapter 4 Editing Paragraphs

Lesson 1 Exercise

1. (1) *Usage/Subject-Verb Agreement/Sentence Correction.* The singular form of the verb is needed because the subject, *U.S. Air Force*, is singular.
2. (3) *Sentence Structure/Run-on Sentence/Sentence Revision.* Divide a run-on sentence into two sentences.
3. (5) *No correction is necessary.* A comma is needed after the introductory phrase.
4. (1) *Mechanics/Punctuation/Sentence Correction.* A sentence interrupter is set off from the rest of the sentence by commas.
5. (3) *Sentence Structure/Coordination/Construction Shift.* The second sentence shows a conflicting idea. Therefore, in the combined sentence, you need a word that keeps the contrast.

Lesson 2 Exercise

1. (5) *Mechanics/Punctuation/Sentence Revision.* Use commas to separate all items in a series.
2. (3) *Usage/Subject-Verb Agreement/Sentence Correction.* The word *salt* is singular, so it takes the singular form of the verb.
3. (4) *Sentence Structure/Run-on Sentence/Sentence Correction.* One way of separating a run-on sentence is by using a semicolon.
4. (5) *Usage/Verb Tense/Sentence Revision.* The paragraph is written in the present tense. The past-tense form of the verb, *had*, is incorrect here.
5. (2) *Usage/Coordinators/Construction Shift.* The word *by* suggests explanatory material will follow.

Lesson 3 Exercise

1. (3) *Usage/Verb Tense/Sentence Correction.* *Increased* is past tense; therefore, its helping verb must also be past tense.
2. (5) *Usage/Subject-Verb Agreement/Sentence Revision.* Use the plural form *travel* to agree with the plural subject, *waves*.
3. (1) *Usage/Verb Form/Construction Shift.* Using the verb form *causing* helps the sentence to relate the first idea to the second.
4. (2) *Usage/Subject-Verb Agreement/Sentence Correction.* Use the singular form *produces* to agree with the singular subject, *motion*.
5. (5) *Usage/Verb Tense/Sentence Correction.* The present-tense form is needed in this sentence.

Lesson 4 Exercise

1. (3) *Sentence Structure/Coordinators/Construction Shift.* The word *by* shows that material will follow that will answer the question *How?*
2. (1) *Sentence Structure/Subordinator/Sentence Correction.* Only one subordinator is needed.
3. (5) *Sentence Structure/Parallel Structure/Sentence Revision.* All items in a series must use the same form in order to have parallel structure. In this sentence, each item is in the noun form.
4. (3) *Sentence Structure/Run-on Sentences/Sentence Revision.* One way to correct a run-on sentence is by using a semicolon.
5. (4) *Sentence Structure/Clarity/Sentence Revision.* The construction is awkward and unclear.

Lesson 5 Exercise

1. (4) *Mechanics/Possessives/Sentence Correction.* Use the possessive pronoun form *their* to modify *shows* rather than the contraction for *they are*.
2. (1) *Mechanics/Capitalization/Sentence Correction.* All the important words in a proper noun should be capitalized.
3. (4) *Mechanics/Spelling/Sentence Correction.* This word is often misspelled.
4. (4) *Mechanics/Punctuation/Sentence Revision.* Use paired commas to set off sentence interrupters.
5. (5) *Mechanics/Possessives/Sentence Revision.* Use an apostrophe to show possession.

Lesson 6 Exercise

1. (3) *Mechanics/Spelling/Sentence Correction.* This word is often misspelled.
2. (2) *Usage/Verb Forms/Sentence Correction.* Use the correct verb form with a helping verb.
3. (4) *Mechanics/Punctuation/Sentence Revision.* Set off a sentence interrupter with a comma.
4. (5) *Mechanics/Possessives/Sentence Correction.* Use the possessive pronoun form *whose* rather than the contraction for *who is*.
5. (1) The sentence is correct as written.
6. (1) *Sentence Structure/Sentence Fragments/Sentence Correction.* Using a subordinator at the beginning of this group of words makes a sentence fragment. Eliminate it to make a well-written sentence.
7. (3) *Sentence Structure/Coordinators/Construction Shift.* The word *because* tells the reader that a reason will follow.
8. (3) *Sentence Structure/Subordinators/Sentence Revision.* Only one subordinator is needed.
9. (4) *Usage/Verb Form/Sentence Correction.* Since the paragraph is not written in the past tense, *can be* is the correct form.

10. (4) *Usage/Subject-Verb Agreement/Sentence Revision.* A verb must agree with its subject. *Have* agrees with the singular subject, *U.S. News and World Report.*

Chapter 4 Quiz

1. 1. Record
   2. Revise
   3. Read
   4. Reread
   5. Reflect
2. 1. Read
   2. Reflect
   3. Revise
   4. Reread
   5. Record
3. (3) *Usage/Subject-Verb Agreement/Sentence Correction.* Change *eat* to *eats* to agree with *American,* which is the subject.
4. (5) *Usage/Pronouns/Sentence Correction.* A pronoun must match the word it refers to. *Restaurants* is plural; therefore, *they,* a plural pronoun, is correct.
5. (1) *Sentence Structure/Sentence Fragment/Sentence Correction.* This sentence fragment can be made into a complete sentence.
6. (4) *Sentence Structure/Parallel Structure/Sentence Correction.* All the items in a series must be expressed using the same form, in order to have correct parallel construction.
7. (1) *Mechanics/Punctuation/Sentence Correction.* Set off sentence interrupters with paired commas.
8. (1) *This sentence is correct as written.* The connector *and* joins two ideas, not two complete sentences; therefore, a comma is not needed.
9. (1) *Mechanics/Capitalization/Sentence Correction.* All important words in a proper name should be capitalized.
10. (2) *Sentence Structure/Coordinators/Construction Shift.* The use of these words in the combined sentences would illustrate how the second idea contrasts with the first idea.
11. (2) *Mechanics/Capitalization/Sentence Correction.* The word *summer* is not used as a proper noun here; it does not need a capital letter.
12. (1) *No correction is necessary.* A comma is needed after the introductory phrase.
13. (5) *Sentence Structure/Coordinators/Construction.* The words *such as* indicate that a list of items will follow.
14. (3) *Usage/Subject-Verb Agreement/Sentence Correction.* *Someone* is singular and takes the singular form, *is.*
15. (1) *Mechanics/Spelling/Sentence Correction.* This word is often misspelled.
16. (5) *Usage/Verb Form/Sentence Revision.* The paragraph is written in the present tense; therefore, *is* is the correct choice.
17. (1) *Usage/Pronoun Reference/Sentence Correction.* The pronoun refers to *Hydrogen peroxide* in the previous sentence. A singular pronoun, *It,* is needed.
18. (2) *Sentence Structure/Run-on Sentence/Sentence Revision.* One way to correct a run-on sentence is to make two separate, complete sentences.
19. (5) *No correction is necessary.* The verb *have* agrees with the subject, *you.*
20. (3) *Mechanics/Spelling/Sentence Correction.* The word *accidents* is a plural, not a possessive. It does not need an apostrophe.

UNIT I Test

1. (3) *Usage/Subject-Verb Agreement/Sentence Correction.* The compound subject, *home computers* and *television,* requires a plural verb.
2. (4) *Sentence Structure/Subordination/Sentence Revision.* Use only one subordinator at a time. The subordinator *while* makes the most sense in this sentence.
3. (1) *Mechanics/Punctuation/Construction Shift. A 1985 survey, conducted by the President's Council on Physical Fitness and Sports, showed the results of a lack of enough active participation in exercise.* Use commas to set off a sentence interrupter.
4. (5) *Mechanics/Spelling/Sentence Correction.* Do not confuse the troublesome words *though* and *through.*
5. *Mechanics/Punctuation—Overuse of Commas. Of these, 40 percent of the boys and 70 percent of the girls could not do more than one pull-up.* Do not use a comma before a coordinator that connects a compound subject.
6. *Mechanics/Capitalization. In addition, about 50 percent of the girls and 30 percent of the boys, ages 6–12, couldn't run a mile in less than 10 minutes.* Do not capitalize a common noun that is not the first word of the sentence.
7. *Usage/Verb Tense. Medically, these results illustrate a problem because poor fitness in childhood increases the likelihood of heart attacks and other health-related problems in adulthood.* Verb tenses in a sentence should be consistent. Change *increased* to the present tense, *increases,* to agree with the tense of the other verb, *illustrate.*
8. *Usage/Pronoun Reference—Agreement with Antecedent. Accordingly, we need to educate children's bodies as well as their minds.* The pronoun, *their,* agrees with the plural antecedent, *children's.*
9. (2) *Sentence Structure/Sentence Fragment/Sentence Correction.* Removing the relative pronoun, *who,* changes this sentence fragment into a complete sentence.
10. (4) *Usage/Verb Tense/Sentence Revision.* Change *became* to the present tense, *become,* to agree with the tense of the paragraph.
11. (5) *Sentence Structure/Coordination/Sentence Correction.* The coordinators *neither* and *nor* are used correctly to connect the two verbs, *meets* and *uses.*
12. (3) *Usage/Subject-Verb Agreement/Sentence Revision.* Change the verb, *provide,* to *provides* to agree with its singular subject, *book.*
13. (4) *Sentence Structure/Subordination/Construction Shift. As you gather information about a particular job, you should think about these ideas.* A coordinator is not needed when ideas of unequal rank are joined by a subordinator.
14. *Sentence Structure/Comma Splice. First, (P) position is important; know the job description and its duties.* Do not use a comma between two complete ideas that are not joined by a coordinator. Replace the comma with a semicolon, as shown above, or create two separate sentences by changing the comma to a period and capitalizing the first word of the second complete idea.
15. *Mechanics/Punctuation—Overuse of Commas. Second, (L) location should be considered for both the geograph-*

ical locale and the physical working environment. Do not use a comma before a coordinator that connects two items in a listing.

16. Sentence Structure/Run-on Sentence. *Fifth, (E) entry skills must be known. They include specific education and training requirements.* Eliminate the run-on sentence by making two separate sentences, as shown above, or by inserting a semicolon after *known*.
17. Mechanics/Spelling—Troublesome Homonyms. *This data will help you evaluate whether or not a specific job meets your expectations and goals.* Change the contraction *you're* to the possessive pronoun *your*.
18. (5) Usage/Subject-Verb Agreement and Pronoun Reference/Sentence Correction. The verb, *are*, agrees with its subject, *languages*, and the pronoun, *themselves*, agrees with its antecedent, *computers*.
19. (2) Usage/Subject-Verb Agreement/Sentence Revision. Change *are* to *is* to agree with the singular subject, *each*.
20. (4) Mechanics/Punctuation/Construction Shift. *LOGO, a specialized language that uses both graphics and words, is used to teach programming to children.* The idea in sentence 5 is changed into an interrupting phrase that describes the noun *LOGO* in the new sentence. Sentence interrupters are set off by commas.
21. (3) Mechanics/Capitalization/Sentence Correction. Do not capitalize *mathematician* because it is a common noun and not a title that is part of a person's name.
22. Usage/Pronoun Reference. No correction is necessary. The relative pronoun *which* is used correctly because it refers to things, "*acronyms*."
23. Mechanics/Punctuation. *Commonly used with smaller computers, this versatile language is noted for being easy to learn and use.* An introductory phrase is followed by a comma.
24. Sentence Structure/Misplaced Modifier. *FORTRAN, an acronym for Formula Translator, is used for mathematical and scientific applications.* A modifier should be placed as close as possible to the word being described. The modifying phrase *an acronym for Formula Translator* describes *FORTRAN*, not *applications*.
25. Usage/Verb Tense. *As different needs arise, different languages evolve.* Keep verb tenses consistent. Change *evolved* to the present tense, *evolve*, to agree with the verb *arise*.
26. (5) Mechanic/Sentence Correction. The sentence is correct as written.
27. (3) Sentence Structure/Run-on Sentence/Sentence Revision. Sentence 8 is a run-on sentence. A period should follow *separately* and the first word of the second complete idea should be capitalized.
28. (2) Usage/Subject-Verb Agreement/Sentence Revision. The subject, *programs*, is plural. It should agree with the plural form of the verb *here*.

UNIT II Essay Writing Unit II Test

Introduction to Holistic Scoring

The following GED Essay Scoring Guide provides a general description of the characteristics found in GED essays scored by the Holistic Method.

GED ESSAY SCORING GUIDE

Papers will show *some or all* of the following characteristics.

Upper-half papers make clear a definite purpose, pursued with varying degrees of effectiveness. They also have a structure that shows evidence of some deliberate planning. The writer's control of English usage ranges from fairly reliable at 4 to confident and accomplished at 6.

6 Papers scored as a 6 tend to offer sophisticated ideas within an organizational framework that is clear and appropriate for the topic. The supporting statements are particularly effective because of their substance, specificity, or illustrative quality. The writing is vivid and precise, though it may contain an occasional flaw.

5 Papers scored as a 5 are clearly organized with effective support for each of the writer's major points. The writing offers substantive ideas, though the paper may lack the flair or grace of a 6 paper. The surface features are consistently under control, despite an occasional lapse in usage.

4 Papers scored as a 4 show evidence of the writer's organizational plan. Support, though sufficient, tends to be less extensive or convincing than that found in papers scored as a 5 or 6. The writer generally observes the conventions of accepted English usage. Some errors are usually present, but they are not severe enough to interfere significantly with the writer's main purpose.

Lower-half papers either fail to convey a purpose sufficiently or lack one entirely. Consequently, their structure ranges from rudimentary at 3, to random at 2, to absent at 1. Control of the conventions of English usage tends to follow this same gradient.

3 Papers scored as a 3 usually show some evidence of planning or development. However, the organization is often limited to a simple listing or haphazard recitation of ideas about the topic, leaving an impression of insufficiency. The 3 papers often demonstrate repeated weaknesses in accepted English usage and are generally ineffective in accomplishing the writer's purpose.

2 Papers scored as a 2 are characterized by a marked lack of development or inadequate support for ideas. The level of thought apparent in the writing is frequently unsophisticated or superficial, often marked by a listing of unsupported generalizations. Instead of suggesting a clear purpose, these papers often present conflicting purposes. Errors in accepted English usage may seriously interfere with the overall effectiveness of these papers.

1 Papers scored as a 1 leave the impression that the writer has not only *not* accomplished a purpose, but has not made any purpose apparent. The dominant feature of these papers is the lack of control. The writer stumbles both in conveying a clear plan for the paper and in expressing ideas according to the conventions of accepted English usage.

0 The zero score is reserved for papers which are blank, illegible, or written on a topic other than the one assigned.

Source: *The 1988 Tests of General Educational Development: A Preview*, American Council on Education, 1985. Used with permission.

HOW TO SCORE YOUR ESSAY

To score your essay, compare it with the following model essays. These model essays represent scores of 3 and 5 respectively.

Compare your essay with the model essay scored 3. If it is as good as that essay, assign your essay a score of 3. If it is not as good as the 3 essay, refer to the answers for the Writing Skills Predictor Test (pages 14–19). Use the descriptions of the 1 and 2 essays there to evaluate your essay.

If your essay is better than the 3 essay, compare it to the model essay scored 5. If yours is better than the 3, but not as good as the 5, score your essay a 4. If your essay is better than the 5 model essay, score it a 6.

In addition, look at the notes with, and the character trait analyses following, each model essay. They comment on the strengths and weaknesses of the models.

Model Essay—Holistic Score 3

Too many key points—lack of focus
Disorganized, illogical flow of ideas
No paragraphs in the middle to explain the points made in the introduction
Undeveloped ideas that don't lead to a point
Concluding statement weak—needs support

Voting is a rigt everyone should have. It is important to vote because thats how people get elected. Voting was not always given to everyone. There were times when not every person could vote. Without everyone voting we cannot have a complete democracy. Voting is everyones right and everyone should exercise this right.

Secondly, voting is important for our government to act right. The people need to let the senators and presidents and congressman know what they think about things. What better way to do that than to vote in all the elections and let them know what you feel about different issues that are important in an election. In summary, it is important for everyone to vote rich people and poor people too. If everyone voted it would be a better world to live in today.

Character Trait Analysis

1. The essay is organized into two paragraphs, an introduction and a conclusion.
2. Within those two paragraphs, many different points are made, but none are supported with examples or details. The total effect is one of disorganization and illogical flow of ideas. Points made do not lead logically to a conclusion.
3. The conclusion that is made is not explained or supported.
4. The essay is shorter than the required 200 words.
5. Errors in spelling, punctuation, sentence structure, and grammar detract from the essay's effectiveness.

Model Essay—Holistic Score 5

Essay begins with an interesting fact
Introduction states point of view

Before a major election is held in the United States, efforts are sometimes made to register more voters. However, the number of people who do vote in an election is often small. I believe that all eligible citizens should vote in every election.

Explains one key idea introduced in first paragraph
Uses facts to support argument

The right to vote is a freedom that we should not take for granted. In some parts of the world, people do not have this right. Even in this country, everyone could not always vote. For example, black men could not vote until after the Civil War. Women could not vote until early in this century. Thus, the right to vote is a freedom we all should cherish.

More facts supporting argument
Uses appropriate transition words to move from point to point

Although people may argue that their votes do not matter, a few votes can sometimes make a real difference. History tells of several presidential elections that were determined by no more than 100,000 votes. That may sound like a lot, but out of millions of voters, it is really a very small percentage.

Summarizes ideas; Concludes with important statement about the topic that is in keeping with point of view

Even when an election is not close, it gives us a chance to state our views about government. Every vote is private, and every vote counts equally. Therefore, an important way to be involved in our government and to preserve democracy is to vote.

Character Trait Analysis

1. The essay is well organized. Ideas flow logically and lead to a conclusion.
2. Point of view is supported by details and facts.
3. All details and facts are consistent with the point of view and make the writer's opinion clear.
4. The essay reads well, although there are a few structural weaknesses and minor mechanical errors.

PRACTICE
Practice Items, Part I

1. (4) *Usage/Subject-Verb Agreement—Interrupting Phrase/Construction Shift.* *The history of sports is often fascinating.* The singular subject, *history*, requires a singular verb, *is*.
2. (3) *Usage/Verb Tense—Clues Within Sentence/Sentence Revision.* The phrase *in 1895* indicates that the verb should be in the past tense.
3. (1) *Usage/Verb Form/Sentence Correction.* Be careful when expressing the forms of irregular verbs, such as *to see*.
4. (2) *Mechanics/Spelling/Sentence Correction.* Remember to drop the *e* in *strike* before adding *-ing*.
5. (4) *Sentence Structure/Sentence Fragment/Sentence Revision.* The subject, *team*, requires a verb, *scores*, to correct the fragment.
6. (4) *Sentence Structure/Comma Splice/Sentence Correction.* In the original sentence, two complete ideas are incorrectly joined with a comma. Since the sentence is also wordy, the error is best corrected by removing ideas that are repeated.
7. (4) *Sentence Structure/Run-On Sentence/Sentence Correction.* The original sentence contains two complete ideas that are run together without punctuation. The error is eliminated by forming two separate sentences.
8. (2) *Mechanics/Capitalization—Proper Nouns/Sentence Correction.* Capitalize the names of countries.
9. (4) *Mechanics/Punctuation/Sentence Revision.* Use a comma to separate two complete ideas joined by connecting words such as *but, and, or, for*.
10. (5) *Mechanics/Spelling—Homonyms/Sentence Correction.* *Role* and *roll* sound alike but have different meanings.
11. (4) *Usage/Verb Tense/Sentence Correction.* The present tense is used throughout the paragraph.
12. (1) *Sentence Structure/Subordination/Construction Shift.* *As November of any election year approaches, we see the faces of candidates frequently on TV.* Use a comma to set off the subordinate idea when it comes first in the sentence.
13. (5) *Sentence Structure/Parallelism/Sentence Correction.* Use parallel structures to express similar ideas.
14. (3) *Usage/Relative Pronoun/Sentence Revision.* Use *who* to refer to people and *which* to refer to things.
15. (4) *Usage/Subject-Verb Agreement—Interrupting Phrase/Sentence Correction.* The plural subject, *Those*, requires a plural verb, *tend*. Do not be confused by the description following the subject.
16. (5) *Usage/Subject-Verb Agreement—Interrupting Phrase/Sentence Revision.* The plural subject, *people*, requires a plural verb, *are*.
17. (4) *Sentence Structure/Coordination/Construction Shift.* *There were some past American presidents who probably would have seemed awkward and plain on television, yet they made excellent leaders.* The original sentences are choppy; the combination makes the relationship between ideas more clear.
18. (2) *Sentence Structure/Sentence Fragment/Sentence Correction.* The fragment is corrected by providing a verb phrase, *do make*, for the subject, *people*.
19. (3) *Sentence Structure/Dangling Modifier/Sentence Revision.* *It* does not watch television; *we* do. Use a word that can logically be modified by *Watching television*.
20. (5) *Sentence Structure/Parallelism/Sentence Correction.* When you join two verbs with *and*, they should be in the same form: *take* and *inject*.
21. (2) *Sentence Structure/Subordination/Sentence Correction.* Use only one subordinator to introduce a subordinate idea.
22. (4) *Sentence Structure/Clarity—Wordiness/Construction Shift.* *In the early 1900s some doctors discovered that patients given shots of cowpox virus were protected from smallpox.* The new construction eliminates the vague word *something*.
23. (4) *Usage/Pronouns—Agreement with Antecedent/Sentence Revision.* The pronoun, *them*, must agree with the antecedent, *patients*.
24. (5) *Usage/Subject-Verb Agreement—Expletive/Sentence Correction.* This sentence has inverted structure. The verb, *have been*, agrees with the subject, *deaths*, even though the subject follows the verb.
25. (1) *Mechanics/Spelling/Sentence Correction.* *Believe* is a commonly misspelled word.
26. (4) *Usage/Subject-Verb Agreement—Interrupting Phrases/Sentence Revision.* The singular subject, *vaccination*, requires a singular verb, *is given*.
27. (1) *Mechanics/Capitalization/Sentence Correction.* Titles are capitalized only when they are used with a person's name.
28. (1) *Mechanics/Punctuation—Overuse of Commas/Sentence Correction.* Do not separate the subject, *vaccines*, from the verb, *are being developed*, with a comma.
29. (5) *Mechanics/Spelling/Sentence Correction.* *Together* is a frequently misspelled word.
30. (3) *Sentence Structure/Run-On Sentence/Sentence Revision.* Two complete ideas that could stand alone are incorrectly run together. The error is corrected by forming two separate sentences.
31. (4) *Mechanics/Punctuation—Items in a Series/Sentence Correction.* Use commas to separate three or more items in a series.
32. (3) *Sentence Structure/Parallelism/Sentence Correction.* When you connect two verbs with *and*, they should be in the same form: *stop* and *talk*.
33. (1) *Usage/Relative Pronoun/Construction Shift.* *Many children who refuse to read much on their own are often willing to read for quite a while if you offer to take turns with them.* Remember to use *who* when referring to people and *which* when referring to things.

34. (4) *Sentence Structure/Sentence Fragment/Sentence Revision.* When a semicolon is used, it should separate two complete ideas. The second idea in this sentence is a fragment. Both the subject, *he,* and the verb, *begins,* must be supplied to make the second idea complete.
35. (5) *Usage/Subject-Verb Agreement/Sentence Revision.* When the connecting words, *either . . . or,* join singular and plural nouns, the verb agrees with the closer noun. The plural verb, *are,* agrees with the closer noun, *bookstores.*
36. (2) *Usage/Subject-Verb Agreement—Inverted Structure/Sentence Correction.* Although the usual order is reversed, the singular subject, *half,* requires a singular verb, *is.*
37. (5) *Mechanics/Capitalization/Sentence Correction.* Names of holidays, months, and days of the week are capitalized.
38. (4) *Usage/Verb Tense—Irregular Verbs/Sentence Revision.* With the keeping verb, *has,* use the past participle. The past participle of *grow* is *grown.*
39. (5) *Usage/Verb Tense—Clues Within Paragraph/Sentence Correction.* The verb tense used, the present, is correct because it is consistent with that used throughout the paragraph.
40. (5) *Mechanics/Punctuation—Sentence Interrupters/Sentence Revision.* Descriptions that are not essential to the meaning of a sentence are set off by commas. Here, *especially in the middle of the year* explains *Having to change schools* but is not essential to the sentence's meaning.
41. (5) *Sentence Structure/Subordination/Construction Shift. Take the case of a child who is learning to do long division when his father is transferred from Germany to California.* In the original sentences, *is learning division* and *is being taught this* refer to the same idea; the new construction eliminates the wordiness.
42. (4) *Sentence Structure/Comma Splice/Sentence Correction.* Use a connecting word, such as *and,* or a semicolon to join two complete ideas. A comma alone is not enough.
43. (4) *Mechanics/Capitalization—Proper Adjectives/Sentence Correction.* Capitalize adjectives that are formed from proper nouns.
44. (4) *Usage/Vague Pronoun Reference/Sentence Correction.* In the original, it is not clear whether *they* refers to the parents, the parents and the child, or many such families.
45. (4) *Mechanics/Spelling/Sentence Correction. Period* is a frequently misspelled word.
46. (3) *Sentence Structure/Comma Splice/Sentence Revision.* A semicolon can be used to separate two complete ideas; a comma may not be used in this way.
47. (4) *Sentence Structure/Clarity/Construction Shift. Each branch of the military has set up family service centers to assist with a variety of problems.* Of all the choices, this one is the most concise way of eliminating confusion over to what *It* refers.
48. (4) *Usage/Verb Tense/Sentence Revision.* Look within a sentence for clues to verb tense. *When computers were invented* should be followed by *people were frightened.*
49. (5) *Usage/Verb Form—Irregular Verbs/Sentence Revision. To take* is an irregular verb. With the helping verbs, *would be,* use the past participle, *taken.*
50. (3) *Mechanics/Punctuation—Overuse of Commas/Sentence Correction.* Do not separate the subject, *thought,* from its verb, *made,* with a comma.
51. (5) *Sentence Structure/Coordination/Sentence Correction.* Two complete ideas are correctly separated by a semicolon. The second idea provides evidence supporting the first.
52. (2) *Mechanics/Capitalization—Proper Nouns/Sentence Correction.* Capitalize the names of cities, counties, states, countries, continents, and planets.
53. (1) *Usage/Relative Pronoun/Sentence Correction.* Use *that* or *which* when referring to things and *who* when referring to people.
54. (1) *Sentence Structure/Clarity/Construction Shift. Fortunately, the workplace has been made safer by computers.* The new construction is clearer and more precise than the original.
55. (3) *Mechanics/Spelling/Sentence Revision. Accident* is a frequently misspelled word.

Practice Items, Part II

Introduction to Holistic Scoring

The following GED Essay Scoring Guide provides a general description of the characteristics found in GED essays scored by the Holistic Method.

GED ESSAY SCORING GUIDE

Papers will show *some or all* of the following characteristics.

Upper-half papers make clear a definite purpose, pursued with varying degrees of effectiveness. They also have a structure that shows evidence of some deliberate planning. The writer's control of English usage ranges from fairly reliable at 4 to confident and accomplished at 6.

6 Papers scored as a 6 tend to offer sophisticated ideas within an organizational framework that is clear and appropriate for the topic. The supporting statements are particularly effective because of their substance, specificity, or illustrative quality. The writing is vivid and precise, though it may contain an occasional flaw.

5 Papers scored as a 5 are clearly organized with effective support for each of the writer's major points. The writing offers substantive ideas, though the paper may lack the flair or grace of a 6 paper. The surface features are consistently under control, despite an occasional lapse in usage.

4 Papers scored as a 4 show evidence of the writer's organizational plan. Support, though sufficient, tends to be less extensive or convincing than that found in papers scored as a 5 or 6. The writer generally observes the conventions of accepted English usage. Some errors are usually present, but they are not severe enough to interfere significantly with the writer's main purpose.

Lower-half papers either fail to convey a purpose sufficiently or lack one entirely. Consequently, their structure ranges from rudimentary at 3, to random at 2, to absent at 1. Control of the conventions of English usage tends to follow this same gradient.

3 Papers scored as a 3 usually show some evidence of planning or development. However, the organization is often limited to a simple listing or haphazard recitation of ideas about the topic, leaving an impression of insufficiency. The 3 papers often demonstrate repeated weaknesses in accepted English usage and are generally ineffective in accomplishing the writer's purpose.

2 Papers scored as a 2 are characterized by a marked lack of development or inadequate support for ideas. The level of thought apparent in the writing is frequently unsophisticated or superficial, often marked by a listing of unsupported generalizations. Instead of suggesting a clear purpose, these papers often present conflicting purposes. Errors in accepted English usage may seriously interfere with the overall effectiveness of these papers.

1 Papers scored as a 1 leave the impression that the writer has not only *not* accomplished a purpose, but has not made any purpose apparent. The dominant feature of these papers is the lack of control. The writer stumbles both in conveying a clear plan for the paper and in expressing ideas according to the conventions of accepted English usage.

0 The zero score is reserved for papers which are blank, illegible, or written on a topic other than the one assigned.

HOW TO SCORE YOUR ESSAY

To score your essay, compare it with the following model essays. These model essays received scores of 3 and 5, respectively.

Compare your essay with the 3 model essay. If it is as good as the 3 model essay, then assign your essay a score of 3. If it is not as good as the 3 model essay, then refer back to the answer key of the Writing Skills Predictor Test and use the descriptions of the 1 and 2 model essays to evaluate your essay. It should be easy to assign a score to your essay if you compare your essay with these model essays and their character trait analyses.

If your essay is better than the 3 model essay, compare it to the model essay that received a 5. If it is better than the 3, but not as good as the 5, then score your essay a 4. If your essay is better than the 5 model essay, then score your essay a 6.

In addition, look at the notes and character trait analyses that accompany the model essays. These comments explain the strengths and weaknesses of these essays.

Model Essay—Holistic Score 3

Weak statement of point of view, vague generalizations

I think having a hobby is a very important way of doing that for several reasons. Many people like to do things that don't have anything to do with their work. They like to get away from their work for a change and find something different to think about.

Undeveloped ideas that don't support the writer's point of view

First, if you have a hobby like jewelry making it can help you see some talent you never knew you had. This might be a good way of making a living that you never thought of before.

Second, a hobby is a grate way to forget about all the worries of the day. It can give you something to think about other than work. Thinking about the bracelets or rings you made is a lot better way to fall asleep than thinking about a fight you had with your boss. Hobbies breaks up your routine. It gives you something different to talk about at the dinner table.

Weak conclusion

In the end people think they don't have time for a hobby but it is important for everybody to have a hobby. When you make the time, you will find out that it is worth it. Weather you try jewelry making or something else, you will find out that it relaxes you and it helps you to face going to work a lot easier.

Character Trait Analysis

1. The essay is organized in three parts: an introduction, the body, and a conclusion.
2. An attempt is made at supporting points with examples and reasons, though they are not clearly stated. Other points are made without supporting detail. The overall effect is one of disorganization and an uneven flow of ideas.
3. Inconcise language makes the purpose of the essay unclear and the conclusion less effective.
4. Errors in spelling, punctuation, sentence structure, and grammar detract from the essay's effectiveness.

Model Essay—Holistic Score 5

States point of view

Finding time for activities outside of work and home is difficult in this fast paced world we live in. It seems as though there is always more work to be done. Making time for yourself is more important than ever, and having a hobby lets you do just that.

Develops key ideas and uses specific, personal examples to support the writer's point of view

Uses appropriate transitional words

Your hobby might be gardening, hang gliding, fishing, or collecting stamps. You might work much harder at any of these than you do at your regular job. But time spent doing something you find pleasurable is rewarding. It will make those jobs at work and home much easier.

For example I spend every Saturday working in my yard. I get up early to pull weeds, mow the lawn, and water the flowers. I work out in the sun all day, but I am never tired in the same way that I am after a regular day's work. In fact, I sometimes continue working after dark. My Saturdays make my Monday mornings much easier. I don't mind getting up to go to work because I've spent time doing something that was important to me.

Summarizes ideas and restates point of view

Having some activity to look forward to is extremly important for adults today. One day or even a few hours spent enjoyably working at a hobby can make every other day of the week much richer. When you find a hobby you also find a part of yourself you never knew you had before.

Character Trait Analysis

1. This essay is well organized. Ideas flow logically and support the conclusion.
2. The point of view is supported by specific details.
3. Sentences are smooth and controlled.
4. Though there are a few structural weaknesses and minor mechanical errors, the essay reads well.

Practice Test, Part I

1. (3) *Sentence Structure/Parallelism/Sentence Correction.* Express similar ideas in similar form. The words *graduations, birthdays,* and *wedding celebrations* are all in the plural form in the corrected sentence.
2. (1) *Mechanics/Spelling/Sentence Correction.* The words *presents* and *presence* sound alike but mean different things.
3. (2) *Usage/Subject–Verb Agreement/Sentence Correction.* The subject of this sentence is a plural noun—*members.* The verb must be changed to the plural form to agree with the subject.
4. (4) *Sentence Structure/Clarity/Sentence Revision.* In the original sentence, *Using a calculator* is a dangling modifier.
5. (3) *Usage/Verb Tense/Sentence Revision.* The phrase *Before they decide* provides a clue that the past tense of *use* is inappropriate.
6. (4) *Sentence Structure/Clarity/Construction Shift. Determining how much paint to buy is no problem with a calculator.* The new organization eliminates repetition of the pronoun *they,* and the overall wordiness of the sentence.
7. (4) *Mechanics/Capitalization—Proper Nouns/Sentence Correction.* Capitalize the names of specific places.
8. (5) *Mechanics/Punctuation—Items in a Series/Sentence Revision.* Separate three or more items in a series with commas.
9. (4) *Sentence Structure/Coordination/Sentence Revision.* Only one connecting word—*but* or *however*—should be used to show how the two parts of this sentence are related. When *however* is used as a connecting word, it is preceded by a semicolon.
10. (2) *Sentence Structure/Comma Splice/Sentence Revision.* A comma is used incorrectly to join two complete sentences. A question mark must be added at the end of the first sentence.
11. (4) *Usage/Pronoun Reference—Agreement With Antecedent/Sentence Revision.* Make sure that a pronoun agrees with the word it replaces. The pronoun in sentence 3, *they,* does not agree in number with its antecedent, *Occupational Outlook Handbook,* in the previous sentence.
12. (1) *Sentence Structure/Subordination/Sentence Correction.* Only one subordinator should be used to connect the subordinate idea with the main idea. In the original sentence, two subordinators, *if* and *in case,* are used.
13. (2) *Usage/Subject–Verb Agreement—Inverted Structure/Sentence Correction.* The plural subject, *cards,* requires a plural verb, *are,* even though the verb comes before the subject.
14. (2) *Mechanics/Spelling/Sentence Correction. Journels* is spelled incorrectly. The endings *al, el, le, il,* and *ile* often sound alike.
15. (2) *Usage/Verb Tense/Sentence Correction.* The present tense is appropriate; throughout the paragraph, the writer discusses sources of information that exist right now.
16. (1) *Usage/Pronoun Reference/Sentence Revision.* To be consistent with the implied subject (*You*), use *yourself. Who,* not *whom,* is required as the subject with the verb *wrote.*
17. (3) *Sentence Structure/Clarity/Construction Shift. Sometimes, for example, employers pay writers to write pamphlets about a company.* The new construction improves the wordy original by using the word *for.*
18. (5) *Sentence Structure/Coordination/Construction Shift. The pamphlets may exaggerate job benefits and fail to mention problems with the job.* Two sentences are combined by joining the verbs in each sentence—*may exaggerate* and *may fail*—to form the phrase *may exaggerate and fail.*
19. (4) *Sentence Structure/Parallelism/Sentence Revision.* Similar ideas in a sentence should be expressed in a similar form. In the underlined portion of the sentence, *discovering* should be changed to *to discover* to correspond in form with *to find out.*
20. (4) *Sentence Structure/Clarity—Modification/Sentence Revision. To make sure that high school graduates have basic computer skills* is used as a modifier. In the original sentence, the word modified is unclear. *School officials,* not *computer literacy,* want *to make sure that . . .*
21. (4) *Mechanics/Spelling/Sentence Correction.* Remember the *d* in knowledge. The endings *age, ege, edge, idge,* and *ige* all sound alike.
22. (4) *Usage/Verb Tense/Sentence Revision.* The word *future* provides the clue that the future tense, *will be,* is needed.
23. (3) *Mechanics/Punctuation—Commas With a Series/Sentence Correction.* A comma is never used before the last item in a series.
24. (3) *Sentence Structure/Coordination/Construction Shift. Students learn about computers in both special computer classes and regular classes.* The new construction avoids repetition by using a coordinator to join similar elements.
25. (2) *Mechanics/Punctuation—Commas After Introductory Elements/Sentence Correction.* When the subject comes in the middle of a sentence, use a comma to separate the introductory words from the subject.
26. (1) *Mechanics/Capitalization/Sentence Correction.* The names of languages are proper nouns and should therefore be capitalized.
27. (2) *Usage/Subject–Verb Agreement—Expletives/Sentence Revision.* The plural subject, *programs,* requires a plural verb, *are.* The word *there* is an expletive; an expletive is never the subject of a sentence.
28. (5) *Usage/Subject–Verb Agreement/Sentence Correction.*

The singular subject in the second part of the sentence—*use*—requires a singular verb, despite the interrupting phrase, *in a variety of areas.*

29. (4) *Usage/Pronoun Reference—Pronoun Shift/Sentence Revision.* Use pronouns consistently within a sentence. The pronoun *you* is used in the second part of the sentence (in *you've won*), as well as throughout the paragraph.
30. (5) *Sentence Structure/Parallelism/Sentence Correction.* Express similar ideas in similar form. The news comes in three ways: *in a letter, on a post card,* or *on a computer form.*
31. (2) *Usage/Pronoun Reference—Agreement With Antecedent/Sentence Correction.* The plural pronoun *they* in the original sentence is incorrect because it does not agree in number with its antecedent, *someone.*
32. (4) *Sentence Structure/Comma Splice/Sentence Correction.* Two complete sentences are incorrectly joined by a comma. The run-on sentence is corrected by replacing it with two separate sentences.
33. (2) *Mechanics/Punctuation—Overuse of Commas/Sentence Correction.* Do not use a comma between the subject and verb of a sentence.
34. (5) *Sentence Structure/Sentence Fragment/Sentence Revision.* The fragment is corrected by adding the verb *is* and creating a subject, *description,* from *describing.*
35. (5) *Mechanics/Capitalization—Proper Nouns/Sentence Correction.* Words such as *County* and *Mountains* should be capitalized when they are part of specific place names.
36. (3) *Sentence Structure/Parallelism/Sentence Revision.* Express similar ideas in similar form. The sales pitch may be about *buying land* or *renting vacation property.*
37. (2) *Usage/Pronoun Reference/Construction Shift.* *Don't be one of those unfortunate people who waste their time and money on these scams.*
38. (5) *Sentence Structure/Sentence Fragment/Sentence Revision.* The fragment is corrected by providing a verb, *last,* for the subject, *jobs.*
39. (2) *Mechanics/Spelling/Sentence Correction.* The endings *int, ent,* and *ant* are frequently confused.
40. (5) *Sentence Structure/Coordination/Construction Shift.* *Agencies that handle temporary jobs are advertised in the telephone book and in the classified section of your newspaper.*
41. (2) *Mechanics/Capitalization/Sentence Correction.* Capitalize words such as *agency* or *company* only if they are part of a proper noun.
42. (4) *Usage/Verb Tense/Sentence Correction.* Keep the tense of verbs consistent throughout the paragraph. *An agency that handles . . . will probably test . . .*
43. (5) *Usage/Pronoun Reference—Pronoun Shift/Sentence Revision.* The pronoun *you* should be used to be consistent with the understood subject of the sentence and with the other sentences in the paragraph.
44. (1) *Usage/Subject-Verb Agreement/Construction Shift.* *One of the advantages is that you are usually paid within a week or two of the week you work.* Make sure that the verb agrees with the subject of the sentence. The subject of the rewritten sentence, *One,* is singular.
45. (3) *Sentence Structure/Clarity/Sentence Correction.* Eliminate unnecessary words. Words such as *because* or *although* are sufficient to express a relationship between two ideas in a sentence.
46. (3) *Mechanics/Punctuation/Sentence Revision.* Use a comma after the coordinating word in a compound sentence.
47. (4) *Sentence Structure/Clarity—Dangling Modifier/Sentence Revision.* The first part of this sentence, *Having decided . . . the drawbacks,* does not clearly modify any of the words in the sentence.
48. (4) *Usage/Pronoun Shift/Sentence Correction.* The sentence shifts from the second person (*you*) to the third person (*we*). Since the rest of the paragraph is written in the second person, use the second person consistently in this sentence.
49. (1) *Sentence Structure/Subordination/Sentence Revision.* The comma correctly separates the subordinate idea from the main idea. The verb in the subordinate idea, *grows,* agrees with the subject, *chick.*
50. (5) *Usage/Relative Pronoun/Construction Shift.* *You might think that your elderly aunt who lives alone needs a guard dog.* The relative pronoun *who* refers to a person.
51. (2) *Mechanics/Capitalization/Sentence Correction.* Capitalize the names of holidays.
52. (4) *Sentence Structure/Misplaced Modifier/Sentence Revision.* The words *that crawled into your yard* modify, or describe, *turtle,* not *brother.* Place the description as close as possible to the word it modifies.
53. (5) *Usage/Verb Tense—Irregular Verbs/Sentence Revision.* With the helping verb *have,* use a past participle as the main verb. The past participle of *think* is *thought.*
54. (2) *Mechanics/Punctuation—Items in a Series/Sentence Correction.* Separate three or more items in a series with commas: *food, vaccinations, and emergency trips . . .*
55. (2) *Sentence Structure/Subordination/Sentence Correction.* Use a comma to separate the subordinate idea from the main idea.

Practice Test, Part II

Introduction to Holistic Scoring

The following GED Essay Scoring Guide provides a general description of the characteristics found in GED essays that are scored by the Holistic Method.

GED ESSAY SCORING GUIDE

Papers will show *some or all* of the following characteristics.

Upper-half papers make clear a definite purpose, pursued with varying degrees of effectiveness. They also have a structure that shows evidence of some deliberate planning. The writer's control of English usage ranges from fairly reliable at 4 to confident and accomplished at 6.

6 Papers scored as a 6 tend to offer sophisticated ideas within an organizational framework that is clear and appropriate for the topic. The supporting statements are particularly effective because of their substance, specificity, or illustrative quality. The writing is vivid and precise, though it may contain an occasional flaw.

5 Papers scored as a 5 are clearly organized with effective support for each of the writer's major points. The writing offers substantive ideas, though the paper may lack the flair or grace of a 6 paper. The surface features are consistently under control, despite an occasional lapse in usage.

4 Papers scored as a 4 show evidence of the writer's organizational plan. Support, though sufficient, tends to be less extensive or convincing than that found in papers scored as a 5 or 6. The writer generally observes the conventions of accepted English usage. Some errors are usually present, but they are not severe enough to interfere significantly with the writer's main purpose.

Lower-half papers either fail to convey a purpose sufficiently or lack one entirely. Consequently, their structure ranges from rudimentary at 3, to random at 2, to absent at 1. Control of the conventions of English usage tends to follow this same gradient.

3 Papers scored as a 3 usually show some evidence of planning or development. However, the organization is often limited to a simple listing or haphazard recitation of ideas about the topic, leaving an impression of insufficiency. The 3 papers often demonstrate repeated weaknesses in accepted English usage and are generally ineffective in accomplishing the writer's purpose.

2 Papers scored as a 2 are characterized by a marked lack of development or inadequate support for ideas. The level of thought apparent in the writing is frequently unsophisticated or superficial, often marked by a listing of unsupported generalizations. Instead of suggesting a clear purpose, these papers often present conflicting purposes. Errors in accepted English usage may seriously interfere with the overall effectiveness of these papers.

1 Papers scored as a 1 leave the impression that the writer has not only *not* accomplished a purpose, but has not made any purpose apparent. The dominant feature of these papers is the lack of control. The writer stumbles both in conveying a clear plan for the paper and in expressing ideas according to the conventions of accepted English usage.

0 The zero score is reserved for papers which are blank, illegible, or written on a topic other than the one assigned.

Source: *The 1988 Tests of General Educational Development: A Preview*, American Council on Education, 1985. Used with permission.

HOW TO SCORE YOUR ESSAY

To score your essay, compare it with the following model essays. These model essays received scores of 3 and 5, respectively.

Compare your essay with the 3 model essay. If it is as good as the 3 model essay, then assign your essay a score of 3. If it is not as good as the 3 model essay, then refer back to the answer key of the Writing Skills Predictor Test and use the descriptions of the 1 and 2 model essays to evaluate your essay. It should be easy to assign a score to your essay if you compare your essay with these model essays and their character trait analyses.

If your essay is better than the 3 model essay, compare it to the model essay that received a 5. If it is better than the 3, but not as good as the 5, then score your essay a 4. If your essay is better than the 5 model essay, then score your essay a 6.

In addition, look at the notes and character trait analyses that accompany the model essays. These comments explain the strengths and weaknesses of these essays.

Model Essay—Holistic Score 3

Point of view is unclear

Sometimes consumers buy products because they are influenced by the way it is packaged. In this essay I will tell why that is so.

When people go to the grocery store they usually have a pretty good idea of what they want to buy there. Sometimes something may catch their eye that they have not planned on buying. For example they could see a new kind of spagetti sauce in a fancy jar. They could use the jar to store other foods in later. Even if they weren't planning on having spagetti they will put it into their shopping cart anyway.

Haphazard listing of details rather than clear examples that support a point of view

As they go threw the store they may forget their shopping list all together. They can buy canned goods because the labels are pretty. They can buy one brand of vitamins because they think thier getting a smaller bottle for free. they can buy four bars of soap when they only need three because they want to get one for free.

Weak unsupported conclusion

Shoppers should be careful because sometimes they will buy things they don't really want to buy. They will only get them because they look good on the shelf.

Character Trait Analysis

1. The essay is organized into three parts: an introduction, the body, and a conclusion.
2. The writer does not clearly state his or her point of view on the topic.
3. Specific examples and details are used to support the writer's points, but the haphazard listing of examples doesn't lead to a logical conclusion.
4. Errors in spelling, punctuation, sentence structure, and grammar detract from the essay's effectiveness.

Model Essay—Holistic Score 5

Strong introduction, clear point of view

Manufacturers know that the more attractive their products look, the more attractive they will be to customers. In my opinion, consumers may want to buy quality products, but they can be influenced to buy an inferior product because of the way its packaged.

Uses a specific example to support writer's point of view

For example, when I buy bread, I want to be sure that it is fresh. If the package is made of good quality material and well—sealed, then I should be able to assume that it is probably protected from going bad. But without a sale date that is clear to read, I can't really tell for sure just how fresh it is.

Explains idea introduced earlier

More supporting details

Many consumers will think that a manufacturer cares about producing a quality product if the packaging is attractively designed. Often this is true. But it takes using the product at least once to tell whether or not it is all that it appears to be. This is true of all products, but it is especially true of cosmetics. Too often, consumers think that the attractiveness of the package will rub off them and make them more attractive too. For instance, if all the anti-wrinkle creams really worked, no one would have wrinkles. Consumers have to try products out for themselves and judge how well they do what they're supposed to do.

Summarizes ideas, concludes with important statement about the topic that is in keeping with point of view

You cannot always tell a book by it's cover. The same is true with packaging. It is difficult for consumers today not to be drawn in by fancy packaging. Products that have proven their quality, even if they are well-presented, are the ones that will survive in the marketplace.

Character Trait Analysis

1. The essay is well organized. Ideas flow logically and lead to a strong conclusion.
2. The point of view is supported by examples and reasons.
3. The examples and reasons are consistent with the writer's point of view.
4. The essay reads well, although there are a few errors in sentence structure mechanics.

SIMULATION
Simulated Test, Part I

1. (5) *Usage/Pronoun Reference—Agreement with Antecedent/Sentence Correction.* The pronoun *them* does not agree with the word it replaces, a *lunch*.
2. (2) *Mechanics/Punctuation—Overuse of Commas/Sentence Revision.* Commas should be used to separate items in a series, with the final comma appearing before the *and*, *or*, or *nor* preceding the last word in the series.
3. (2) *Sentence Structure/Comma Splice/Sentence Correction.* Use a semicolon, not a comma, to separate complete ideas that are connected by *nevertheless*, *however*, *thus*, or *therefore*.
4. (1) *Usage/Subject–Verb Agreement/Construction Shift.* *Meat, fish, chicken, nuts, and beans contain protein.* The plural subject requires a plural verb.
5. (4) *Mechanics/Capitalization/Proper Nouns/Sentence Correction.* Capitalize the names of regions of the world.
6. (2) *Sentence Structure/Comma Splice/Sentence Revision.* Do not use a comma to separate two complete ideas. The error is corrected here by forming two sentences.
7. (3) *Usage/Subject–Verb Agreement/Sentence Revision.* When both subject words connected by *either . . . or* are singular, use a singular verb.
8. (2) *Mechanics/Spelling—Frequently Misspelled Words/Sentence Correction.* The *-ing* form of *proceed* is *proceeding*; the *-ing* form of *precede* is *preceding*.
9. (3) *Sentence Structure/Parallelism/Sentence Correction.* Ideas of equal importance connected by *or* or *and* should be expressed in similar, or parallel, form. . . . *a plain paper bag or in a lunch box . . .*
10. (3) *Sentence Structure/Parallelism/Sentence Correction.* When ideas have similar roles in a sentence, they should be worded with similar, or parallel, structures.
11. (4) *Usage/Vague Pronoun Reference/Sentence Correction.* Make sure that the antecedent of a pronoun is clear. It is not clear whether the pronoun *they* refers to the *Democrats*, the *Republicans*, or both.
12. (1) *Mechanics/Punctuation—Commas with Sentence Interrupters/Construction Shift.* *Economic issues, those financial matters concerning goods and services, have gotten less attention.* Use commas to set off an interrupting phrase from the rest of the sentence.
13. (4) *Sentence Structure/Sentence Fragment/Sentence Correction.* The sentence fragment is corrected by providing a verb, *receive*, that agrees with the subject, *issues*.
14. (4) *Usage/Verb Tense Error—Clues to Tense in Paragraph/Sentence Revision.* The present tense is used consistently throughout the paragraph.
15. (5) *Sentence Structure/Dangling Modifier/Sentence Revision.* A sentence should be worded so that a modifier clearly and logically modifies a word in the sentence. *The U.S.*, not *drugs*, *works with Mexico . . .*
16. (5) *Mechanics/Spelling—Homonyms/Sentence Correction.* Use the possessive *their* when referring to ownership.
17. (3) *Usage/Subject–Verb Agreement—Expletives/Sentence Correction.* Although *there* precedes the verb, it is not the subject of the sentence. The plural subject, *areas*, needs the plural verb *are*.
18. (1) *Sentence Structure/Subordination/Construction Shift.* *For example, they feel that keeping peace in the Middle East should take priority over the question of whether or not to raise our minimum wage a few cents.*
19. (5) *Usage/Vague Pronoun Reference/Sentence Correction.* Make sure that the antecedent of a pronoun is clear. It is not clear whether *they* refers to *Many people*, *presidents*, or general disagreement.
20. (5) *Sentence Structure/Run-On Sentence/Sentence Correction.* The run-on sentence is corrected here by rewriting it as two sentences.
21. (3) *Mechanics/Punctuation—Comma After Introductory Elements/Sentence Correction.* When a subordinate idea appears at the beginning of the sentence, it is followed by a comma.
22. (4) *Mechanics/Spelling—Contractions/Sentence Correction.* In a contraction, put the apostrophe (') where the missing letter should be.
23. (1) *Sentence Structure/Subordination/Construction Shift.* *Studies show that the more television children watch, the worse they are likely to do on reading tests.*
24. (5) *Usage/Subject–Verb Agreement—Interrupting Phrase/Sentence Correction.* The singular subject, *Television*, requires the singular verb, *is*, despite the phrase that separates the two.
25. (2) *Mechanics/Capitalization/Sentence Correction.* Capitalize the names of days of the week.
26. (2) *Usage/Verb Tense/Sentence Revision.* *To lie* is one of those irregular verbs whose forms you must memorize. Today they sit and lie; yesterday they sat and lay.
27. (2) *Usage/Pronoun Reference/Sentence Revision.* Do not shift pronouns within a sentence or paragraph. Continue with *you*, to be consistent.
28. (3) *Sentence Structure/Sentence Fragment/Sentence Revision.* The sentence fragment is corrected by supplying the verb, *should control*, required by the subject, *Parents*.
29. (3) *Mechanics/Punctuation—Commas in Compound Sentences/Sentence Correction.* Use a comma before the coordinator that connects two complete ideas in a compound sentence.
30. (3) *Usage/Relative Pronoun/Construction Shift.* *Before doing anything for someone who is choking on something, wait a moment to see if he coughs it up himself.* Remember to use *who* when referring to people and *which* when referring to things.

31. (2) *Mechanics/Spelling—Frequently Misspelled Words/Sentence Correction.* Don't confuse the spellings of *breathe* and *breath.* When you breathe, you take a breath.
32. (5) *Mechanics/Capitalization—Titles of People/Sentence Correction.* The title *Dr.* is correctly capitalized because it precedes a particular name.
33. (4) *Usage/Subject–Verb Agreement/Sentence Revision.* The singular subject, *One*, requires a singular verb, *is*, despite the interrupting phrase, *of the most common ways to start.*
34. (4) *Sentence Structure/Subordination/Sentence Revision.* Don't forget to include both words of the subordinator in such combinations as *so/that, such/that, as/as, more/than.*
35. (4) *Usage/Subject–Verb Agreement—Inverted Structure/Sentence Correction.* The subject determines the form of the verb, even when it follows the verb. Here, the singular subject, *thumb*, requires a singular verb, *is*.
36. (3) *Sentence Structure/Comma Splice/Sentence Revision.* Do not use a comma to separate two complete ideas. Here, the error is corrected by making the first idea, *With your other hand cupped over the fist*, subordinate to the second, *give a hard upward pull.*
37. (4) *Sentence Structure/Run-On Sentence/Sentence Correction.* If the two ideas in a run-on sentence are closely related, a semicolon may be used at the end of the first complete sentence.
38. (1) *Usage/Verb Tense—Word Clue to Tense in Sentence/Sentence Revision.* The words *have* and *usually* indicate that a present-tense verb, *has*, is required.
39. (2) *Usage/Verb Tense—Word Clue to Tense in Paragraph/Sentence Correction.* Use the present tense to be consistent with that used throughout the paragraph.
40. (2) *Usage/Subject–Verb Agreement/Sentence Revision.* The verb form that agrees with the singular subject, *arguing*, is *takes*.
41. (3) *Sentence Structure/Subordination/Construction Shift.* *Anger that has been suppressed for months or even years may erupt when family members see each other again.* The new construction makes the relationship between ideas clearer.
42. (2) *Usage/Subject–Verb Agreement—Compound Subjects/Sentence Correction.* The compound subject, *Fatigue and irritability*, requires a plural verb, *go*.
43. (4) *Mechanics/Spelling—Homonyms/Sentence Correction.* The words *brake* and *break* sound the same but have different meanings.
44. (3) *Mechanics/Capitalization/Sentence Correction.* Capitalize words such as *Island* and *City* when they are part of the name of a place.
45. (2) *Usage/Subject–Verb Agreement/Construction Shift.* *Neither waiting in line to buy six pumpkin pies nor baking six of them leads to feeling very relaxed.* Since *neither* and *nor* join singular nouns (*waiting* and *baking*), a singular verb, *leads*, is required.
46. (3) *Mechanics/Punctuation—Contractions/Sentence Revision.* *You're* is a contraction that means *you are.*
47. (4) *Sentence Structure/Run-On Sentence/Sentence Correction.* The first complete idea ends with the word *however.* A semicolon should be placed after *however* to correct the run-on sentence.
48. (3) *Sentence Structure/Subordination/Construction Shift.* *Although dentists' offices have changed in appearance over the years, the dentist's role is basically unchanged.*
49. (3) *Usage/Verb Tense—Clues within Sentence/Sentence Correction.* The words *goes around . . . while* provide the clue that the present tense, *are taken*, should follow.
50. (5) *Usage/Verb Tense/Clues within Sentence/Sentence Revision.* The word *now* provides the clue that the present tense, *uses*, should follow.
51. (4) *Usage/Ambiguous Pronoun Reference/Sentence Revision.* It is not clear whether *their teeth* refers to dentists' teeth or children's. The ambiguity is cleared up by eliminating the unnecessary words *who work with children.*
52. (3) *Mechanics/Spelling/Sentence Correction.* *Procedure* is a frequently misspelled word.
53. (3) *Sentence Structure/Parallelism/Sentence Revision.* A verb that is parallel to *brush* is needed in the second part of the sentence. *Use* is parallel to *brush*.
54. (3) *Sentence Structure/Subordination/Sentence Correction.* Use only one subordinator to introduce a subordinate idea.
55. (1) *Mechanics/Capitalization—Proper Nouns/Sentence Correction.* Capitalize words such as *Association* or *Company* if they are part of the name of a group.

Simulated Test, Part II

Introduction to Holistic Scoring

The following GED Essay Scoring Guide provides a general description of the characteristics found in GED essays that are scored by the Holistic Method.

GED ESSAY SCORING GUIDE

Papers will show *some or all* of the following characteristics.

Upper-half papers make clear a definite purpose, pursued with varying degrees of effectiveness. They also have a structure that shows evidence of some deliberate planning. The writer's control of English usage ranges from fairly reliable at 4 to confident and accomplished at 6.

6 Papers scored as a 6 tend to offer sophisticated ideas within an organizational framework that is clear and appropriate for the topic. The supporting statements are particularly effective because of their substance, specificity, or illustrative quality. The writing is vivid and precise, though it may contain an occasional flaw.

5 Papers scored as a 5 are clearly organized with effective support for each of the writer's major points. The writing offers substantive ideas, though the paper may lack the flair or grace of a 6 paper. The surface features are consistently under control, despite an occasional lapse in usage.

4 Papers scored as a 4 show evidence of the writer's organizational plan. Support, though sufficient, tends to be less extensive or convincing than that found in papers scored as a 5 or 6. The writer generally observes the conventions of accepted English usage. Some errors are usually present, but they are not severe enough to interfere significantly with the writer's main purpose.

Lower-half papers either fail to convey a purpose sufficiently or lack one entirely. Consequently, their structure ranges from rudimentary at 3, to random at 2, to absent at 1. Control of the conventions of English usage tends to follow this same gradient.

3 Papers scored as a 3 usually show some evidence of planning or development. However, the organization is often limited to a simple listing or haphazard recitation of ideas about the topic, leaving an impression of insufficiency. The 3 papers often demonstrate repeated weaknesses in accepted English usage and are generally ineffective in accomplishing the writer's purpose.

2 Papers scored as a 2 are characterized by a marked lack of development or inadequate support for ideas. The level of thought apparent in the writing is frequently unsophisticated or superficial, often marked by a listing of unsupported generalizations. Instead of suggesting a clear purpose, these papers often present conflicting purposes. Errors in accepted English usage may seriously interfere with the overall effectiveness of these papers.

1 Papers scored as a 1 leave the impression that the writer has not only *not* accomplished a purpose, but has not made any purpose apparent. The dominant feature of these papers is the lack of control. The writer stumbles both in conveying a clear plan for the paper and in expressing ideas according to the conventions of accepted English usage.

0 The zero score is reserved for papers which are blank, illegible, or written on a topic other than the one assigned.

Source: *The 1988 Tests of General Educational Development: A Preview*, American Council on Education, 1985. Used with permission.

HOW TO SCORE YOUR ESSAY

To score your essay, compare it with the following model essays. These model essays received scores of 3 and 5, respectively.

Compare your essay with the 3 model essay. If it is as good as the 3 model essay, then assign your essay a score of 3. If it is not as good as the 3 model essay, then refer back to the answer key of the Writing Skills Predictor Test and use the descriptions of the 1 and 2 model essays to evaluate your essay. It should be easy to assign a score to your essay if you compare your essay with these model essays and their character trait analyses.

If your essay is better than the 3 model essay, compare it to the model essay that received a 5. If it is better than the 3, but not as good as the 5, then score your essay a 4. If your essay is better than the 5 model essay, then score your essay a 6.

In addition, look at the notes and character trait analyses that accompany the model essays. These comments explain the strengths and weaknesses of these essays.

Model Essay—Holistic Score 3

Weak, impersonal point of view. The essay topic asks for the writer's opinion, not vague generalizations about life today

List of undeveloped, unconnected ideas that don't support a personal point of view; needs specific examples

Weak conclusion—unsupported by examples in essay

Having a role-model is especialy important for young people today. Each year the world seems to get more and more confusing and it is important for young people to know that there are individual people out there who can achieve success.

These role-models may be parents, grandparents, a relative, someone you know, or someone you read about in the paper. These role-models show young people that they can make a contrabution to the world. They show that it is possible to make your dreams come true. They show that not all rock stars are bad.

Young people today get so much information thrown at them mainly from the media that it can be confusing. A role-model can be someone who shows them how they handle living in a complacated world, and still manage to be successful.

It is important that young people today have role-models all people should have them for that matter. If everybody had a role-model then they would find comfort knowing that success in the modern world is really possible, not just some dream.

Character Trait Analysis

1. The essay has been organized into three parts: an introduction, the body, and a conclusion.
2. The point of view is weak and impersonal throughout the essay.
3. Several different points are made, though none are backed up with specific supporting examples and reasons. Total effect is one of disorganization and illogical flow of ideas.
4. The conclusion could have been made stronger with supporting details.
5. Errors in spelling, punctuation, sentence structure, and grammar detract from the essay's effectiveness.

Model Essay—Holistic Score 5

Point of view is clearly stated

Key idea is explained using general examples

Another key idea is explained; uses a specific example to support the idea

Another key idea is explained; a specific example is used to support the idea

Uses appropriate transition words to move to final point

Summarizes ideas

Concludes with important statement that is in keeping with the point of view

I believe that it is still very important that young people have role-models. Without strong individuals to look up to, the next generation may be defeated before it has even given the future a chance.

Role-models help define the choices young people have. By being an excelent biochemist, gym instructor, or astronaut, they are showing young possible roads their own careers could take. These could be careers a young person never would have thought of if they hadn't been introduced to the role-model.

Young people also need to know that success is possible. They need to know that someone has come along before them and achieved goals that might seem impossible to the rest of the population. Helen Keller was a role-model for many young people. Though she was heavily handicapped when she was born, she learned to read and write. She became a famous writer.

Role-models also help show young people how to get where they want to go. Their own careers can be like charts or maps for young people to follow. Knowing how Gary Carter worked hard to become the excellent baseball player he is shows young people how they can accomplish this, too.

But most importantly, role-models show young people that they are not alone in their dreams. Someone else has dreamed something similar to their dream before them. Our young people need to get to know the courage, strength, and other good qualities role-models have had. Unless they discover how individuals have striven to succeed, they may never achieve their dreams. And there may be no role-model candidates for future generations.

Character Trait Analysis

1. The essay is well organized. Ideas flow logically and lead to a conclusion.
2. Point of view is supported by substantive ideas.
3. Specific examples have been used to support these ideas in the essay.
4. Though there are a few structural weaknesses and minor mechanical errors, the essay reads well.